Attention, Perception and Memory

Although attention, perception and memory can be identified as separable components of the human cognitive system, this book argues that for a complete understanding of any of them it is necessary to appreciate the way they interact and depend upon one another. Using evidence from experimental psychology, cognitive neuroscience and neuropsychological patients, aspects of attention, perception and memory are related together. Written by an established author, this text clearly explains and evaluates key theories and puts different approaches to this field in context.

Attention, Perception and Memory: An Integrated Introduction contains introductory, yet comprehensive chapters on key topics of cognitive psychology and will be of interest to first and second year undergraduates studying psychology and, more specifically, cognitive psychology.

Elizabeth A. Styles Senior Lecturer in Psychology at St Edmund Hall, Oxford, UK.

Psychology Focus

Series editor: Perry Hinton, Oxford Brookes University

The Psychology Focus series provides students with a new focus on key topic areas in psychology. It supports students taking modules in psychology, whether for a psychology degree or a combined programme, and those renewing their qualification in a related discipline. Each short book:

- presents clear, in-depth coverage of a discrete area with many applied examples
- assumes no prior knowledge of psychology
- has been written by an experienced teacher
- has chapter summaries, annotated further reading and a glossary of key terms.

Also available in this series:

Attention, Perception and Memory

An integrated introduction

■ Elizabeth A. Styles

Psychology Press
Taylor & Francis Group
HOVE AND NEW YORK

First published 2005
by Psychology Press
27 Church Road, Hove, East Sussex,
BN3 2FA

Simultaneously published in the
USA and Canada
by Psychology Press
270 Madison Avenue, New York,
NY 10016

*Psychology Press is a part of the Taylor
& Francis Group*

Copyright © 2005 Psychology Press

Typeset in Sabon and Futura by
RefineCatch Ltd, Bungay, Suffolk

Printed and bound in Great Britain by
TJ International Ltd, Padstow,
Cornwall

This publication has been produced
with paper manufactured to strict
environmental standards and with
pulp derived from sustainable forests.

*British Library Cataloguing in
Publication Data*
A catalogue record for this book is
available from the British Library

*Library of Congress Cataloging-in-
Publication Data*
Styles, Elizabeth A.
    Attention, perception, and memory :
an integrated introduction /
Elizabeth A. Styles.
        p.   cm.
    Includes bibliographical references
and index.
    ISBN 0-86377-658-2 −
    ISBN 0-86377-659-0 (pbk.)
    1. Cognition.   2. Attention.
    3. Visual perception.   4. Memory.
    I. Title.
    BF311.S78 2005
    153−dc22   2004018457

ISBN 0-86377-658-2 (hbk)
ISBN 0-86377-659-0 (pbk)

Contents

Illustrations

Series preface

The Psychology Focus series provides short, up-to-date accounts of key areas in psychology without assuming the reader's prior knowledge in the subject. Psychology is often a favoured subject area for study, since it is relevant to a wide range of disciplines such as Sociology, Education, Nursing and Business Studies. These relatively inexpensive but focused short texts combine sufficient detail for psychology specialists with sufficient clarity for non-specialists.

The series authors are academics experienced in undergraduate teaching as well as research. Each takes a topic within their area of psychological expertise and presents a short review, highlighting important themes and including both theory and research findings. Each aspect of the topic is clearly explained with supporting glossaries to elucidate technical terms.

The series has been conceived within the context of the increasing modularisation which has been developed in higher education over the last decade and fulfils the consequent need for clear, focused, topic-based course material. Instead of following one course of study, students on a modularisation programme are often able to choose modules from a wide range of disciplines to complement the modules they are required to study for a specific degree. It can no longer be assumed that students studying a particular module will necessarily have the same background knowledge (or lack of it!) in that subject. But they will need to familiarise themselves with a particular topic rapidly since a single module in a single topic may be only 15 weeks long, with assessments arising during that period. They may have to combine eight or more modules in a single year to obtain a degree at the end of their programme of study.

One possible problem with studying a range of separate modules is that the relevance of a particular topic or the relationship between topics may not always be apparent. In the Psychology Focus series, authors have drawn where possible on practical and applied examples to support the points being made so that readers can see the wider relevance of the topic under study. Also, the study of psychology is usually broken up into separate areas, such as social psychology, developmental psychology and cognitive psychology, to take three examples. Whilst the books in the Psychology Focus series will provide excellent coverage of certain key topics within these 'traditional' areas, the authors have not been constrained in their examples and explanations and may draw on material across the whole field of psychology to help explain the topic under study more fully.

Each text in the series provides the reader with a range of important material on a specific topic. They are suitably comprehensive and give a clear account of the important issues involved. The authors analyse and interpret the material as well as present an up-to-date and detailed review of key work. Recent references are provided along with suggested further reading to allow readers to investigate the topic in more depth. It is hoped, therefore, that after following the informative review of a key topic in a Psychology Focus text, readers not only will have a clear understanding of the issues in question but will be intrigued and challenged to investigate the topic further.

Acknowledgements

This book was written while I was Senior Lecturer at Buckinghamshire Chilterns University College. I am grateful for the resources and study time made available to me as well as the good company of my colleagues there. I must also thank the editorial staff at Taylor and Francis for their help and forebearance and the reviewers for their helpful suggestions.

To my Mother, Gwen

Prologue

When psychology first began it was believed that it should be the study of conscious experience. The early psychologists such as William James (1890) appreciated the intimate relationship between attention, perception and memory, and produced some of the best subjective descriptions of the contents and operations of the mind. Even before James, other researchers attempted to measure the units of sensation that they believed made up the primitive units of experience. For many years the study of the contents of mind were abandoned as impossible to measure scientifically while the Behaviourist movement concentrated on stimulus–response relationships. However, in the middle of the 20th century, cognitive psychology began the scientific investigation of the internal processes that lay between stimulation and response. The first models in cognitive psychology included attention, perception and memory, but as research expanded, psychologists increasingly concentrated on smaller and smaller aspects of these. This was because it is too difficult to investigate all aspects of human cognition at once, and large problems and questions need to be broken down into small ones to make them possible to answer. Whilst this approach has led to great advances in understanding, it can sometimes lead to the important relationships between attention, perception and memory being played down. The development of connectionist and parallel distributed models in the last 20 years has begun to bring back the relationship between perception, attention and memory.

In this book I shall try to show that although a great deal can be understood about components of cognition in isolation, and although the brain has an organisation that is specialised, it must be remembered that the outcome of many processes are involved in producing coherent behaviour, and that we must not forget that attention, perception and memory are all involved in even apparently simple tasks. I have chosen to include sections on measuring sensation, hearing and touch, and cross-modal studies, as these are often not included in similar texts, and as we live in a multidimensional environment, I felt these topics were important. Of necessity I have omitted topics that others might think essential.

In the first chapter I shall outline some of the questions for psychology; the development of the cognitive approach and some of its assumptions are explained in Chapter 2. Chapter 3 is concerned with some of the early work on sensation and demonstrates that even the measurement of sensation can be influenced by other processes. It also shows that the relation between the physical world and the experienced world is neither simple nor reliable. This chapter also explains some methods that will be referred to in other chapters. The next three chapters are about visual perception, visual attention and recognising objects and faces. Although divided for convenience, these chapters involve attention, perception and memory for the visual world. Chapters 7, 8 and 9 deal with the world of sound, touch and pain, and attention to sounds, and then consider the way that information from vision, hearing and the other senses interacts in studies of cross-modal effects. As our interaction with the world involves the processing of information from all sources, it is important to understand cross-modal studies. Next, we shall consider how attention is involved in the control, planning and monitoring of behaviour, and

Chapter 10 considers how learning leads to skills and automatic behaviour, and how actions can go wrong. Finally, Chapters 11 and 12 deal with different types of memory and how knowledge about the past and the present is represented.

Introduction

WELL, HERE YOU ARE: sitting down, reading a book. Not really very remarkable, you might think—initially. What's more, the book is about cognitive psychology, a topic you might be expecting to find dull and hardly relevant to what people usually expect psychology to be about. Are attention, perception and memory really that important? If so, are they really as interesting as other aspects of psychology such as social interaction or developmental psychology? Let us consider this by asking some questions. How did you get hold of this book? Why did you decide to read it? Perhaps someone told you about it. How do you remember who told you? Would you recognise that person if you saw them again? How did you understand what they said to you? If you had to go to the library, how did you know what to do there, or how use the catalogue? How did you know what a bookcase looked like and how did you avoid walking into desks and other people on your route? How did you read the words on the spine of the book to see if they matched the title you remembered, and how did you manage to reach for the book you wanted rather than another book nearby? The answers to these few questions involve attention, perception and memory. Now, while you are reading, you are moving your eyes along the lines of text— effortlessly. You are paying attention to reading; you perceive the words and know what they mean because you have learnt them and they are stored in your memory. As you read on you may learn new things that will also become stored in memory, but how will you be able to recall what you have learned when it comes to the exam? Whether or not you do well in a test, I hope you will have gained some insight into the importance of attention, perception and memory for daily living.

As we go about our everyday business, we move about the world, recognise people and objects, make plans and actions, and remember what we did yesterday and what we must do today. The environment provides a rich source of sights, sounds and smells, and we perceive it all around us. We attend to parts that interest us, look around it, make actions in it and upon it. We can remember what we did and what we heard and who we saw some time later. In this complex environment we need to know who we are, where we are, what is around us and where things are in relation to each other and to us. We need to decide whether what we detect is important, and how we should respond to it. All these things seem so familiar, simple and effortless it would be easy to think there is little to explain—we just 'do' them. However, the way we are able to encode, interpret and respond to the complexity of stimuli around us does need explanation. This is an exciting and challenging task, and it is at the heart of the questions asked by cognitive psychology.

Let us take an apparently simple example. You step out into the garden on a sunny morning. You experience a world in which the flowers and shrubs are brightly coloured and the sun is warm on your back. There is the sound of birds singing; the wind rustles the leaves on the trees and brushes your hair against your face. The hum of traffic buzzes in the background. As you stand there, you catch the smell of last night's barbecue. You laugh again as the joke that your friend told you comes into your mind, and you try to remember the name of the person they brought with them, but fail. This shows that as well as sensing the external world via the sensory systems, this sensory information may also trigger internal events, or stored memories. All around there are sources of sensation, which are perceived, attended to and transformed by complex processing sequences to construct your total experience of the garden scene and all its associated memories. Somehow, the external physical world has been translated into what you are experiencing. The brain has produced an internal, mental representation of the physical world that enables you to see, hear, smell and feel it and remember events related to it.

Apart from being able to experience the world, we also act on the information it provides. If the mobile phone in your pocket rings, you automatically reach into your pocket and press the buttons necessary to answer it. As you talk, you walk around, avoiding obstacles. An insect lands on your face and you immediately make a rapid movement to brush it away. How do you know where to place each step, reach, what to press or where to brush your face? How much of this do you do without thinking? These are all questions addressed by cognitive psychology.

Curiously, if you *really* step out into the garden and do what I have just described, the experience you have is that the world really *is* 'out there'. It is not experienced as being inside your head, but as displayed around you. You can walk around in it, point to parts of it and touch other parts. In this example, I expect you will have imagined the experience. When you imagine something, knowledge is retrieved about previous experiences stored in long-term memory to construct what it would be like if you really were to do it. This construction is held in conscious memory while you think about it, or attend to it. However, when you are imagining the garden scene there really is nothing 'out there', so the image must be in your mind. Of course, in reality, the image of the scene is only in your mind in both cases. Cognitive psychologists are interested in discovering the processes that allow us to perceive and attend to the world around us as well as explaining how what we have learnt is used in making sense of what we find there.

The problem

Attention, perception and memory are central topics in cognitive psychology; if you look in any textbook on cognitive psychology you will usually find a separate chapter on each of them, together with chapters on other aspects of cognitive psychology. These chapters are usually subdivided into smaller sections, each looking at component processes and theories of different aspects of attention, perception and memory. This approach is taken to aid clarity of explanation, but in so doing, can give the impression that individual aspects of cognition can be understood in isolation from each other. However, it is always important to remember that to properly understand the role of any single aspect of cognition we must appreciate how that role is dependent upon and interacts with other aspects.

In this book I shall attempt to demonstrate that although we can consider attention, perception and memory as identifiable components of the human cognitive system, for a complete understanding of any of them it is necessary to appreciate the way they interact and depend on each other. I shall have to divide what is explained into chapters, but will try all the time to relate one to another, and demonstrate the interrelationships with everyday examples. We all know, at a subjective level, that unless we pay attention to something we neither perceive it nor remember it. 'Pay attention to what I am saying or you will not be able to remember it later!' 'I am sorry, I was not paying attention and did not see what you were doing.' These examples show what we all know; that attention leads to better perception and memory. However, these words do not explain anything. They are simply labels that represent what we do; they do not explain what is actually involved when we attend, perceive or remember. The challenge for cognitive psychologists is to specify fully and explain all the processes involved.

Attention, perception and memory

Although not independent, attention, perception and memory can be identified as different cognitive activities that are involved in identifiable aspects of cognitive behaviour. In the chapters that follow we go into the details of experiments, studies of patients and evidence from cognitive neuroscience that have refined our understanding of these fundamental concepts. Here I shall attempt to characterise what is meant by each term so that we can refer to them as we go along.

Attention

There are many varieties of attention, but in most cases it is involved in the selection of a subset of information for further processing by another part of the information processing system. Selection from a subset of the sensory input or sense data may be required for perceptual processing; we can call this 'attention for perception', for example, looking at something to see what it is. Alternatively, selection of one or another form of response may be required; we can call this 'attention for action', for example, do you want to take the call on your mobile? You will press different buttons depending on your decision.

Attentional selection is deemed necessary because the rest of the processing system cannot process all stimulus inputs or all response outputs simultaneously. Both these varieties of attention give it the role of an active agent that does something, i.e., selects. Alternatively, attention is described as a pool, or pools, of processing *resources* that can be allocated to perform cognitive tasks. The attentional resources can be allocated to a single task, and may have to be increased as the task becomes more demanding, or the resources can be divided between tasks according to individual task demands. For example, if the call you are taking is very important you may stop walking to devote all your attention to it. Here again, attention is an active agent; this time it does the information processing, rather than select information for processing elsewhere. When we need to maintain attention over a period of time to, for example, detect an intermittent signal appearing at a particular location, this involves sustained attention and vigilance. For example, you may have been intending to listen in case the phone indoors rings, but after a while in the garden you forget you should be monitoring for a distant sound. If we become tired or bored, maintaining this kind of task can be difficult. Attention may wander; we need to be able to keep our attention on the task at hand. The control of attention, either to determine what is to be selected or how to divide resources or maintain vigilance, also involves attention; in this case, executive attention is involved in the supervision of selectivity or resource allocation.

A rather different view of attention is that, rather than an active agent, it is the outcome of processing. Rather than a cause, it is an effect. This is related to the subjective experience of what is being attended as the focus of conscious experience. In this case, attention is not an active processing agent but simply an outcome of processing that allows us to 'know' what we are doing; we 'see' the object of attention. In one influential theory of attention, focal attention is used to bind visual features together into objects.

The relation between conscious experience and attention brings us to the distinction between processes that do or do not require attention. Most of the processing in the brain is not available to conscious inspection; it is unconscious and proceeds automatically, without requiring any attentional processes. Processes that require attention in some form or other are called controlled processes, while those that do not are called automatic processes. Even when we are attending consciously on a task, attention can be *captured* automatically by a sudden change in the environment. In this case the control of attention is dictated by unconscious processes.

Perception

The most general meaning of the term perception is sensory processing. The sense organs transduce physical energy from the outside world, which is encoded and delivered to the brain via sensory neurons for interpretation by the perceptual system. For example, the pattern of light on the retina is encoded by rods and cones; this data is transmitted through the pathways that deal with visual input and distributed to the cortical areas of the brain that are specialised for representing edges, colour, shape, location, movement, etc. Perceptual analysis is refined as it moves through the visual pathways. This information can be used to judge distance, specify the spatial layout of a scene, identify faces and objects, or guide eye movements or reaching. Most early stages of perceptual processing are automatic and unconscious. We prevent ourselves from knowing the colour of an object or the movement of a car as it goes past us. A more specific definition of perception refers to this conscious, or phenomenal, experience of seeing, hearing, touching, etc. We do not perceive a fragmented pattern of light, shade and edges, we 'see' a face or 'hear' a voice. In fact we 'see' a girl in a red car, going fast, in the distance. This is the perceptual experience that is the final output of perceptual processing.

Although the perceptual systems encode the environment around us, attention may be necessary for binding together the individual perceptual properties of an object such as its colour, shape and location, and for selecting aspects of the environment for perceptual processes to act on. For us to identify the information that represents the objects formed from perceptual data by attentional processing, that representation must be able to contact stored knowledge in the memory system.

Memory

The simple definition of memory is a store of information. It is a result of learning. However, psychologists have been able to distinguish many varieties of memory, with different capacities, that endure for different periods of time and store different kinds of knowledge information using different representations. Furthermore, some memories can be recalled into consciousness while other memories store knowledge that can only demonstrated by the performance of actions. In addition to the storage components of memory, psychologists must also identify and be able to explain all the operations involved in encoding information into memory and retrieving information from memory as and when it is required.

The duration of memory gives us one way of partitioning it. Very brief duration sensory memories, with high capacity and fast decay, act as buffers from which information selected by attentional processes can be encoded into a more durable form. Examples of these are iconic memory for visual information and echoic memory for auditory information. It is iconic memory that allows you to see the patterns made by sparklers on firework night. Each spark is very short-lived, but iconic memory holds the information long enough for it to be related to the movement of all the other sparks. Then there is short-term or working memory, which holds information arriving from perceptual processing and retrieved from longer-term memory stores while we perform ongoing tasks such as mental arithmetic or problem solving. This memory contains what we are currently thinking about, is limited in processing capacity, and remains active in consciousness as long as it is attended. We can appreciate the limitation by trying to multiply two large numbers, say 142×317, in our head. Most of our short-term memory is immediately used up in remembering the question. Once we try to do the multiplication and have to also remember the products, the capacity of memory is overloaded and we probably lose the very numbers we were trying to multiply! There appear to be separate short-term stores for visuospatial, verbal and auditory information. Apart from the storage components of working memory there is also an executive control system that can move information between stores; for example, naming the letter 'R' requires us to recognise it visually, but produce a spoken response. The central executive is also important in maintaining order and is involved in planning and decision making, so would be involved in keeping track of numbers used in a mental arithmetic problem.

The most durable long-term memory stores are the repository for all other stored knowledge. A major distinction is between semantic memory for facts, and episodic memory for personal experiences. Both semantic and episodic memory stores are declarative, which means we are able to tell someone else their contents. So, if I ask you 'Where is Paris?' you can retrieve the fact that it is in France, and may also know that it is the capital city. If you then go on tell me what the view was like from the top of the Eiffel tower when you went up it last summer, you are then retrieving and telling me about something from your episodic memory. Autobiographical memory is related to episodic memory and provides us with self-identity and our life history.

Other memories are not declarative—you are unable to explain them in words but can demonstrate them by actions. These memories are stored in procedural memory and specify how to do something. Although you know how to ride a bicycle you cannot explain to another person how you do it. It might be possible to describe some of the actions, such as 'get hold of the handlebars, put one foot on the pedal and scoot along until you are going fast enough to get on . . .' etc., but these instructions do not convey the knowledge necessary for successful cycling. Anyone may be able to explain how to ride a bicycle, but it would only be possible to find out if they really did 'know' how to do it by asking them to demonstrate this skill.

Another distinction between memory types, similar to the procedural/declarative distinction, is the difference between implicit and explicit memory. Again, people can learn and demonstrate knowledge implicitly, but without knowing they have that knowledge.

Another important issue in memory theory is the question of whether memory is better thought of as different stores or different processes. The argument here is that, depending on the kind of processing engaged in during learning, a different kind of memory will result. There certainly are many different processes involved in learning and memory, but the process account of memory has been difficult to prove. What is definitely true is that unless a stimulus is consciously perceived and attended to, it does not leave a memory trace that can be explicitly retrieved. However, there is evidence that stimuli that have not been attended and cannot be consciously recalled are able to affect subsequent processing. This is evident in studies of subliminal perception and in patients with amnesia, who show preserved learning from experiences they cannot recall.

The philosopher Kant (1724–1804) argued that the only things about which we can have knowledge are 'phenomena', and the physical world of real objects can only be known indirectly. MacPhail (1998) points out that as we do not perceive the external world directly, then 'in order to know what is "out there" we need to understand the nature of the transformations wrought upon it by our minds. And that is a psychological issue' (p. 63). The questions that modern psychologists attempt to answer have been around for thousands of years and have been debated by philosophers, but philosophers are not scientists.

Psychology, however, can be considered 'the science of mental life' (James, 1890), and as Miller (1962) points out, the key words are 'science' and 'mental'. In the example of stepping into the garden, the mental experience is evident, but to explain how this experience is arrived at is a question requiring scientific explanation. Before psychologists can begin their scientific study they must try to define aspects of mental life into smaller, manageable and potentially answerable questions, and to develop methods that allow them to measure and quantify components of 'mental life'. As psychology has evolved the questions asked and the methods used have changed, as we shall see.

Chapter 2

So what must be explained, and how can we find the answer?

Introduction

WHEN PSYCHOLOGY WAS FIRST FOUNDED, conscious experience was its central, most important area of enquiry. Wundt (1873) said that one of the principal aims for psychology was to investigate consciousness, which he saw as standing between the internal and the external world. Some of Wundt's other aims were to investigate the physiological conditions of conscious events and to try and understand human existence. For Wundt, and his student Titchener, psychology was the scientific study of immediate experience, and therefore consciousness, which was the 'totality of experience at a given moment'; just like your experience when you stepped (or imagined stepping) into the garden. Other early psychologists, including William James and Sigmund Freud, also saw the study of consciousness as the heart of what research in psychology should be concerned with.

In the early days of psychology, the preferred method for discovering the basic elements of conscious experience was *introspection*. Introspection involves the subjective examination of mental contents and introspectors had to reduce their experience into the most basic elements and carefully avoid what Titchener called the 'stimulus error', which was the imposition of meaning or interpretation onto the stimulus. Of course, this is what we normally do. We 'see' a tree, not a pattern of colours, shapes and intensities distributed in time and space. Titchener's introspection attempted to avoid any interpretations based on learned categories or concepts that are usually the basis for our everyday interpretation of the world. He was trying to separate perception from attention and memory. However, it will become evident that the interaction between sensory data and stored knowledge is an essential process in cognitive psychology. Today the distinction between *bottom-up* sensory-driven processing and *top-down*, knowledge-driven processing is involved in many cognitive explanations, and is central to understanding the relationships between attention perception and memory.

Early psychologists liked the idea of being able to explain consciousness in terms of fundamental neural mechanisms such as excitation and inhibition, but the danger they saw was that if consciousness could be reduced to neural processes, then psychology would be neurology and have no place of its own in science—so they rejected this way of accounting for consciousness. Today, new computational modelling techniques are able to explain some psychological processes in terms of excitation and inhibition, that is, similar to neural processes. These *connectionist* or *parallel distributed processing* accounts of cognition will be discussed later, and are believed to be powerful because they are based on similar principles to those on which neurons in the brain operate.

In the early to mid 20th century, psychology became the study of 'behaviour', conscious experience was believed to be an impossible area of study, and introspection was disregarded as an unreliable source of data. The Behaviourists, as they were called, for example Watson (1916) and Skinner (1938), took the view that only observable behaviour should be used as data. They believed that only stimulus inputs and response outputs could be objectively observed, and that it was not scientific to talk about unobservable, hypothetical stages such as attention, perception or memory, in the way we do now. The study of internal mental processes and consciousness was unscientific as it could not be objectively measured. However, it became increasing clear that not all behaviour could be explained in terms of stimulus and response, in particular how the same stimulus could give rise to different behaviours, or how humans could control complex situations. A new approach was needed, and in the mid 1950s the approach we now call cognitive psychology began to dominate research into psychology as it allowed psychologists to study scientifically the hidden processes that operate between a stimulus and a response. In the following sections, the cognitive approach and its development will be explained. More recently, psychologists have become increasingly interested in consciousness again and are beginning to give accounts of cognition and consciousness that are entirely based on neurological events. This view is not a threat to psychology today and psychologists work together with neurologists, neuroscientists, radiographers, computer scientists, cognitive neuropsychologists and others in a combined effort to understand the brain and how it gives rise to our astonishing capabilities, including conscious experience. Marcel (1988) says, 'Psychology without consciousness, without phenomenal experience or the personal level, may be biology or cybernetic, but it is not psychology' (p. 121).

Cognitive psychology and the cognitive approach

In the preceding paragraphs I have used the term cognitive psychology without defining what it means, and as yet have not attempted to define attention, perception or memory. First let us consider what we mean by cognition and cognitive psychology, and then turn to the individual terms. Basically, cognition means knowing about something; it is the act of knowing. Cognitive psychology, therefore, is the branch of psychology that is concerned with understanding how it is we come to know about things, how we are able to make sense of the world around us and interact with it in a meaningful way. It is hard to improve on the definition given by one of the most important contributors to the development of cognitive psychology, Ulric Neisser. In his book *Cognitive Psychology*, Neisser (1967, p. 4) explained that 'cognition refers to all the processes by which the sensory input is transformed, reduced, elaborated, stored, recovered and used. It is concerned with these processes even when they operate in the absence of relevant stimulation, as in images and hallucinations. Such terms as sensation, perception retention recall, problem solving and thinking, among many others, refer to hypothetical stages or aspects of cognition'. We can include attention amongst the other processes not specifically mentioned. Neisser goes on to say that 'Given such a sweeping definition, it is apparent that cognition is involved in everything a human being might possibly do; that every psychological phenomenon is a cognitive phenomenon'.

Human information processing

In the preceding quotations Neisser refers to *hypothetical stages*; these are stages of information processing that are hypothesised to be necessary to perform a cognitive task, and arise from the distinctive approach used by cognitive psychologists in trying to understand the hidden workings of the mind. Early psychologists such as Wundt and James had studied cognitive psychology inasmuch as they were concerned with the conscious experience of what was known to the person introspecting, but they were not able to study processes that took place at unconscious levels.

In 1958 Broadbent proposed a new conception of human performance in terms of information processing, and together with the work of others at the time, this view led to what we can call the birth of cognitive psychology. This new conception of the mind allowed early cognitive psychologists to begin to consider the unobservable, hypothetical, internal processes that were believed to underlie all cognition.

Varieties of processing

Although everything we do can be considered cognitive, not all cognitive processes are the same. When considering how to partition human information processing into hypothetical stages, there are processes that can be considered to involve selecting a particular location of the environment or aspect of the sense data for further processing; we could think of these as involving attentional processes. Other processes may be concerned with encoding information at the attended location and could be considered perceptual processing. Then again, recognising what the attentional and perceptual processes produce would involve matching the incoming data to representations of knowledge stored in memory. As explained here, these different processes appear to be distinct operations, and would seem to proceed in a sequence of stages; attend, perceive, recognise. Because cognitive psychologists take the view that the human information processing system is similar to any system that processes information, they have adopted the computer

15

metaphor for attempting to understand and model cognition. So, in addition to the subject matter of cognitive psychology, it also adopts a distinctive approach in trying to understand how we operate. The human being is thought of as an active processor of information. This information may arrive as sense data, or be generated internally from stored knowledge. Information is processed in different ways by different information processing systems to enable us to, for example, attend, perceive or remember. Some information is consciously manipulated, as for example in mental arithmetic. Other processing takes place outside conscious awareness; for example, when you say 'hello' to a friend you recognise, you are only aware *that* you recognise them, not *how* your brain enabled you to recognise them. Similarly, when you produce the word 'hello', you cannot explain how you found the word, or how you moved your vocal apparatus to pronounce it.

The computer metaphor

Following the acceptance that information processing underlies cognition, the computer is now widely adopted as the most promising metaphor for modelling and understanding human cognition, and computer technology has developed, so the sophistication and usefulness of the metaphor has increased. Initially computers were slow, limited-capacity, serial devices, not very similar to the human brain. Modern computers, however, are fast and parallel with enormous computational power, much more like our own computer, the brain. One advantage of the computer metaphor is that it has suggested, by analogy, a number of hypotheses about human information processing. When designing a computational device it is better to have one component that analyses the input, one that stores information in a memory buffer, another that executes particular subroutines depending on the input, a memory for previously entered information and so forth. However, despite advances in computer technology, we are different from most computers. We are animate, rather than inanimate beings, we can move around our environment and act upon it, we can catch a ball and throw it back; not only do we respond to environmental stimuli, we can also modify them.

In writing computer programs, or attempting to analyse the steps and stages involved in a cognitive task, flowcharts are often produced that specify the operations necessary to achieve a particular goal. The flowchart is a sequence of interconnected boxes and arrows, and each box on the chart represents a component process or stage of the overall task that must be completed before the next stage can be moved to. In Broadbent's 1958 model (see Figure 2.1) you can see these hypothetical stages quite clearly.

Although this model is most frequently described as a model of attention, it also includes perception and memory. One advantage of a flowchart is that its boxes specify what needs to be computed in order for a particular behaviour to be achieved. However, questions such as what moves along the arrows that connect the boxes and how this takes place must not be ignored. Another problem is that there is a danger of forgetting the importance of the interaction between stages of processing. Whilst Broadbent's model includes attention, perception and memory in the same model, the drive to understand the workings of each component part has led to psychologists specialising in the study of attention, perception or memory. This

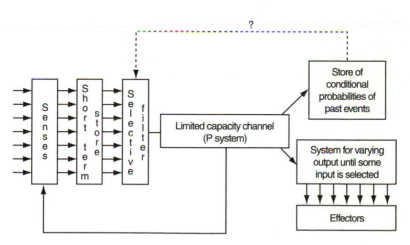

FIGURE 2.1 Broadbent's (1958) model of human information process-ing. From Broadbent (1970).

specialisation is necessary because it is impossible to experiment on all aspects of the processing system at the same time, and within each area research has focused down even further to answer more specific questions. However, it is important to remember that the fully functioning brain will be attending, perceiving and remembering all at once, with each component contributing to 'mental life'. Let us consider the important interaction between attention, perception and memory.

Bottom-up and top-down processing

Broadbent (1958) initially proposed that most cognitive processing proceeds in a staged sequence. On the presentation of a stimulus, perceptual processes act on the input, then attentional processes transfer some of the perceptual information to a short-term, transitory memory store, then if the material is *rehearsed*, it could be translated into a more permanent long-term memory. A sequence of processing stages that proceeds from sense data to further stages is called *bottom-up*; however, our expectations of what the sense data contains can influence the way we interpret it *top-down*. Bottom-up processing is said to be stimulus-driven because it is directly affected by the stimulus input. On the other hand, top-down processing is said to be conceptually driven as it is affected by existing knowledge derived from past experience. An example of top-down processing would be listening to a conversation in a noisy room. Although the sound stimulus is degraded and incomplete, our knowledge of language allows us to complete what we fail to hear, top-down, and follow the conversation quite easily. Most cognition involves this interaction between stimuli and stored knowledge, and demonstrates that the hypothetical stages of attention, perception and memory must be interactive during cognitive activities.

Experimental psychology

Experiments are carried out to test hypotheses derived from a theory. In a typical experiment the psychologist will design a task that is intended to manipulate a variable affecting one hypothetical stage of processing and will then measure response time or accuracy to determine the effect of that variable on performance. For example, the ability of the participant to select information from a visual display may be manipulated by providing a cue as to where in the visual field the target will arrive. Posner (1978) found that a brief light flashed at the location where a target subsequently appears will speed the detection of a target, but if the cue is in the wrong location the participant cannot ignore the flash and is therefore slower to respond to the target. This experiment on visual orienting of attention will be discussed in detail when we look at visual attention. Another example, in the area of memory, is that the number of items that can be remembered in the short term is limited to the number of 'chunks' rather than the absolute amount of information. (Miller, 1956). Although measuring cognitive performance in controlled laboratory conditions is not the same as observing cognitive performance in the uncontrolled natural environment, it can be argued that the control that experiments impose has allowed the identification of many fundamental cognitive processes. Experimental psychologists have developed many of the basic paradigms that examine cognitive processes at the behavioural level. Throughout this book we shall see that the experimental paradigms, the theories they were designed to test and the results they have discovered have been applied by other psychologists using other methods of investigation. These other methods, discussed in later sections, include cognitive neuropsychology, computational modelling, and cognitive neuroscience. Different methods approach the problem of cognitive psychology at different levels of analysis and explanation.

Levels of explanation

Marr (1982) believed that theories need to be defined at different levels of analysis to provide a complete and overarching account of intelligent behaviour. He argued that there are three levels of explanation to be considered.

1   The implementational level, i.e., the 'hardware' that does the job.

2   The algorithmic level, i.e., the set of procedures or rules that need to be carried out by the hardware in order to achieve the required computations.

3   The computational level, i.e., what the system actually needs to compute in order to achieve the purpose for which is designed.

To make these levels clear, Marr used the analogy of a cash register in a supermarket. Over the years, cash registers have changed substantially. Initially they were entirely mechanical devices with series of ratchets that clocked up numbers and were worked by hand; later they became electronic, and now we have the laser bar code readers that derive the cost of each item! So, although at the hardware or implementational level these machines are different, at the computational level they do exactly the same thing, i.e., add up your shopping bill. The algorithm used by the machines may also be different, but not necessarily. Experimental cognitive psychology and cognitive neuropsychology are interested in the algorithmic and computational levels, while cognitive neuroscientists, physiologists and neuroanatomists are concerned with the hardware, or underlying brain and neural mechanisms. Increasingly these initially different disciplines are working together, along with computational modellers and philosophers to provide explanations of cognitive behaviour at all levels, and are informing each others' ideas in the way Marr suggested.

Modularity of mind

The sort of computer we are most familiar with, a PC, is made of components that work together to achieve a particular task such as word processing, playing games, surfing the net and so on. These different tasks run on the same computer, but require the use of different programs and components in different combinations at different times. Nevertheless, it is possible to specify what is required and when. Although we accept that all the parts are necessary, the designer can produce one part of the system in isolation, provided it is specified how that part interfaces with the others so that the output from one component can communicate with the remainder of the system. In this sense we can identify components of human information processing, but the psychologist must also specify the ways in which the outcome of processing in one system affects and is affected by the other systems.

One of the most important assumptions in psychology today is that the human brain is modular. This assumption stems from the very influential ideas of Marr (1976) and Fodor (1983). In a modular system, large and complicated computations are achieved by lots of 'modules'. These modules perform particular processing operations on particular domain-specific kinds of information. Together they form the whole system, but each module acts as an independent processor for its own particular purpose. Fodor (1983) argues that modules are innately specified, hard-wired and autonomous, in that the functioning of the module is not under conscious control. In a modular system the failure of one module does not prevent the remaining modules from working. Such a system would seem advisable in terms of survival; we would be severely disadvantaged if damage to one small part of the brain resulted in all of the rest of the undamaged brain ceasing to work. Not only is a modular system a sensible design, but there is good evidence that when patients suffer local damage to particular brain regions, only certain computational functions are lost.

Cognitive neuropsychology

Not only is a modular system based on a good design principle, but evidence from neuropsychological patients who have suffered brain damage supports this assumption. Damage to one part of the brain may lead to the loss of one function, such as the ability to recognise faces, but leave the ability to read and recognise words intact. This dissociation between the processing of different stimuli supports the idea that one module is responsible for face processing while another is responsible for reading. However, it could simply be that reading is less difficult than recognising a face, so if another patient with different brain damage can be found who shows the reverse pattern of behaviour, i.e., who can read but not recognise faces, then a double dissociation is found. This is strong evidence for the independence of the processes underlying reading and face recognition. Studies of patients suggest that there is a meaningful relationship between the location of brain damage and the function that is lost. Work by cognitive neuropsychologists on people who have lost particular abilities can help to clarify models and theories of normal cognitive functioning. Any model or theory must be able not only to account for normal behaviour, but also to explain what has gone wrong for the patient. In the flowchart approach to modelling cognition, it is often the case that the patient appears to have lost the processing capability of one box of the flowchart, or that the information is not able to flow from one stage to another—as if an arrow has been lost. Throughout this book we shall meet a number of examples where neuropsychological evidence has furthered our understanding of normal cognitive processing. *Cognitive neuropsychology* provides evidence that the brain appears to break down as if it were a modular system.

Computational modelling

Since the beginning of cognitive psychology as a distinct approach to psychology, researchers have tested their ideas and models of human behaviour using computational modelling. We shall meet a variety of these models in different chapters. Some of the earliest models were semantic networks, such as that of Collins and Quillian (1969), which were devised to help understand how knowledge is represented and can be retrieved from *semantic memory*. Another kind of model is a *production system*, and in Chapter 9 we shall consider Anderson's ACT*, with respect to learning skills. In production systems, rules for the operation of a procedure are represented as IF–THEN rules, so IF a set of conditions are present in working memory, THEN the rule is applied. These systems are also useful for modelling logical cognitive processes such as reasoning and problem solving, but we shall not consider these cognitive processes here. The most recent computational techniques use *connectionist* networks, or *parallel distributed processing* models. The power of these models is that rather than having to be explicitly programmed, the networks can learn and to some extent program themselves. Another property of connectionist models is that they are composed of elementary units or nodes that are highly interconnected and have excitatory and inhibitory connections between them. In this sense they are more like the brain than previous models. The complexity of connectionist models is outside the scope of this book, but we shall meet some early versions of this type in their application to pattern recognition and knowledge representation.

Cognitive neuroscience

Over the past few years technological developments have allowed psychologists to actually 'see' the working human brain in action. Techniques such as functional magnetic resonance imaging (fMRI), positron emission tomography (PET), magneto-encephalography (MEG) and event-related potentials (ERPs) can be used to discover important information about the brain's activity during cognitive tasks. It has become possible to see where and when particular brain areas become active during task performance. This information, as suggested by Marr when he discussed levels of explanation, has contributed to and constrained theory-building in cognitive psychology. With the techniques of *cognitive neuroscience*, psychologists do not have to rely on the breakdown of ability following brain damage in neuropsychological patients, but can observe the workings of the intact brain.

Evidence shows that the human brain is made up of millions of neurons that intercommunicate with each other via numerous connections, tracts and pathways that feed backward and forward through the brain to form a highly interconnected, complex system. The brain receives information from the sense organs and stores a vast amount of knowledge gained from past experience. By combining selected data from the outside world with stored knowledge, the component parts of the brain work together to produce coherent and purposeful behaviour. So, although we may think of attention, perception and memory as being independent in terms of the chapters in a book, in reality they cannot be entirely independent because of the nature of the human brain.

Cognitive neuroscience is concerned with bringing together a deeper understanding of psychology using modern techniques of brain imaging, which allow us to see the brain at work; using data from neuropsychological patients who have selectively lost abilities they once had; modelling psychological processes using computers; and traditional experimental psychology. A good overview of the approaches to cognitive psychology can be found in Eysenck and Keane (2000), and an introduction to cortical functions and brain imaging in Stirling (2000).

Summary

Early psychologists believed that introspecting on the contents of consciousness could provide evidence, but this method was rejected as too subjective and replaced by Behaviourism, which rejected the study of mind. The new approach of cognitive psychology provided a model of the human mind as an information processing system that could be considered to process information in a similar way to a computer. Within this approach it became possible to analyse the processing components that were necessary to perform cognitive tasks and to proposed hypothetical stages for experimental investigation. Early models and theories of human information processing incorporated perceptual, attentional and memory processes and appreciated their interaction. Theories can be defined at different levels of explanation, and advances in cognitive neuropsychology, cognitive neuroscience and computational modelling can aid understanding at different levels. Although the mind is generally considered to be modular, and although attention, perception and memory are different components of the cognitive system, they do not work in isolation; the cognitive tasks they perform are complementary and interactive.

Self-assessment questions (Solutions on p. 319)

1 What is introspection and what are its disadvantages?
2 What is the information processing approach and what are its advantages?
3 Distinguish between top-down and bottom-up processing.
4 Give two characteristics each for attention, perception and memory.

Further reading

Eysenck, M. and Keane, M. (2000) *Cognitve psychology: A student's handbook* (4th ed.). Hove, UK: Psychology Press. See Chapter 1 for an overview and more detail of the cognitive approach.

Gross, R. and McIlveen, R. (1999) *Perspectives in psychology*. London: Hodder and Stoughton. A useful introduction to the history of psychology.

Jarvis, M. (2000) *Theoretical approaches to psychology*. London: Routledge. A useful introduction to the history of psychology.

Chapter 3

Sensation

A starry night

Y OUR FRIEND IS LATE. You are watching TV while you wait, but are listening for the sound of someone coming up the path, or the slam of a car door. Now and again you think you hear her coming, but on looking out discover you were wrong. At last you are fairly sure you really do hear her, and go out; this time you are right, and your friend is outside. It is a clear frosty night, and you both look up to admire the stars. Although there are many bright stars, there seem to be more to the edges of the sky, but as you move your eyes to look directly at them they seem to disappear. Sometimes you think you see a faint star, but sometimes you are not sure if it really there or not. 'One of those stars is moving, it must be a satellite or a planet,' your friend says. You ask 'where?', and try to detect if one of the lights in the group pointed out is moving or not. 'Well, I can't see anything moving!', you say, but you friend is quite certain that she is not imagining it. Who is right, and how can we explain some of these examples?

The beginnings of psychological experience

So that we can interact effectively with objects that really exist and events that are detected in the world around us, it is essential that we know what is going on 'out there'. The physical world is represented in the brain, and we shall discuss representation in Chapter 12. The brain is safely packed away inside the protection of the skull and consequently is not directly in contact with the environment. Therefore information from the physical world has to be detected, encoded, stored and translated into a 'language' or neural code that the brain can understand. The process of informing the brain begins with stimulation of a sense organ by some physical or chemical energy. This energy is detected by the sense organs, which contain specialised sensory neurons that encode physical and chemical properties as neural impulses. By a series of relays and recoding these messages are sent to the brain. Having interpreted the input from the sensory systems, the brain must make that knowledge available to other parts of the brain for further encoding, recognition and interpretation and for making or planning responses. It is the interpretation of physical data by the senses that ultimately gives rise to the perception of sensations, which are the beginning of our psychological or 'conscious experience' of the environment. The chapters following this will examine the senses separately in more detail, but first we shall consider some of the methods that have been used to discover the relationship between physical energy and psychological experience. Some of the earliest work done under the auspices of 'psychology' concerned the search for basic units of sensation and conscious experience, and was at the heart of the questions asked by some of the first experimental psychologists working in the 19th century.

Detection and sensation

Going back in history, Johannes Muller (1838–1948) formulated one of the earliest principles of sensory coding. This principle of specific nerve energies states that sensory nerves can only transmit one specific type of sensation. Thus the optic nerves from the eyes can only transmit the sensation of light, the auditory nerves only the sensation of sound and so forth. If you are hit in the eye you may 'see stars'. In this case the sensory neurons have been stimulated by pressure, but as they project (or transmit their impulses) to the visual cortex of the brain, it is a visual experience that results. Although pressure may give rise to the sensation of seeing stars, the only stimulation of the visual system that provides reliable information about the world is light. The type of physical stimulus to which a sense organ normally responds is called the *adequate stimulus*. Human sense organs can detect a range of physical and chemical energies, but outside their range of response we have no sensation. For example, dogs and cats can hear high-frequency sounds to which we are deaf. Bees can detect colours in the ultraviolet area of the spectrum, but we can only see the colours of the rainbow, which we call the visible spectrum. This limitation of our sensory apparatus means that anything in the physical world that cannot be detected by our sense organs is 'not there' for us. We may be able to detect and measure these physical properties of the world using mechanical or electronic instruments, for example by using an infrared camera to see in the dark, but as far as our day-to-day experiences are concerned, we are not conscious of them. For detailed descriptions of the human nervous system and sensory organs, Carlson (1999) is an excellent source.

Measuring sensation — classical psychophysics

Many of the early experimental works in psychology were concerned with discovering basic mental elements of conscious experience, rather like searching for the basic elements in chemistry. Sensations were thought to be some of these most basic elements. In the late 19th century psychology was a fledgling science, very much concerned with gaining credibility by using accepted scientific methods. If psychologists could *measure* something that could be considered fundamental to the human mind, this would be a step forward toward the acceptance of psychology as proper science. This search for ways of measuring mental elements was most evident in the area of psychology we call psychophysics. The name sums up the intended parallel between psychology and physics (a 'real' science).

Classical psychophysics is the branch of psychology concerned with discovering the relationship between perceived or subjective magnitude and physical magnitude. However, whilst it is relatively simple to measure the brightness of a light using a light meter (your automatic camera does this for you when you take a photograph and adjusts the timing of the exposure accordingly), it is much more difficult to measure the subjective experience of brightness. The problem was, and still is for psychology today, how internal, private events of conscious experience can be measured objectively. Although a lot of this work was done a long time ago, many of the principles, methods and discoveries are still used, and we shall refer back to them several times.

How bright is the light?

Let us think about how you could find out how bright I think a light is. Well, the obvious way would simply be to ask me. I might reply that the light is very bright, or rather dim, or not as bright as the last light you asked me about. This method is not very useful, and relies entirely on subjective, loose descriptions of my experience of the light. The psychophysical techniques used by psychophysicists have been developed to restrict the responses the observer can make in describing their experience by forcing them to make simple discriminations. Classical psychophysics is the area of psychology within which the most precise and careful methods of measurement are used and it has allowed psychologists to produce mathematical formulae that relate mental and physical events fairly accurately.

Sensory scaling

If you have a piece of string you can measure it with a ruler. The string physically exists, and one of its physical properties is its length. It also has other physical properties such as width, mass and colour. As a physical object it can be seen by many independent people who will agree it to be a piece of string and who can all measure it using a ruler. A ruler has equally spaced marks on one of its edges that are labelled from zero to, say, 15 centimetres. On the other edge the spacings of the marks might be different, and labelled from zero to 6 inches. Either way, whichever scale is used there is an objective method of verifying the answer to the question 'How long is the piece of string?'.

If you want to discover which of two pieces of string is the longest, you could simply compare them. This would allow you to say that one piece is longer than the other piece. However, if you wanted to know how much longer one was than the other you would reach for the ruler again. The ruler has a dimension scale along its edge, which is evenly divided into units such that two centimetres are twice as long as one centimetre and ten centimetres are ten times as long as one centimetre. You could then discover the difference in length between the two pieces of string in terms of units on the scale. This kind of scale is called a ratio scale. Ratio scales for physical dimensions such as length or weight have a zero point—the start of the ruler, for example, says 0. Classical psychophysicists wanted to be able to produce a scale with which to measure sensory properties such as brightness, heaviness or loudness. To do this they needed measurements to allow precise description of people's sensations. Sensory qualities differ quantitatively—a light may be bright or very bright—and qualitatively—a light may be green or blue. Normally we describe these sensory properties on a nominal scale, where we assign names to properties. To be able to measure how much brighter one light appears to the observer in comparison to another light, some sort of sensory scale is necessary. As we have seen, a good scale like the ruler has a zero point and equally spaced intervals.

Like the physical properties of a piece of string, physical properties of light, sound, heat, etc. can be measured using suitable instruments of physics. Sensations of brightness, loudness and warmth cannot be measured so easily. It would be tempting to imagine that if a light were physically twice as intense, it would be sensed subjectively as twice as bright. However, we know this is not the case, because early psychologists devised ways of measuring sensation. Of course, measuring very simple sensations such as the minimum change in light intensity you can detect does not seem close to helping us understand how you interpreted the visual scene that confronted you in the garden, but such work was very important in helping psychologists understand the relationship between the physical and psychological scales.

The need to produce a scale for measuring subjective magnitudes led to the development of the concept of thresholds, which are very important in psychophysics. If there is a point at which the level of energy in the physical stimulus produces conscious experience, but below which the observer is unable to report any subjective experience of it, this point could be called the beginning of perceptual experience, or the absolute threshold. For example, a light may be 'on' in terms of physics, but the intensity too low for the photodetectors in the retina to respond. Increasing the physical intensity by just a very small amount may enable a photoreceptor to 'fire' and a subjective experience of a dim light to be triggered. Therefore, the *absolute threshold* can be considered the point at which no perception becomes perception; it is the beginning of our psychological experience of the physical world.

Similarly, if the observer is asked to try to detect a difference between two stimuli, for example the point at which a change in the physical stimulus produces a change in subjective experience, this is a *difference threshold*, or a *just-noticeable difference*. Again, to use light as an example, consider adjusting a dimmer switch. You may have to turn the knob for some distance before you notice a change in the brightness of the light, so although the physical electrical power has increased, your sensation of brightness does not change in the same proportion. Only after you have increased the power by a certain amount will you notice a difference. You will be familiar with similar effects when adjusting the loudness of a music system. Early classical psychophysicists realised that if they could measure these thresholds, the increments in subjective experience might be able to be used as intervals along the scale of psychophysical measurement.

Can you see the light? Finding the beginning of the scale

The beginning, or zero point, on a sensory scale is the absolute threshold. In theory, below this point there is no conscious experience of stimulation and hence no awareness of the event, while above the absolute threshold the stimulus is always experienced. Sometimes, thresholds are called 'limen'. Thus events that are below threshold are called subliminal and events above threshold are called supraliminal. Psychologists now know that despite the inability of an observer to report anything about a stimulus event, there is some evidence for processing below the level of conscious awareness, or subliminal perception.

If it is the case that above the absolute threshold a stimulus is always detected and below the absolute threshold the stimulus is never detected, there should be a step function change in the observer's behaviour, as shown in Figure 3.1.

How could you design an experiment to test this? You might very well come up with the same ideas as the early psychophysicists such as

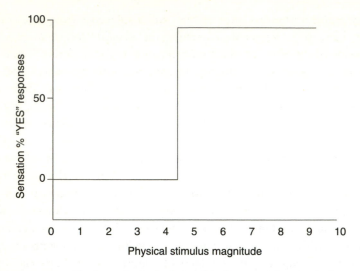

FIGURE 3.1 The hypothetical relationship between the physical magnitude of a stimulus and sensation that would be expected if a single threshold was always applied.

Weber, Fechner and Helmholtz. Suppose you set the intensity of a tone at a level below that at which you can hear it. Gradually you turn up the volume until the tone can be heard. Next you turn the volume down again until you can no longer hear the tone. If you record the intensity, or volume, at each of the levels, that point of transition from not hearing to hearing, or hearing to not hearing, is your 'absolute threshold' for sound intensity. You could do the same with a light source, again increasing or decreasing the intensity of the physical stimulus until you could or could not see it. Well, that all seems rather easy, and of course things are never that straightforward. Unfortunately, the data you generate in trying to determine absolute threshold does not give a step function. If it did, you would only need to do the experiment once. Like all good psychologists, you would do the experiment many times to be sure of your accuracy. What you would find is actually a shallow S-shaped curve, as shown in Figure 3.2. This function, relating stimulus intensity to subjective experience, is curved because there are many other variables at work that may

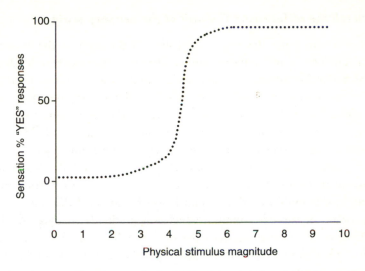

FIGURE 3.2 The observed relationship between the physical magnitude of a stimulus and sensation. The shape of the curve reveals that there is no single threshold, rather an increase in the likelihood of reporting a sensation as physical magnitude is increased. The 50% point is taken as the absolute threshold.

influence your judgement. For example, if you are looking for a dim light, it is detected best in peripheral vision, and your eyes will become more sensitive to light as they adapt to the darkness over a period of time. You may become fatigued or lose confidence in your judgement. When stimulus energy is very low, there may be fluctuations in the number of photons actually produced in a given pulse of light, or there could be slight variations in the amplifier producing a sound stimulus. Thus both the stimulus and you yourself may be changing slightly all the time. If you were to do the experiment on a friend, he may not wish to make errors and so wait until he is absolutely certain until he says he has seen or heard the stimulus. On the other hand, he may want to make sure he does not miss any stimuli at all and guess when he is not really sure. Depending on the criterion people set themselves, they will perform differently. Because of all these uncertainties in the data obtained in absolute threshold experiments, psychophysicists have adopted the 50% point on the curve as defining the absolute threshold.

Can you tell the difference? The unit of the sensory scale

Once a zero point has been established as the start of the sensory scale, we need a unit of measurement. Here the difference threshold, or just noticeable difference (jnd), can be used. Once you have initially detected a tone or a light, how much louder or brighter does the stimulus have to be before you can notice a difference? Using a similar experiment to the one used for determining absolute thresholds, you could continue to increase the stimulus energy until you or your friend were able to detect a noticeable change. Weber (1834) did many experiments on difference thresholds. He presented his participants with two stimuli, one the standard, which remained the same, and the other the variable stimulus, which was gradually changed. As the difference of intensity between the two stimuli becomes smaller and smaller it becomes less and less likely that the participant will be able to notice a difference between the two intensities. A point will come at which no difference can be subjectively detected; this is the threshold for the jnd. Weber discovered that as the standard stimulus became stronger and stronger, the jnd became bigger and bigger. Imagine you had to detect a change in brightness and that only one light was on in the room. If you turned on one more light the difference would be easily noticed. However, if there were ten lights already on and one more was added, the difference would be much less noticeable. This, basically, is Weber's law, which states that the ratio of the difference threshold, or jnd, to the intensity of the strongest stimulus is a constant. Psychologists now know that this law is not reliable at very high or very low intensities, but over most values the law is a good one and holds for a number of senses.

Using the psychological scale

Fechner (1860) decided that as there is a zero point to sensation, the absolute threshold, this could be the start of the psychological scale, the start of the ruler. The units of measurement along the scale would then be the just noticeable difference, or differential threshold, which are subjectively equal changes in the magnitude of sensation. With the psychological magnitude scale, it was possible to begin to find out more about the way the physical intensity of a stimulus related to the perceived psychological magnitude. As a consequence of Weber's law, when physical intensity is plotted against the observer's perception, Fechner found that small changes at low intensities produce large changes in psychological magnitude, and at high intensities there are small changes in perceived magnitude. That is to say, if the light is turned up at an even rate, at the beginning, the light has to increase only a small amount before the observer notices a change. However, as the light becomes more intense, there needs to be a greater and greater change before a difference is noticed. Fechner's law states that the subjective magnitude of a sensation is the logarithm of the physical magnitude of the stimulus. However, Fechner's law has been shown to have flaws.

Measuring sensation directly

S. S. Stevens (1936, 1956, 1957) did a series of experiments in which participants were asked to estimate their subjective experience of a stimulus by assigning it a number. For example, he might show them a light and tell them it had a brightness of 10. Then he would present another light, and if it seemed to be twice as bright the participant should say 20, if it were half as bright they should say 5, and so forth. Using this method, Stevens found similar results as Fechner for lights, but for other kinds of stimuli the relationship did not hold. For example, as an electric shock increases, the participants notice only small changes in sensation at low intensities of shock, but as the shock increases in physical energy, only a small change results in a change of sensation. Thus, sensitivity to electric shock behaves in the reverse manner to sensitivity to light (see Figure 3.3).

Stevens proposed that subjective magnitude and stimulus intensity are related in different ways for each of the different sensory systems, although within each sense the relationship is constant. Stevens' power law states that the magnitude of sensation is equal to the physical intensity of the stimulus, raised to a power that depends on the sensation being measured.

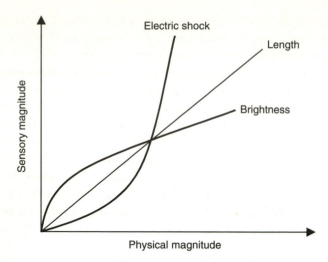

FIGURE 3.3 The relationship between physical and psychological magnitude. The sensation of electric shock increases far more rapidly than physical intensity, while the brightness sensation of a light increases more slowly than the physical change. Length is perceived to change in direct proportion to the physical stimulus.

Psychophysical methods

Generally, psychophysics experiments involve hundreds of trials on a small number of participants. They tend to be very demanding experiments as not only are there lots of trials, but also the discriminations are very subtle. You have to concentrate very hard and deciding what to report is very difficult. I remember volunteering to do a psychophysical experiment that required me to make same–different judgements on pairs of sounds. The experiment was carried out in a darkened room to avoid me being distracted by anything visual and there seemed to be hundreds and hundreds of trials. I never volunteered again!

Four main methods have been developed by psychophysicists in an attempt to gather precise information on sensory thresholds. These are the method of adjustment, the method of limits, the method of constant stimuli—all invented by Fechner in the mid-19th century—and the staircase method. We shall not go into any detail of these methods here, but anyone serious about carrying out experiments on thresholds would need to be aware of them as, depending on the method used, a different value of the threshold might be obtained. In the examples I talked about earlier I did not always know who was adjusting the stimuli, or whether the stimuli were adjusted continuously. The method of adjustment involves the participant adjusting the knob controlling the source of the stimulus, say a light source, until they detect a change. Sometimes the light is set at a high level and the participant adjusts it downwards and sometimes the light is set at a very low level and the participant adjusts it upwards. The experimenter records the settings of the knob each time, and resets it for the next trial. The method of limits is very similar to the method of adjustment, except in this case it is the experimenter who does the adjusting, and records the participant's response as to whether or not the light was seen. Also the adjustments are not continuous, and the participant is not monitoring for a change, but asked if they see anything now? and now? etc. In the method of constant stimuli the range of stimuli to be used are planned by the experimenter, but presented in random order, so that the participant will sometimes get a very weak stimulus, then a strong one, then a moderate one and so forth until all the stimulus values have been tested. The staircase method is similar to the methods of limits, but omits trials in the region where there is not expected to be any change in the participant's response.

The problems of subjective report

As we said earlier, there are all sorts of variables that influence a perceiver's verbal report of their subjective experience. One of the most important influences is confidence in their own judgement. When a participant is uncertain about whether or not they have detected a change, or indeed detected a signal at all, what do they do? Some will take a cautious approach and always wait until they are very sure; others will take more risks. Consequently, different people will appear to have different thresholds, and the same person may give different values for their own threshold on different occasions, depending on their mood. One way of controlling for variations in confidence is to use a different type of experiment. Consider the determination of the absolute threshold. In the example given earlier, the participant knew that a light was always presented and their task was to say if they could see it or not. Likewise, in the measurement of jnds, the participant knew the physical stimulus had been changed and their task was to say 'yes' if they could detect that change, and 'no' if they couldn't. Green and Swets (1966) added another dimension to the absolute threshold experiment by including trials on which there was no stimulus at all. Now the participant never knows whether there is a stimulus or not, and to be correct needs not only to detect presence, but also absence. This means there are now four possible outcomes on each trial; two correct and two incorrect. The correct responses are when a stimulus is present and the participant correctly detects it, and also when there is no stimulus and they correctly state it to be absent. The incorrect responses arise when there is a stimulus but the subject misses it and when no stimulus is presented but the participant says there is, giving a false alarm.

Let us imagine what it would be like to take part in such an experiment. There you are, sitting in complete darkness, gazing ahead and expecting a very dim light. You hear a tone, and know that in a moment a light will or will not be presented. We all know that when our eyes are closed, even in the dark, there are visual sensations. These result from random activity in the nervous system and provide a background of noise. So even when there is no light stimulus presented, but we are expecting one, we might confuse some of this random neural excitation with a very low intensity stimulus event. However, if a stimulus (signal) really is presented, it will add its activity to the background neural noise, and as the stimulus becomes more and more intense it will become more and more discriminable. Now, if we are to make a response, we need to set some sort of criterion for deciding if we really did see something or not. If we are too lax, we will make a lot of false alarms, and say there is a light when in fact it is only noise in the system. On the other hand, if we are too cautious we will miss a lot of lights that are really there. So, there will be a pay-off between being right and being wrong, which can be measured by the proportion of the kinds of errors we make. The attraction of what is called signal detection theory (SDT) is that by looking at the relationship between the number of correct detections (hits), correct rejections, false alarms and misses, it is possible to work out the criterion that a participant is using and how sensitive they are to the difference between just noise and noise plus the signal. Figure 3.4 shows how we can represent the distribution of activity in the nervous system that is due to neural noise alone when no signal is present, and the distribution of neural activity when a signal is added to the underlying activity.

In Figure 3.4, you can see that there is an overlap between distributions of noise alone and signal plus noise. The distribution of noise alone is to the left, which is towards the lower end of the activity range. When a signal is presented, the distribution of noise plus the signal produces more excitation and moves the distribution towards

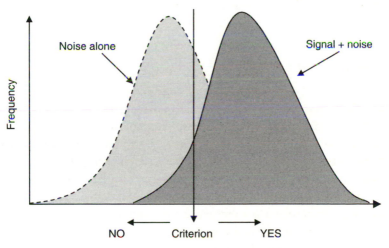

FIGURE 3.4 The overlapping distributions of noise alone, and signal plus noise shown as excitation of the nervous system. C represents the criterion chosen by the observer above which they consider they have detected a signal. Any signal below criterion will be missed, but the overlap of the distributions shows that with a criterion set at this point, there is noise that will be accepted as signal, leading to false alarms.

the higher end of the activity range. The difference between the mean of the two distributions is called *d prime*. If the participant sets a criterion shown by the line labelled C, then you can see that some of the real signals will be missed, because they fall below the activity level the participant had decided to accept. At the same time, some of the neural noise activity overlaps with the signal plus noise, and so there will be occasions when noise will be accepted as a real signal. A stricter criterion would result in fewer false alarms but more misses. A more lax criterion would mean more false alarms but fewer misses.

Once the false alarm and hit rates have been worked out for a participant, we can use tables of probability to work out how much the distributions overlap, and therefore d prime, or the difference between noise alone and the signal plus noise. This tells us how sensitive the participant really is to the presence of a signal, whatever criterion they have chosen for their decisions. As the signal becomes more and more intense the difference between noise alone and signal plus noise increases until there is no overlap at all and no judgement criterion is needed.

Is this really a simple task?

Let's step back for a moment and consider the complexity of this apparently simple task. We have said that sensation is the beginning of psychological experience, and have seen how we might be able to measure the relationships between physical properties of our environment and our experience of it. However, even when the task only requires us to detect the presence or absence of a light, a lot more is involved. What you are doing is really rather remarkable. Although the aim of the experiment is to measure a threshold, you have to be able to understand the experimenter's instructions. To do this you will have analysed the sound of language, known what the words mean, and translated them into a state of readiness to respond. Somehow your brain has got ready—become tuned to the task at hand—so that what you are 'tuned into' is looking for a dim light, rather than listening for a tone. Your attention is directed into the darkness in front of you. We shall discuss selective attention and attentional control in later chapters. Then you will have to decide on the criterion you are going to use to accept whether a light was there or not. The trials begin, and each time there is an opportunity to respond you have to translate your sensory experience of, say, having detected a light, into a verbal reply 'Yes' or 'No', or perhaps pressing one or other of two response buttons. To make this apparently trivial and effortless response, the information about whether or not there was a light needs to be coded and re-coded through pathways in the brain, into either speaking or moving your finger. A response is an action that requires planning and executing, and involves moving the muscles used for speech or pressing buttons. When the next trial starts you must still remember the instructions, forget the last trial and get ready for the next. This memory for what is to be done in future is called *prospective memory* (see Chapter 11). At the same time you must remain vigilant, and not miss a signal due to a lapse of attention. You must maintain your posture, fix your gaze and try not to think about other things, such as when it will be time for lunch. Altogether, although the experiments to measure the most basic elements of sensation are concerned with small changes, that fact that you can do the task at all is astonishing. It is the complexity of the rest of the participant's mental apparatus that has made sensory scaling difficult for psychophysicists. All these aspects of cognition are the subject of the rest of this book.

A troubling example

The philosopher John Locke (1690/1929) pointed out the problem that sensation is not as simple as we might first think. You see it all depends . . . If you have been playing snowballs with bare hands and come in to wash your hands, the water from the cold tap feels warm. Usually, the water from the cold tap feels cold. Locke gave the example of three bowls of water—one hot, one cold and one tepid. Put one hand in the hot water and the other in the cold water, and wait for a few minutes. Then put both hands into the tepid water. To the hand that was in the cold water, the tepid water feel hot; to the hand that was in the hot water, the tepid water feels cold. How can this be? You have two different sensations arising from the same stimulus. Is the tepid water cold or hot? How can we rely on our senses to tell us about the world 'out there' if, as in this case, they are giving us conflicting information? Locke used this example to make clear the difference between the real world and the subjective, experienced world—the difference between sensation and perception. In fact it is known that there is a process called adaptation, which sense organs undergo when stimulated; for example, the smell of onions cooking will be powerful to someone just entering the house, but if you have been doing the cooking, then you do not smell onions after a while. So does the house smell of onions? Well, it depends on who is doing the smelling, or, more precisely, it depends on what your sensory apparatus has been exposed to and for how long. Despite the careful work by psychophysicists on just-noticeable differences and thresholds, our perception of the world is open to distortion. In the following sections we shall be looking more closely at our how our visual, auditory and tactile sensations are constructed into our perceptions of the world. These rely not only on bottom-up sensory data, but also on the way in which sections of the brain communicate with each other, and the top-down action of previous experience, or stored knowledge.

Summary

The senses code physical energy into neural codes, which are the beginning of psychological experience of the outside world. Early psychologists used psychophysical methods in an attempt to measure the relationship between changes in physical energy and changes in psychological sensation. In deriving a sensory scale, the start point is the absolute threshold, and units on the scale are just-noticeable differences. There are problems in all psychophysical experiments because observers vary in the criteria they use, or their willingness to guess when uncertain. They may also become bored or fatigued. Signal detection theory is a method that can avoid some of these difficulties by using data from errors as well as correct responses. Although detection is superficially simple, it actually involves many other psychological processes including attention, memory and response organisation. The experience we have of a physical stimulus is relative, as water of the same temperature will feel hot or cold depending on whether our hand has previously been in cold or hot water. All this evidence suggests a variable relationship between the physical environment and subjective experience.

Self-assessment questions (Solutions on p. 320)

1 What is the difference between the absolute threshold and a just-noticeable difference?
2 Give five reasons why thresholds are variable.
3 Why is signal detection theory an improvement on other methods for measuring signal detection?
4 Explain the events described in the first paragraph of this chapter in terms of what you have learned in this chapter.

Further reading

Laming. D. (1994) Psychophysics. In R. L. Gregory and A. M. Coleman (Eds.), *Sensation and perception*. Harlow, UK: Longman. For an up-to-date, more detailed overview of psychophysics and psychophysical methods.

Levine, M. W. and Shefner, J. M. (2000) *Fundamentals of sensation and perception, 3rd ed.* Oxford: Oxford University Press.

Woodworth, R. S. and Schlosberg, H. (1955) *Experimental psychology*. London: Methuen. For a comprehensive overview of classic work in psychophysics.

Chapter 4

Visual perception and memory: Making sense of the visual environment

A walk in the park

A S YOU WALK THROUGH THE PARK you see the grass stretching out into the distance in front of you with trees and plants distributed in it. Your impression is not of a flat picture, but of a three-dimensional space within which you can move. There are children playing in the distance and a jogger running toward you. As you continue walking, you notice birds picking through the litter under the trees: they are well camouflaged; it is not until they move that you can pick out their shapes. As you walk along you spot something on the ground. Initially it is not clear what it is, then you realise it is a milk carton that has fallen at an odd angle.

The problem for perception

The processes involved in visual perception enable us to act and react to the visual environment safely and accurately. We need to know what things are and where things are, and where we are in relation to them. The problem for visual perception is to make sense of the sensory data that is detected as patterns of light falling on the retina. The retina is a two-dimensional, flat surface, yet we perceive the world in three dimensions: how is this achieved? Some perceptual processing is a direct outcome of the biological and physiological nature of the visual system, whereas other perceptual processes involve the use of knowledge gained from experience with the visual world. Together with attentional and memory processes, perceptual processing gives rise to our experience of the visual objects and events around us. Although we are only concerned with vision in this chapter, it is important to remember that many objects in the environment have perceptual properties from other modalities, in that they possess auditory, tactile and other sensory properties as well. In later chapters we shall examine hearing and touch and cross-modal effects in perception. So, another problem for perception is to combine information about the properties of objects and the environment.

Biological bases of visual perception

The visual cortex receives information from the retinae of the eyes, via a number of staging posts. The light energy entering the eye activates millions of neuron-like light-sensitive cells, which are the light receptors for vision lining the retina. There are two main types of cells, rods and cones. Cones provide colour vision and are most dense on the fovea, which is the part of the retina over which vision is most acute. Rods are more sensitive to light than cones and are present not only on the fovea, but also in the less acute peripheral areas of the retina. When you go from a well-lit room into a dark place, you can see very little to start with. However, within a few minutes you begin to be able to see more detail. This is because the rods and cones adapt to the darkness. Cones adapt rapidly, but only have a small capacity for adaptation.

Rods adapt much more but take longer to do so, and after half an hour or so your night vision will not improve any more. However, you will probably have noticed that a star that you can see 'out of the corner of your eye' seems to disappear every time you look at it. This is because there are many more rods in peripheral vision than on the fovea, so that as soon as you fixate the position of the star, you are focusing on a less light-sensitive area of the fovea. The fovea is composed of several layers of cells, which transmit the information from the rods and cones to bipolar cells and then ganglion cells. The ganglion cells are bundled together in the optic nerve, which takes information from each eye, through the visual pathways to the visual cortex. The place on the retina where the optic nerve leaves the eye is called the *blind spot*, as there are no light receptive cells at that point. So, why do we not notice this gap in visual information? First, because we have two eyes: when the image falls on the blind spot of one eye it falls on receptors on the other eye. However, what if you close one eye? As the blind spot is toward the edge of the visual field we do not see it in sharp focus, but more important than that that there is a poorly understood process that is capable of 'filling in' the missing information. You can find your blind spot by closing one eye and looking at Figure 4.1. Move the page toward and away from you while you fixate on the cross, and at about 30 cm from your eye, you should find that the spot disappears.

The biological and physiological bases of visual perception is a huge area of study, beyond the scope of this book. For those interested in the complexities of specialisation within the visual system, Bruce, Green and Georgeson (1996) provide a full account.

Knowing what, where and how

To enable us to interact safely with real objects in the environment, the brain encodes and makes available many sources of information about the properties of objects. We want to pick the red, ripe apple

FIGURE 4.1   Test stimulus for finding your blind spot (see text for details).

that we can reach without falling out of the tree. We must know what things are, where they are and how to reach for them, look for them or run away from them.

There are two parallel streams of visual information analysis in the visual cortex. The first, a *ventral stream*, analyses 'what' an object is; the other, a *dorsal stream*, analyses 'where' an object is located (Posner and Petersen, 1990; Ungerleider and Mishkin, 1982; Zeki, 1980). However, each stream knows nothing about the analysis achieved by the other. Goodale and Milner (1992) propose that the main function of the dorsal stream is to guide actions—it specifies 'how', or what action to make to the object; for example, reach for it, move the fovea toward it. Milner and Goodale (1995) identify selective links to separate areas of pre-motor cortex, which is the brain area concerned with making movements, and pre-frontal cortex, which is involved in planning and intentional behaviour. There are also different brain pathways that carry information involved in transforming spatial information from vision into information that can be used as a basis for making spatial movements. In addition, different brain areas code for colour, orientation and other properties of objects. Livingstone and Hubel (1987) found cells that are sensitive to movement but relatively insensitive to form and cells that are sensitive to form but relatively insensitive to movement.

The binding problem

Quite clearly, the biological evidence indicates a very complex, yet selective processing system. Properties of the visual world are coded by specialised cells, pathways and brain regions. The problem that arises from this division of labour is how attributes belonging to the same object are accurately combined to control response. This is the *binding problem*. One influential theory is feature integration theory of focal attention, (FIT), proposed originally by Treisman and Gelade (1980). Although we shall discuss this theory in detail in the next chapter, it is important to note at this point that a cognitive theory of attention is important for attempting to understand how the biologically separate sources of visual information might be combined into objects so that we can recognise and identify them, and FIT takes account of the visual system. This is an example of how understanding the implementational level (the brain) can inform and constrain theorising at the another level, as Marr (1982) suggested (see Chapter 2).

Cognitive aspects of visual perception

The pattern of stimulation falls onto the retina and forms the retinal image. This image is similar to that formed on the film in the back of a camera. However, a camera only takes static shots; even a movie is essentially lots of rapid static shots very close together, and our perception of the visual environment involves much, much more. For example, have you ever taken a photograph of something, only to discover it is just a tiny speck on the developed photograph? To you as the observer, that object was the centre of attention, and you were ignoring much of the other information in the scene. The camera does not 'pay attention' and just represents the whole of the area to which it was exposed. Likewise, you might have taken a photograph of some scenery, only to find that the result is rather disappointing. When you are in the environment you have a sense of the total surroundings, and the angle of vision that your eye has is much wider than that of the camera lens. Also, and very importantly, you have two eyes, whereas the camera has only one. However, we can take satisfactory photographs and in them we can see again the world as we saw it for real. We shall now discuss some of the ways in which your eyes work together using binocular vision to interpret a visual scene. We shall also examine some of the ways we can use monocular vision (which does not depend on using both eyes) and can be used in pictures as well as real life. Richard Gregory (1977) says that perception is 'a dynamic searching for the best interpretation of the available data'. This interpretation includes using our expectations based on memory for previous experiences, as well as what are called visual cues. As the retina is essentially flat, the brain has to use clues and cues to construct a three-dimensional world. The two-dimensional retina has only length and breadth; the third dimension is depth.

Depth perception — binocular cues

Animals that hunt, move by arm-swinging through trees, or make fine manipulative movements with their forepaws or hands, have eyes that face forward, on the front of the face. Prey animals tend to have their eyes on the sides of their heads to give them better all-round vision. Humans have evolved along the first route and have forward-facing eyes that provide a number of cues to depth. Having two eyes facing forward gives an animal overlapping visual fields. That is, both eyes can see the same object or view, but from slightly different angles. When we look at, or fixate, an object or a point in space, our eyes automatically move so that the area of maximum sensitivity, the *fovea*, is where the image is focused. As the two eyes are separated on the face, each eye will be angled slightly differently, but the image of the point will be focused on the fovea of each eye. If you alternately close one eye and then the other you can notice these slightly different views, and the object you are looking at seems to be more to the left or the right depending on which eye is looking. This difference between the views is called horizontal disparity. Next, try this. Get a friend to hold their index finger in front of them at arm's length, then ask them to gradually bring their finger toward their nose, and keep it in focus as they do so. If you watch their eyes you will see that their eyes move more and more inwards towards each other as the finger approaches the nose. This *convergence* of the eyes provides some information to the brain about how far away the object is that is being focused on. The lens of the eye is soft, and can be made thinner or thicker by the muscles that squeeze it, in order to keep an image in focus. The closer an object is, the thicker the lens needs to be; this is called *accommodation*. Convergence and accommodation are only useful for providing information about depth over rather short distances, and there is some controversy over whether they are very much use at all (e.g., Foley, 1980; Kunnapas, 1968; Lovinenko and Belpolskii, 1994).

Stereopsis

As the eyes move inwards toward each other, the disparity or difference between the corresponding images on each retina changes. *Stereopsis* is a cue to depth that uses disparity. Wheatstone (1838) invented a piece of apparatus known as the Wheatstone stereoscope. The principle of the stereoscope is to project a picture to each eye separately. Each picture is a slightly different view of the same object, just as it would appear if each eye was really viewing the object, and so they simulate the retinal disparity. The observer perceives a strong sense of depth, despite the two separate pictures only being flat. A similar principle is used to produce the illusion of depth in stereograms. You are probably familiar with the red and green pictures that appear flat and blurred until you put on spectacles that have one red and one green celluloid lens. When you look through the spectacle, the red image is directed to one eye, and the green image directed to the other. A sense of depth is achieved because the red and green images have been designed to show the different views that would normally be seen when you view a real object with both eyes.

Although the eyes encode the initial environmental information separately, we are not subjectively aware of two visual images. We are only aware of a single, unified percept that is perceived as if there were a single 'Cyclopean' eye. Cyclops, remember, was a monster with just one eye in the centre of his forehead, so he would not have had stereoscopic vision, would he? Anyway, the Cyclopean eye has only one direction for each point in visual space. It is the point located between the eyes where the different directions of each eye appear to converge; the subjective visual direction. For the brain to achieve this subjective experience of where a point or an object is located in the depth plane, a considerable amount of processing must take place and psychologists have found it difficult to understand exactly how this happens.

Basically, the brain has to establish the correspondence between the information coming from the two eyes for stereoscopic vision to emerge. Obviously a comparison between the two sources of information cannot happen until that information arrives in the same part of the brain. Examination of the way that information passes from the retina along the visual pathways and relay stations en route has shown that the first place where this can take place is in primary visual cortex area V1. Here there are many simple and complex cells that are responsive to information arising from disparate areas of the two retinae. Hubel and Wiesel (1962) won the Nobel prize for their work on recording from cells in the visual cortex. Among other things, they found that cells in the cat cortex are selectively responsive to lines of different orientations or moving in particular directions, and that most of these cells are driven by binocular information. More important for our discussion here, Hubel and Wiesel (1970) also found some cells that are particularly responsive to a stimulus presented at a particular distance. These cells would be useful for coding depth. More recent work by Poggio and Fischer (1977) and Poggio and Poggio (1984) has indicated a variety of specialised cells that act together to encode depth more precisely.

Random dot stereograms

One of the most powerful and interesting demonstrations of the way in which information from two eyes can give rise to the perception of depth can be found when we view a random dot stereogram. Bela Julesz's (1971) book is well worth getting hold of if you can find it. It includes very fine examples of *random dot stereograms*, which were developed by Julesz to help him understand how information from the separate eyes becomes integrated.

Julesz's work shows that rather than each eye recognising an image independently, and the brain synthesising a match from disparity between monocular images, the form of the image itself is computed using information from both eyes. Considering the number of dots in a random dot stereogram, it becomes clear that working out the correspondence between all the dots is a mammoth task, leading to millions of possible comparisons being necessary. Given this problem, a number of possibilities have been put forward to account for stereo matching for depth. Julesz (1971) suggested that just as there are systems to detect edges and contours, there is also a stereo-detection code built into the visual system. An alternative suggestion is that depth can be computed without having to find the correspondence for each disparate dot individually, but this involves computing other visual properties such as phase difference between the information from each eye. Oshawa, De Angelis and Freeman (1990) have discovered that neurons are able to do this. Discovery of disparity from phase difference does not require the matching of any individual point or object, but can proceed over all locations in the receptive field at once.

Binocular rivalry: The role of attention in perception

Usually the two eyes receive information, albeit from slightly different viewpoints, of the same scene. However, when the eyes are presented with dissimilar scenes, we do not perceive the two different images superimposed on each other, but instead perceive the images alternately; this cannot be controlled by the observer. The eye whose image is momentarily perceived is called the dominant eye and the other, the suppressed eye. This phenomenon is called binocular rivalry; it was first noticed over 100 years ago, and has intrigued scientists ever since. A number of stimulus properties effect binocular rivalry; for example, if the image to one eye is brighter, or has more contrast, that image will tend to dominate more of the time. The question that binocular rivalry raises is how one image rather than the other becomes selected for perceptual awareness, or conscious experience. A number of hypotheses have been proposed that involve attentional processes. Posner (1980) differentiated between two types of attention, which he called *endogenous* and *exogenous*. Endogenous attention is controlled by voluntary intentions, and internally driven top-down, whereas exogenous attention is captured by a novel, external stimulus, and is stimulus-driven bottom-up. In a recent study, Ooi and He (1999) demonstrated two aspects of attentional involvement in binocular rivalry. First, they found that the dominant image is less likely to become suppressed if voluntary attention is directed to it, and they suggest that this endogenous attention is important for giving a visual percept access to conscious awareness. Second, they found that the scene to one eye was more likely to become dominant if attention was drawn to it by a cue that attracted attention to it exogenously. This example demonstrates the close and interactive links between attention, perception and conscious awareness.

Pictorial or monocular cues to depth, size and distance

Convergence, accommodation and binocular stereopsis are reliant upon the physiology of the nervous system. There are many other sources of information available that help us perceive depth, size and distance, to which we shall now turn. Although the difference between the information arriving from the two eyes is important, it is only useful for judging depth within a close range of the observer. Fortunately there are many more sources of information about depth, size and distance that do not require us to use both eyes at once and that are useful for much greater distances from the observer. For example, pictures are only two-dimensional yet we can gain the impression of depth; these *pictorial cues* are *monocular cues* to depth and are often used by artists to give the illusion of three-dimensional space.

Familiar size

You see your friend running towards you. As they approach they get larger and larger: however, you know your friend is coming closer, not actually growing. This is because you have knowledge in your memory about the size of people and know that people do not rapidly change size. In fact, the retinal image is expanding, and the rate of expansion is an indication of how fast something, in this case your friend, is approaching. Likewise, as a car passes you and moves off into the distance, it appears to get smaller. However, it is known that perception of size does not vary as much as would be expected from the change in size of the retinal image. This is an example of *perceptual constancy*, in this case *size constancy*. Basically we experience a car moving away, or a person coming nearer. We do not concern ourselves with the changing size; we interpret the information as giving movement in the depth plane. It is very important that we have stored knowledge about the size of objects, because the retinal image is ambiguous. We can see this in Figure 4.2.

The human figure appears to be small, but because we know the normal size of a human we infer it is in the distance and therefore the statue must be very large. So, what we have here is an example of

FIGURE 4.2 The use of relative size as a cue for distance. The human figure provides information about the size of the colossal stone statues as well as indication distance. The relative height on the horizon of the trees and mountains also provides depth cues.

the way in which non-visual information is added to retinal information to compute size. This adding of additional non-visual information can give rise to a number of visual illusions, and because we know the size of familiar objects, their relative size is an indication of perspective.

Occlusion and texture

Objects in a scene are often overlapping, so that an object in front occludes the contour of the object behind it. We assume that the unbroken contour is the object in front and that the broken contour is the object behind. This assumption can be used to depict depth in pictures but can also give rise to illusory contours. Another pictorial cue to depth is what is known as a *texture density gradient*. If you look at a pebbled beach, or a tiled floor, the elements are all similar, but near you they are fewer and larger than they are further away (see Figure 4.3.

All ground surfaces have texture, but some are clearer than others; plain concrete has a less marked texture than pebbles or tiles. The change in texture provided by the ground surface gives us way of working out depth and distance. As elements of the texture recede into the distance, the texture appears to change in density. Surface textures also reveal shape by the compression and perspective of the texture elements.

Linear perspective

Another pictorial cue to depth and distance is *linear perspective*, which is perhaps the best known and most difficult to get right when drawing a picture. With straight lines like those of a receding railway track it is relatively easy, but when you try to draw a cup you are likely to make the open rim far too round. This is because it can be difficult to draw what you really see rather than what you know to be there. You know the cup is round, so you make it round, and it then looks wrong but

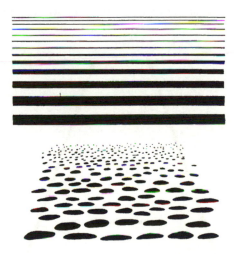

FIGURE 4.3 Schematic diagrams of texture gradients.
Texture gradients can also be seen in the photograph used in Figure 4.2.
From Bruce, Green and Georgeson (1996).

you are not sure why! To draw accurately, you need to draw what you see, not what you know. The understanding of linear perspective was not perfected until the Renaissance in the 15th century, but once it was understood, artists competed to demonstrate their mastery of it. Figure 4.4 shows linear perspective. Relative size and a texture gradient often occur together.

Other cues

Another cue to distance is height in the visual field. Objects nearer to us are lower than those that are further away. Also objects that are some distance away, like hills beyond the fields, are less bright and clear than objects nearer to us. This effect is due to the scattering of light reaching the eyes by particles in the atmosphere and is called atmospheric perspective.

Shape and shading

As the main source of light is from the sun, we are adapted to expect light to come from above. This means that we interpret shapes and

FIGURE 4.4 Linear perspective.

shading as if they are lit in this way. If you look at the shaded discs in Figure 4.5, you will see that although the picture is really flat, some discs look convex, i.e., like bumps, and others look concave, i.e., like dents. However, if you turn the picture through 180 degrees the bumps become dents, and vice versa. This is because the visual areas of the brain assume that the sun is shining from above and you will notice that when the top of the disc is bright the illusion of convexity is present, whereas when the bottom of the disc is bright the illusion of concavity is present. Ramachandran (1988) proposes that during evolution the brain has become adapted to take advantage of the stable properties of the visual environment.

Other information about where objects are can be gleaned from the observation of whether their shadows are attached or not. An object on the ground has its shadow attached to the bottom of it, whereas an object above the ground has its shadow separated from it. The higher the object is from the ground, the greater the distance between the object and its shadow. All these cues combine to provide a rich and detailed description of the visual environment, and can contribute to some of illusions described in these pages.

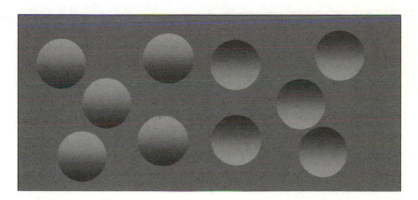

FIGURE 4.5 The discs appear to be lit from above, and are consequently seen as concave or convex. However, if you turn the page round, the convexity or concavity changes. From Ramachandran and Blekeslee (1998).

Depth from motion

You are sitting in a train, quite stationary, then you think you hear the engine engage and look to see if the train is moving. How do you tell? So far we have only considered you to be a static object, perhaps with people or cars moving towards or away from you. However, not only is the world is full of movement, but you move your head and eyes to observe the world. This raises a number of questions. How do you know whether it is you, your eyes or the world that is moving? All of these movements will result in changes on the retina, but such changes are ambiguous without other information. Watching from the train window, you can see that the posts of the fence beside the railway move across the retina faster than the telegraph poles along the road across the more distant field, and that the telegraph poles move faster than the trees. The fact that there is this difference in relative motion of stationary objects not only tells you that train is moving, but also that the fence is nearer than the telegraph poles and the telegraph poles are nearer than the trees. What you observe is called motion parallax.

How do we know what moves?

When sitting in the train, you can feel the vibration of the wheels on the track and hear the sound of the engine, which provide additional, non-visual cues that the train is moving. When you are moving about independently, for example when walking or driving, your movement will mean that the retinal images of objects around you will move. Sometimes an object in the environment will move past your eyes and, furthermore, whether you are walking or standing still you will frequently be moving your eyes. When you make an eye movement the retinal images of objects will move. So there are a number of reasons why the retinal image of objects may move and somehow this information about our own movements and the movements of objects in the environment must be tracked. The eye movements we make to explore the visual world are called saccades, but when you make a saccade you do not have the experience of the world moving past your eyes. Gregory (1998) suggests there are two systems involved in disambiguating retinal information. First the image on the retina, and second a system that knows about the movement of the eyes and the head.

If an object moves across the retina, it could be for two reasons. First your eyes could be stationary and the image of the object has moved across the retina because the object is moving. Alternatively, the object may be stationary but, because the eye has moved, this has caused the image to move across the retina. In addition, there is the case where the object is moving and the eyes are moving at the same time to keep the moving object at fixation. In this last case both the eyes and the object are moving, but the image of the object on the retina is stationary.

When you move your eyes, that part of the brain concerned with initiating eye movements sends an *afferent* signal to the muscles that control movement of the eyes together with another *efferent* signal, an *efference copy*, which is sent to a different brain area and informs the interacting systems of the brain that the eyes are making a movement. You can demonstrate the importance of this efference copy by making your eye move without using the eye muscles. If you gently press the eye sideways while fixating on an object, the object appears to move. As the eye was not moved by its own muscles, no message was sent to the muscles that normally activate an eye movement and there was no corollary discharge. As the brain has received no message to say that the eye is moving, it does not know that the eye has moved and therefore interprets the movement of an image on the retina as a movement of the world. The role of an efference copy for motor commands is implicated in the fact we cannot tickle ourselves very well; we shall discuss this in Chapter 8.

What about the case when the eyes are moving, but are tracking an object so that its image is stable on the retina? Here the eyes are moving but the object should not appear to be, although it is! Now we know the object is moving because although there is no movement across the retina, signals from the eye muscles saying that the eye is moving are sent to the brain. So, information about eye and body movements is also needed to clarify what is moving relative to what.

The constructivist approach to perception

According to the *constructivist approach*, the way we perceive the world is an active, constructive process. We have seen in many of the examples above that our knowledge and expectations influence the way in which stimuli are perceived. Psychologists supporting the constructivist approach include Neisser (1967), who argued 'the mechanisms of visual imagination are continuous with those of visual perception—a fact that strongly implies that all perceiving is a constructive process' (p. 95). Gregory (1998) follows ideas originally proposed by Helmholz, that 'perception is intelligent decision-taking, from limited sensory evidence . . . perceptions are hypotheses of what may be out there' (p. 5). Imagine seeing a single headlight though the fog. Initially you hypothesise that it is a motor bike, but as the vehicle approaches, additional shape information becomes available, and your hypothesis changes to a car with one headlight not working. Once you have decided it might be a car you are able to construct, from very poor visual input, the shape you are expecting. Figure 4.6 shows how we construct a shape according to a hypothesis.

In Figure 4.6, many of the contours of the dog are filled in from the knowledge we have of dog shapes. However, the difficulty of seeing the dog in the static image would be solved if the dog were to move, then, the pattern of dots belonging to the dog would immediately become visible, as the relative motion of the two patterns of dots would make the dog stand out from the background. According to the Gestalt law of 'common fate', groups that move together are likely to belong together, so moving the spots that belong to the dog make it stand out from the background.

The importance of context

Context can influence how we interpret a shape. Palmer (1975) showed that participants were more likely to correctly identify easily confused pictures when these were preceded by brief visual presentation of an appropriate scene, than if no scene was shown, and identification was even worse when inappropriate context was given. Context influenced the hypothesis about what the object was, leading to the participants

FIGURE 4.6 Can you see anything in this picture? (See text for details.) From Gregory (1998).

seeing what they expected rather than what the object really was. For example, the shape of the type of mail-box used in the US is similar to a loaf of bread. When preceded by a picture of a kitchen table laid for breakfast, the mail-box was identified as a loaf. Bruner and Goodman (1947) asked rich and poor children to estimate the size of coins and found that the poor children reliably over-estimated the size of coins in comparison to the rich children. This shows that emotional factors can also influence perception.

A constructivist approach to visual perception explains illusions in terms of false hypotheses. For example, the Ponzo illusion arises from our knowledge of railway tracks, and the Muller-Lyer illusion from our expectations generated from the corners of rooms (see Figure 4.7).

Gregory proposes that the two-dimensional shape is interpreted automatically for depth, and our knowledge of linear perspective gives the impression that the pattern of lines in the right-hand 'arrow' is the inside corner of a room, and therefore near to us, while the 'arrow' on the left like the outside corner of a building and is therefore assumed to be further away and so must be smaller, due to size constancy. This explanation is not universally accepted, and as yet there is no complete account. See Morgan (1996) for a full discussion of the mysteries of visual illusions.

The ecological approach to perception

Unlike the constructivist approach, which emphasises the interaction between top-down and bottom-up processes, J. J. Gibson (1950, 1966, 1979) adopted the *direct perception* approach. According to this view, perception is an entirely bottom-up process and relies only on the

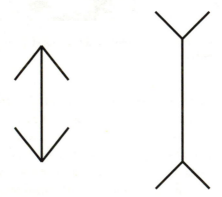

FIGURE 4.7 The Muller-Lyer illusion. The two vertical lines are actually the same length.

pattern of information on the retina, or the *optic array*. The texture gradient we discussed earlier is a prime example illustrating the information in the optic array that, according to Gibson, gives direct information about depth. Equal-sized objects placed one behind each other in a texture gradient are judged to be the same size, because the texture changes as it recedes into the distance at the same rate as the change in size of the objects.

Gibson's approach is called *ecological* as it ties perception very closely to action. That is to say, the way we perceive the world is importantly related to the way we have to interact with or act upon it. Gibson emphasised the importance of surfaces in the environment, and one important surface is the ground we walk on, for example a pebbled beach or a tiled floor. As we move through the environment, visual elements near us move faster than those further away, and the nearer the elements are the clearer they are. According to Gibson, this 'optic flow' determines the accuracy of movements. To explain how we know what different objects in the environment are, Gibson introduced the idea of affordances. The perceptual characteristics of an object suggest its affordance, for example whether it is suitable for walking on, being picked, or for sheltering in. So, the affordance of a chair is 'sit on it'. However, we could use a chair to stand on, or to jam a door closed. Gibson's approach cannot easily explain how different affordances arise depending on the perceiver's current goal or needs, or the effects of context. These difficulties, amongst others, have led to the rejection of the direct approach to perception. However, suggesting the link between perception and action has been important in motivating new research in this area, as has Gibson's emphasis on interactions with a rich visual environment.

The visuo-spatial sketch pad

Baddeley and Hitch (1974) proposed a *visuo-spatial sketch pad* that deals with the temporary *working memory* (WM) for visual information. It is a component of their working memory model, which we shall consider as a whole in Chapter 12. As visual information is distributed in space, the spatial component is perhaps the most important, although we know from our discussions on vision and visual attention that the brain encodes features such as colour, orientation and spatial location separately. In the next chapter we shall discuss Treisman and Gelade's (1980) proposal that focal attention to a spatial location is important for binding features together. We might assume that visual working memory forms a representation of attended objects distributed in space, and that the visuo-spatial sketch pad can be likened to 'the inner eye'. It is evident that we are able to manipulate visual information in order to judge if shapes are similar, and that we can mentally rotate visually presented information in a continuously updatable form. Think of doing a jigsaw puzzle. You look at the space you need to fill, and search the remaining pieces to find one that will fit into the vacant place in the puzzle. Having picked up the piece, you rotate it to fit into the gap; you can 'see' where it fits and which way round it has to be. A classic experiment demonstrating *mental rotation* was reported by Shephard and Metzler (see Figure 4.8 to try mental rotation for yourself).

Shephard and Metzler (1971) presented their participants with two-dimensional drawings of three-dimensional objects that resemble shapes made from Lego bricks. Two shapes were presented, each viewed from a different angle; the task was to work out if the shapes were the same or different. In order to do the mental matching, the visual representation needed to be 'rotated'. The time taken for a judgement to be made was found to be in a direct relationship with the degree of rotation required for the shapes to be matched. It was as if the participant mentally rotated one shape until it was at the same orientation as the other, and then made their response decision. This view of a mental image, or representation, being qualitatively the same as the object in the physical world, is called an 'analogue' view. There is some debate about whether or not this is the correct interpretation, but we shall return to that issue later. For the present, this kind of data provides evidence that visual information can be coded into WM and the resulting image manipulated in some sort of sketch pad.

Further evidence on the nature of short-term visual information processing comes from a study by Brooks (1968). Participants were asked to imagine a letter, such as F, and then imagine an asterisk travelling around the contour of the letter. At each change of direction

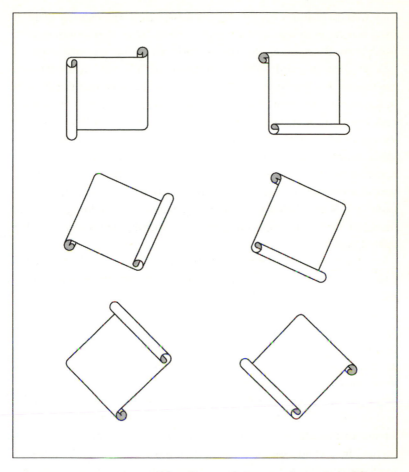

FIGURE 4.8 Can you see if each pair of shapes is the same or different? This task requires mental rotation of the kind measured by Shepard and Metzler (1971).

they were to indicate whether the asterisk was at the extreme edge of the letter or at an intermediate point. Three ways of responding were used; a vocal response, say 'yes' or 'no'; a tapping response, one for 'yes', two for 'no'; and a pointing response to 'Y' or 'N' on a card with Ys and Ns distributed over it, and to choose the next available Y or N in the display. The same response methods were used for a comparison task involving judgements on whether successive words in proverbs were a noun or a verb. In the verbal task there was no effect of response mode on performance, but for the visual imagery task, the pointing response produced far slower reaction times. As the spatial pointing task significantly interfered with the visual task, but not the verbal task, it was concluded that the participants were holding a spatial image of the letter, which was interfered with by performing another spatial task.

Baddeley and Lieberman (1980) studied the visuo-spatial sketch pad in an experiment that required the participants to imagine a 4×4 matrix. They were told that one particular square was the starting square. Next they heard a message that instructed them with the location of the digits 1 to 6 or 1 to 8 within the matrix. Digit 1 was always in the starting position, and then the following digits were always in a square adjacent to where the participant should be imagining they were on the matrix. Two different types of message were used. The first type was an easily visualised message, using the words left/right, and up/down. For example 'in the starting square put a 1, in the next square to the left put a 3, in the next square down put a 6', and so forth. The second type of message was more complicated. Although formally equivalent, the words left/right were replaced by good/bad, and up/down replaced by quick/slow. In the nonsense messages the instructions needed to be translated from a verbal to a visual code to be visualised. So, now the message would be 'in the starting square put a 1, in the next square to the good put a 3, in the next square slow put a 6', and so forth. As if this was not enough, Baddeley and Lieberman asked their participants to do another task at the same time. Half the participants had to make a brightness judgement: this is a 'visual' task. The other half were blindfolded and asked to point a flashlight at a receptive photocell on a swinging pendulum; auditory feedback allowed this group to know if they were keeping track of the pendulum: this is a spatial task. The performance on the matrix task with the easily visualised messages was disrupted by the spatial secondary task. On the other hand, performance of the matrix task with the nonsense messages was impaired by the visual task. Baddeley and Lieberman interpreted these results as evidence for separable visual and spatial processes, but that spatial information rather than visual information was more important for retaining easily visualised messages.

Logie (1986) showed that unattended visual displays interfere with the learning of lists of words using an imagery mnemonic (in which words are associated with visual images), but not with learning by verbal rehearsal. Overall the results from dual-task experiments on working memory suggest that there are modality-specific processing systems that can operate independently, provided there is no competition for the same processing resource.

Summary

The visual system is very complex and codes numerous properties of the visual input with specialised cells, pathways and systems. The problem of combining information from so many different sources is called the 'binding problem'. Deriving a three-dimensional description of the visual world involves some information that results from the physiology of the eye, such as accommodation, and some from having two eyes, such as convergence and stereopsis. Other information comes from our knowledge of the visual environment, such as familiar size and linear perspective. The constructivist view of perception is that hypotheses are formed about the most likely interpretation of the available information, and that these hypotheses act top-down to construct what we 'see'. The direct approach considers that all the information necessary for correct perception is available in the visual environment, and that perception is entirely a bottom-up process. This view links to action but has difficulty in explaining top-down effects of goals on perception. Information derived from perception is represented in the visuo-spatial sketch pad, where it can be manipulated.

> *Self-assessment questions (Solutions on p. 320)*
>
> 1 Can you explain the observations in the scenario at the start of the chapter?
> 2 What is the 'binding problem'?
> 3 What is the constructivist approach to perception?
> 4 Can perception be explained entirely by bottom-up processes?
> 5 Why would the visuo-spatial sketch pad be more spatial than visual?

Further reading

Baddeley, A. D. (1997) *Human memory: Theory and practice*. Hove, UK: Psychology Press. For visual memory.

Bruce, V., Green, P. R. and Georgeson, M. A. (1996) *Visual perception: Physiology, psychology and ecology*. Hove, UK: Psychology Press. For a full account of all aspects of visual perception.

Gregory, R. L. (1998) *Eye and brain*. Oxford: Oxford University Press. For the constructivist view and many interesting findings in the area of visual perception.

Visual attention

Selective visual attention

YOU ARE SITTING AT THE BREAKFAST TABLE, eating your cereal. On the back of the cereal packet is a picture of a bear sitting in the forest, eating honey from a pot. The title of the picture challenges you to find ten honey pots that are hidden in the picture. As you have your breakfast you start to search for the honey pots. Some of them are quite obvious, they pop out from the picture, but others are much harder to find because they are hidden amongst similar shaped objects or are at an orientation you were not expecting. This is an example of visual search, although rather more complex than those that are widely used in the study of visual attention.

To search the visual environment, visual attention must be directed to selected regions of the visual field. As we saw in the previous chapter, the fovea is the most sensitive part of the retina, so to encode detailed visual information, our eyes need to be moved so that this area is focused on the visual location in which we are interested. When viewing a scene, the eyes are reoriented about three times a second by making *saccades*, or eye movements that allow the fovea to focus at one location in the scene after another. In between saccades the eyes are stationary, and during these *fixations* visual information is encoded. These fixations take in snapshots of information about the visual scene. So, one of the first questions that arises is 'How does the eye know where to go, and how does selection take place?' Second, where is the information stored for further processing?

The first problem we meet is that although we usually move our eyes, overtly, to an object or location in space to fixate what we are attending to, we can covertly attend to somewhere else. As early as 1866, Helmholtz recognised this problem. If you fixate on the asterisk here * you will find that you can read surrounding words, or detect colours of surrounding objects, without moving fixation. We seem to be able to look at things out of the corner of our eye. This ability to attend to a location without making an eye movement is called *covert attentional orienting*. In the example of 'looking out of the corner of your eye', the direction of attention is controlled by you, the observer; it is said to be *endogenously* controlled. So, knowing where someone fixates does not tell us where they are attending. On the other hand, a sudden change in the visual environment will *capture* attention. For example, a sudden movement in peripheral vision is immediately noticed. It interrupts what you are currently attending to and draws attention to the novel stimulus. This is due to cells in peripheral vision having the property of interrupting the ongoing processing of information from cells in more central vision. This interruption effect has an obvious benefit for survival. It would be no good if, while we were concentrating on eating our breakfast, focusing on the honey pot puzzle, we did not notice a burglar walking round the room collecting our valuables! Although a sudden movement will capture visual attention, *exogenously*, once we have noted the stimulus that captured attention, we can endogenously orient attention back to what we were previously doing. Usually, we will move our eyes so that the fovea coincides with the attended location, so that attention and fixation are coincident.

Posner (1980) said visual 'attention can be likened to a spotlight that enhances the efficiency of the detection of event within its beam' (p. 173). Taking the spotlight analogy, the objects or events in the centre, or focus of the beam of attention, will be highlighted, whereas those nearer the edge will be less easily detected. We see here that visual attention is considered to be directed in visual space, and much research has been devoted to understanding how attention moves in space, as well as discovering the spatial extent of the spotlight. The link between attending and perceiving is an example of attention for perception.

Moving visual attention without making eye movements

One task, developed by Posner and his colleagues (Posner, Snyder and Davidson 1980), has come to dominate research on orienting attention. The task was originally developed to study visual orienting, but has subsequently been applied to study patients with attentional deficits and adapted for use in other modalities, see Driver and Spence (1999) and Chapter 8. Posner's original experiments (Posner, 1978, 1980; Posner *et al.* (1980) examined the benefit of indicating to the participant, with a visual *cue*, the location at which a target would appear. No overt orienting of attention by eye movements was allowed. Participants made a speeded response as soon as they detected the target. Two types of cue were used; central or peripheral. A *central cue* is presented directly on the fovea at fixation and indicates if the target will arrive on the left or right. It is central in two senses: first, it is centred in the visual field, but second, it requires central processing to interpret a symbol, usually an arrow, into a direction to which visual attention can be endogenously oriented. A peripheral cue is presented in peripheral vision on the side where the target will appear and is usually a brief flash of light. On control trials neither cue is given. Results revealed that targets at the cued location were responded to more quickly than targets arriving at a different location. This showed that visual attention can be covertly oriented in the absence of overt eye movements and led Posner *et al.* (1980) to propose the attention as a spotlight analogy. Of course, unlike a spotlight, attention does not shine out of the eye onto the environment; the enhancement by the spotlight is internal—it acts on the cortex, or cortical space, to prepare the nervous system to be maximally responsive to stimuli coming from a particular external location. In addition, Posner made the distinction between endogenous and exogenous attentional orienting clearer. His experiments showed that the exogenous system automatically shifts attention according to environmental stimuli and is outside the subject's voluntary control—the stimulus cannot be ignored. The endogenous system can also orient attention covertly according to intention, but this system cannot over-rule the attentional capture driven by the exogenous system.

In further experiments, Posner *et al.* (1980) manipulated the likelihood that the cue was a valid indicator of target location.

Participants were given the probability that the cue would be valid or not. For example, they were told there was a 20%, 50% or 80% chance that the cue would be in the position where the target would arrive. If participants could voluntarily control the orienting of attention in the 20% valid case, they should be able to interpret that the target was 80% likely to come on the opposite side of visual space to the cue, and direct attention accordingly. Performance on trials with a central cue indicated that the participant could ignore cues likely to be invalid and direct attention to the other side of visual space. However peripheral cues, although they were known to be improbable indicators of the target location, produced reaction costs, as if they could not be voluntarily over-ruled or ignored. These results (see Figure 5.1), led Posner *et al.* (1980) to suggest that there is a distinction between the endogenous, internal intentional control of visual attention by the participant's interpretation of the central cue, and the exogenous, or stimulus-driven capture of attention by the peripheral cue.

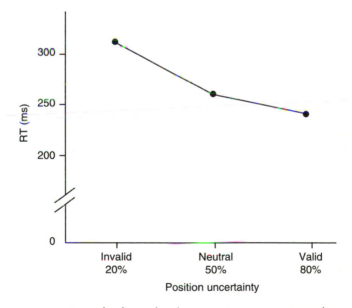

FIGURE 5.1 Typical relationship between response time and position uncertainty in a visual orienting task. A valid cue speeds response but an invalid cue slows response time in comparison to the neutral cue.

Unilateral visual neglect

Further evidence on orienting visual attention has come from studies of patients with *unilateral visual neglect*. These patients typically have right-hemisphere parietal lobe damage (Rizzolatti and Matelli, 2003). They tend to ignore the side of visual space 'contralateral' (on the other side) to their injury; for example, they may neglect to eat food from the left side of the plate, and fail to respond to people on the neglected side. When tested on a variety of visual tasks, patients will copy only one half of a picture, or if given a page of lines to cross out they will ignore the lines on one half of the page. The patients do not seem to think there is anything strange about their drawings or notice that their performance is unusual in any way. However, they are not 'blind' on the side they neglect. Figure 5.2 shows the typical copying performance of neglect patients.

Posner, Walker, Freidrick and Rafal (1984) examined covert orienting in patients with unilateral visual neglect. When tested on Posner's orienting task, these patients were found to have difficulty orienting attention to the neglected side of space. The difficulty is most marked when attention has previously been engaged on a target in the good right visual field but the next target is presented in the neglected left visual field. Posner and Petersen (1990) proposed two independent but interacting attentional systems: first, a posterior, covert orienting system, which directs attention to stimulus locations using the operations 'disengage', 'shift', and 'engage'; a second anterior system is involved in overt orienting and controls the detection of events. Posner and Badgaiyan (1998) provide an overview of the experimental and neurological evidence, which now includes functional magnetic resonance imaging (fMRI) data. They suggest that the *posterior attentional orienting system* is involved in disengagement, engagement and amplification of the attentional target. The second *anterior attentional orienting system*, which includes the frontal lobes, is involved in overt, intentionally controlled orienting and has connections with the supplementary motor area that is involved in making eye movements. It exerts general control over the brain areas involved in target detection and response, and also anticipates the target location. Here again, attention is to facilitate perceptual processing.

Target

Copy

Spontaneous drawing

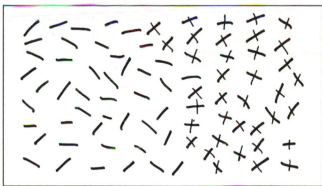

FIGURE 5.2 Examples of drawing and line cancellation typical of patients with visual neglect. From Styles (1997).

Another proposal from the cognitive neuroscience perspective has been put forward, which relates visual orienting behaviour to brain mechanisms. LaBerge (2000) suggests that the selective property of visual attention is expressed as activity in the cortex, by the amplification of neural activity. This expression can be controlled by the stimulus, bottom-up, or by intention, top-down. Jonides (1981) demonstrated that when a secondary memory task is combined with visual cues in an orienting experiment, the memory task interferes with the interpretation of a central cue, suggesting that endogenous orienting competes for central attentional processing. The memory task did not interfere with capture of attention by a peripheral cue, suggesting that exogenous orienting is *automatic*.

Visual extinction

Patients with brain damage may have other visual attention difficulties. Visual extinction is a problem in which the patient can detect a stimulus presented on the contralesional side of space, but cannot detect the same stimulus when another item is presented at the same time in the good, ipsilateral side of space. Although the object in the now-neglected side of visual space can be detected when presented on its own, when another object is presented simultaneously, only the object toward the good side can be seen. The previously seen object is extinguished by the introduction of the new object. An interesting finding is that although the patient is apparently unaware of the extinguished stimulus, they nevertheless have encoded attributes of that stimulus, which can prime or facilitate the processing of other related stimuli (e.g., Berti, Allport, Driver, Dienes, Oxbury and Oxbury, 1992) or be used as the basis for a same–different judgement (Volpe, Ledoux and Gazzaniga, 2000). Simultanagnosia is another attentional problem characterised by the inability to 'see' more than one object concurrently and is a symptom of patients suffering from Balint's syndrome. These patients have bilateral lesions, that is, on both sides of the posterior parietal or occipito-parietal parts of the hemispheres. Humphreys and Riddoch (1993) showed that when presented with a mixture of red and green circles, a Balint's patient could not see both colours simultaneously. However, when the circles were joined together into a single object, both colours could be reported. Treisman (1999) tested a patient, RM, who suffered with simultanagnosia. RM had no difficulty in detecting the target of a red X in visual displays when the distractors differed in either shape (red Os) or colour (blue Xs), but when looking for a red X amongst red Os and blue Xs he was unable to do the task, even in very small displays. It appeared that RM could not form conjunctions of features. Balint's patients like RM have difficulty pointing to and locating oblects in space. We discuss feature integration theory in detail a little later.

Some theoretical explanations that can account not only for normal visual attention and unilateral neglect, but also for *simultanagnosia* and *extinction*, involve the argument that attentional behaviour is a result of an integrated brain state. Duncan (1999) proposes a distributed view of attentional functions in which '. . . generally, attention is seen as a widely distributed state, in which, several brain systems converge to work on different properties and action implications of the same, selected object' (p. 126). The hypothesis is that the multiple sources of information activating different brain systems responsive to visual input are subject to competitive processing. If one source of information is enhanced, than another is inhibited and the most active pattern of activity gains dominance, or control. Duncan suggests that the attentional bias observed in unilateral neglect and the phenomenon of extinction can be explained in terms of damaged areas losing the competition to dominate processing, and so not reaching conscious awareness.

Neglect in other 'spaces'

All the studies so far have only considered retinotopic space, that is, space as represented on the retina. However, selective visual attention and unilateral neglect can operate on the basis of objects, and within other spatial and representational frames. A study by Driver and Halligan (1991), in which they pitted environmental space against object-centred space, provides evidence for the importance of object-based attention. They were able to show that patients with unilateral visual neglect still ignored the neglected side of an object, even when it appeared in the non-neglected side of environmental space. Thus neglect can be of one side of an object's principal axis, not simply of the side of space occupied by that object, and so visual attention can also operate on object-centred space.

Experiments on unilateral neglect in the monkey, have shown that damage to different areas of pre-motor cortex can produce different, dissociable forms of neglect (Rizzolati and Carmada, 1987; Rizzolati and Gallese, 1988; Rizzolati, Gentilucci, and Matelli, 1985). Neglect may be of 'reaching' space, when the animal makes no attempt to reach for an object, of oculo-motor space, when no eye movement is made toward objects, or of orofacial space, where the animal will not lick juice from around one side of the mouth. Similar dissociations between near space and far space have been seen in human patients; for example, patients may respond normally to distant stimuli but not to near stimuli, or vice versa. Neglect of stimuli at a distance is called 'extrapersonal neglect', while inattention to near stimuli is called 'peripersonal neglect' (Rizzolati and Matelli, 2003). Patents with 'personal neglect' neglect their own body, becoming untidy because they do not look after their appearance on the neglected side of the body. Bisiach and Vallar (2000) have shown that such patients are not responsive to tactile stimuli on the side of their body contralateral to their lesion.

These findings are important because they show that the region or sphere of space attended to and the operation of attentional orienting must be considered in terms of the type of action that we might make in response to perceiving a stimulus. So sensation, perception and action are all linked together to enable us to make the right action to the right object in the right place. Selection for action is a topic in Chapter 11.

Attention can also be oriented to an internal representation generated from memory. Bisiach and Luzzatti (1978) asked an Italian patient with unilateral visual neglect to report, from memory, what could he could see if he stood on the cathedral steps in Milan. This was a view with which he was very familiar. Imagining he was standing on the cathedral steps, the patient reported all the buildings on one side of the square and ignored all those on the other side. Then the patient was asked to imagine crossing the square to face the cathedral and report what he could see now. All the buildings previously ignored were reported. Clearly the representation of the square stored in memory was intact, but one side of the imagined space was being neglected. Bisiach (1988) reports another patient who stubbornly refused to acknowledge disability on one side of his body. The patient suffered from left-sided visual neglect and a left-sided paralysis. However, he did not accept that his paralysed arm was anything to do with him; he seemed completely unaware of it. All this evidence suggests a complex variety of 'spatial' frames and representational systems within which attention can be oriented and can operate, and that attention, perception and memory are interdependent.

The nature of the attentional spotlight

William James (1890) described visual attention as having a focus, a margin and a fringe. Is the spotlight referred to by Posner (1980) similar, is it of fixed size, or can it zoom in or out? What is the difference in processing in and out of the spotlight? Where is the margin and the fringe? Laberge (1983) found evidence that the beam of the spotlight could be adjusted according to task demands. He presented people with a series of five-letter words. In one condition the participants were to categorise a letter at the centre of the row of letters; in the other they were to categorise the word. Laberge thought that if the spotlight could be altered in its width, observers would focus attention narrowly in the letter condition, but in the word condition they would distribute attention over the whole row of letters. When attention was focused on the centre letter, responses to that letter were faster than to the other letters, but when attention was directed to the whole word, response time to all letters was equal. In addition, with attention spread over the word, all response times to the central letter were slower than when that letter was the sole focus of attention. This evidence suggests that the breadth of focus for visual attention can be altered, or 'zoomed', according to the size of the attended object. Other evidence for the zoom-lens model was provided by Eriksen and colleagues (Eriksen and Murphy, 1987; Eriksen and St. James, 1986). These experiments examined the interference effects of irrelevant distractors in the visual field. It has long been known that the presence of other visual items with responses that are incompatible with the target response will cause interference on response times (see Styles, 1997, Chapter 3, for a review). Eriksen and Murphy showed that when a pre-cue was given to the target location, interference occurred with a response-incompatible distractor near the target, but with no location, pre-cue interference could occur from more distant distractors. Eriksen and Murphy suggested that, without a cue to target location, attention is initially widely distributed and all items in the display are processed in parallel, leading to interference for more distant distractors. However, with a pre-cue to location, attention can be narrowed down so that only distractors very close to the target will interfere. Lavie (1995) argues that the size to which the spotlight can close down depends on the perceptual load, or demand, of the whole task. In her own experiments she manipulated task difficulty and has shown that 'perceptual load plays a causal role in the efficiency of selective attention' (p. 463). In high load conditions, attention is narrowly focused, but as load reduces, attention may be spread more widely and other information in the display will also be processed. This seems an adaptive strategy; we want to know as much as we can about the visual environment, but at the same time we need to be able to selectively process the most important part. So, if the main task is not demanding all attentional resources, there is capacity available for other processing of less relevant information. According to this account, visual attention can appear to be either a spotlight or a zoom-lens, depending on the task. In Lavie's experiment the task was made more difficult by the complexity of the cue and the responses to be made to the target. Here we can see that the use of memory and the need to programme and control motor responses interact with attentional effects, showing the relationship between attention and other cognitive processes. Lavie *et al.* (2004) have recently proposed the load theory of selective attention and cognitive control which we shall discuss in Chapter 12.

Local and global processing

When we attend to a visual object we can attend at different levels. At the *local processing* level the individual elements can be seen for what they are, independent of the overall configuration. At the *global processing* level, you see a face. In everyday life we sometimes want to attend to the whole object, and sometimes to the detail within it. For example, at the global level we can see a tree, but if we want to discover the species and examine the leaves, attention must be directed to the local level. One question for visual attention is, do we see the tree, and then focus down to examine the local detail, or do we combine the local details into the whole tree? Navon (1977) presented subjects with large letters made up of small letters (see Figure 5.3).

The large letter is the global shape and the small letters are the local shapes. These letters can be constructed so that the large and small letters are the same, or congruent, or so that the large and small letters are different, or incongruent. Navon showed that response to the global letter identity was unaffected by whether the local property was congruent or incongruent, However, response to the local letter identity was interfered with by an incongruent global letter. Navon took these results as evidence for attention being directed to coarse-grained global properties of an object prior to analysis of fine-grained local details.

Stoffer (1993) examined the time course of changing attention between the local and global levels. He suggested that attention not only has to change spatial extent, but also has to change between representational levels. Clearly if attention changes from operating on the global shape to a local element there will have to be a zooming up or down of attentional focus. Central or peripheral cues were given for participants to attend to either the local or global property. This task is similar to Posner's (1980) spatial orienting experiments we discussed earlier. In this case, however, attention is directed to different levels of

```
EEEEE       SSSSS
E           S
E           S
EEEEE       SSSSS
E           S
E           S
EEEEE       SSSSS
```

FIGURE 5.3 Example of the local and global properties of compound letters. From Styles (1997).

representation rather than space. Results showed that attention can be controlled either involuntarily (exogenous cue) or voluntarily (endogenous cue). However, zooming to the local level took longer than zooming to the global level. Stoffer suggests that the global level is usually attended to first but an additional step is required to re-orient attention to the local level of representation.

Visual search : What does the attentional spotlight do?

One of the biggest problems in psychology is the *binding problem*. We have mentioned it before, but now we shall try to understand how it is that we are able to search for and respond to whole visual objects that have their correct properties of colour, shape and location combined. Imagine searching for the honey pots on the back of the cereal packet, or searching for your favourite brand of beans on the supermarket shelf. You search for a set of properties that occur together and specify the target of your search as being different from all the other possible visible objects. Your friend may usually wear a red coat, and as you search the busy street your attention seems to be drawn to anyone with a red coat; red seems to *pop out* from the crowd. However, once you have detected a red coat, further information will allow you to disregard each person until, at last, you recognise your friend. To do this, the combination of information about each person will need to be matched to memory. Of course, we not only need to know the correct combination of visual properties, but also what other sensory and semantic properties belong to that object.

Visual search with focal attention

Perhaps the most influential theory of visual attention in the past 25 years has been *feature integration theory* (FIT), initially proposed by Treisman and Gelade (1980). This theory has undergone many modifications to take into account new data, but the essentials remain. Basically FIT is a theory for the perception of integrated objects. It attempts to account for the binding problem by giving visual attention the role of 'glue' that sticks the separable features of objects together.

We see the round, green letter O because focal visual attention has been directed to the location where 'round' and 'green' are together. The features are combined by attending to that location and 'green O' can then be identified.

In FIT it is assumed, on the basis of what is known about the visual system, that sensory features such as colour, orientation and size are coded automatically without the need for focal attention. Different features are coded onto *feature maps*, so for example the distribution of different colours will be represented in the colour map, while lines of different orientations will be represented in the orientation map. Detection of single features on the maps takes place automatically, without attention, pre-attentively, in parallel. However, to determine if there is a line of a particular orientation and colour in the visual scene, the separately coded features must be accurately combined into a conjunction.

Separate features can be combined in three ways. First, the features that have been coded may fit into predicted object frames according to stored knowledge. Here we see the role of top-down memory processes in interpreting the perceptual features of familiar objects. For example, we expect the sky to be blue and grass to be green; if the colours blue and green are active at the same time, we are unlikely to combine green with the position of the sky. A second way is for focal attention to select a location on the *master map of locations*. This master map represents where all the features are located, but does not 'know' which features are where. In Chapter 3 we note that there are two streams of visual information processing, one that codes 'what' and one that codes 'where', and that these two streams are blind to the information on the other stream. The location maps would be based on the 'where' stream of visual information processing. Figure 5.4 is an illustration of the FIT framework.

When attention is focused on one location in the master map, it allows retrieval of whatever features are currently active at that location and creates a temporary representation of the object in an '*object file*', which can then be used to recognise it. Conscious perception, or recognition, depends on matching the contents of the object file with stored descriptions in long-term visual memory. Finally, if attention is not used, features may conjoin on their own and although

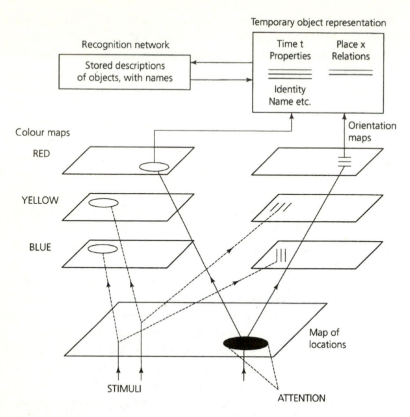

FIGURE 5.4 A version of feature integration theory. From Treisman (1988). Focal attention binds the features present at the location on the map of locations.

the *conjunction* will be sometimes be correct it will often be wrong, which produces an 'illusory conjunction'.

Evidence for feature integration theory

The initial experiments by Treisman and Gelade (1980) showed that when subjects search for a target defined by a conjunction of properties, for example a green T amongst green Xs and brown Ts, search time increases linearly with the number of non-target or distractor items in the display. When the search is for a target defined by a unique feature, for example a blue S set amongst green Xs and brown Ts, search time is independent of the number of distractors. This pattern of performance suggested that to detect a conjunction, attention must be focused serially on each object in turn, but detection of a unique, distinctive feature is parallel. A unique feature can 'call attention' to its location. This is sometimes called the attentional 'pop-out' effect.

Because a distinctive feature will automatically 'pop out', attention does not need to search for the target and so display size will not affect the time needed to detect it. However, if the target is defined by a conjunction of features, it could be that it is the very first or the very last object conjoined by focal attention that contains the target. In this case, on average half of the items in the display will have been searched before a target is detected. When there is no target present, every possible position must be searched. If we plot search times for present and absent responses, against display size, we find that there is a 1:2 ratio between the search rates for present:absent responses. Data of this kind are shown in Figure 5.5. These results suggest that conjunction search is serial and self-terminating and are consistent with the idea that in conjunction search, focal attention moves serially through the display until a target conjunction is found. Targets that are defined by a single feature are found equally quickly irrespective of display size. This fits with the idea of parallel preattentive feature search: as soon as activity for the target feature is detected on the relevant feature map a target must be present; if not, there is no target. Locating the feature is unnecessary.

Treisman and Schmidt (1982) report a divided visual attention task. Participants were shown a row of three coloured letters flanked by two digits. The task was to report three digits, and then the letters and their correct colours. Participants made errors in the letter task, but these were not random. They were 'illusory conjunctions'. Subjects reported letters and colours that had been present in the display, but combined the wrong features. It seems that when there is not enough time for focal attention to search each of the locations occupied by the coloured letters, the features detected are combined in some arbitrary way. However, participants are not guessing the letters and colour; they

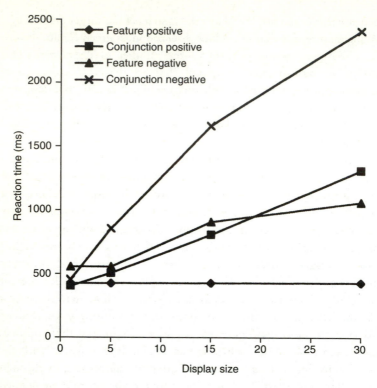

FIGURE 5.5 The relationship between display size and search time for conjunctions and features. From Styles (1997), adapted from Treisman and Gelade (1980).

report the correct letters and the correct colours, but combine them incorrectly.

Treisman (1986) argued that if attention is necessary for detecting a conjunction, then a pre-cue that tells attention where to go first should eliminate the need for serial search of any other display locations. In contrast, as feature search does not require serial search by location, a location cue should provide no benefit. Results showed that valid cues speeded conjunction search, but there was little effect on feature search. Again this suggests an important role for focal attention to location in conjunction search.

Although Treisman (1986) used a similar technique to that used by Posner and his associates, there is an important difference between the simple present/absent detection required of Posner's observers, and the tasks required of Treisman's observers. In Posner's orienting experiments nothing has to be ignored; there is no selection of one item for selective response in preference to other items. Kahneman and Treisman (1984) suggest that 'different processes and mechanisms may be involved in these simple tasks and in the more complex filtering tasks'. This suggestion is supported by experiments reported by Lavie (1995), which were discussed earlier.

Treisman (1999) tested a patient with Balint's syndrome, RM. Patients with Balint's syndrome have bilateral lesions in parietal cortex, but have normal acuity, stereopsis, colour vision and contrast sensitivity. These patients have no fundamental visual deficits, but show neglect, fail to orient head and limbs and make gross errors in reaching and preparatory movements. RM was given a variety of tasks requiring feature integration and it was shown that even when he was given two letters, each in a different colour, he made binding errors, reporting the colour of one letter as the colour of the other. Treisman concluded that RM had lost the master map of locations and was therefore unable to form a stable representation of integrated objects. RM knew what things were, but not where they were.

Some alternatives to feature integration theory

Attentional engagement theory: Visual search and visual similarity

There are a number of demonstrations of 'pop-out' for conjunctions. According to FIT this should not happen. Duncan and Humphreys (1989, 1992) suggest that 'pop-out' can arise because of grouping effects in the display. Rather than being spatially based, where location is all important, attentional engagement theory (AET) holds that selection by visual attention may be object-based. Duncan and Humphreys stress the importance of similarity not only between targets but also between non-targets in the visual environment. Similarity is a powerful grouping factor, and the efficiency of visual search can depend on how easily targets and distractors form into separate groups. This is similar to auditory grouping on Gestalt principles, discussed in Chapter 7 with respect to hearing. Sometimes targets can easily be rejected as irrelevant, but in other displays targets may be much more difficult to reject. As targets become more similar to non-targets, the more difficult it is for selective mechanisms to segregate, or group, the visual display. Beck (1966) had showed that subjects found it easier to detect a visual texture boundary on a page printed with areas of upright letter Ts and Ts that were rotated by 45 degrees, than to detect a boundary between Ts and Ls. The rotation difference between two groups of Ts meant that they shared no features, whereas the letters L and T contained the same features. Shapes that share features are more difficult to segregate into separate groups. In a series of experiments, Duncan and Humphreys (1989) showed that manipulating the heterogeneity of distractors and their relation to the target resulted in large variations in the efficiency of visual search not predicted by FIT. According to FIT, features are coded pre-attentively in parallel over the visual display, and conjunctions of features, which should be necessary to discriminate T from L, require serial search with focal attention. Duncan and Humphreys showed that although in some conditions conjunction search was affected by display size, in other conditions display size effects were reduced or absent. In fact, in conditions where all the distractors were homogeneous, absent responses could be even faster than present responses. Duncan and Humphreys (1989) suggest that selection takes place at the level of the whole display and that visual search for a target can be based on the rapid rejection of the distractor group.

Duncan and Humphreys propose that search efficiency depends on the difference between targets and distractors and, as similarity between distractors increases, search for a target becomes more efficient. Efficiency of target search depends not only upon how similar or different the target is from the distractors, but also upon how similar or different the distractors are to each other. In contrast to FIT, AET is more concerned with the relationship between targets and distractors and the way that information in the visual field can be segregated into perceptual groups, than with spatial mapping. In FIT space can be considered to be more important, whereas in AET, objects as perceptual groups appear to have a special role.

Other theories of visual attention

There are a number of other theories of visual attention that agree that both space and perceptual grouping into objects are important for search with visual attention; for example, guided search theory (Wolfe, Cave and Frantzel, 1989), which is a refinement and extension of FIT and attempts to account for the variability in search times. Many other models are mathematically complex or are computational models, best covered in more specialised books than this. The advantage of mathematical and computational models is their ability to rigorously test ideas by implementing them outside the human brain. Examples of mathematical models are Bundersen's (1990) theory of visual attention (TVA) and Logan's (1996) CTVA theory. CTVA can account for the importance of both space and perceptual grouping in visual attention. For further details of theses theories see Styles (1997).

Reporting brief visual displays: Iconic memory and attention

Imagine walking down a dark country lane during a thunderstorm. Most of the time you are in complete blackness, but as the lightning flashes, you are able to see the whole scene illuminated. You can see the path, the trees and fields around you. Although the flash is extremely brief, it seems to illuminate your path for longer; the image seems to persist. This persistence is also apparent when you draw patterns with sparklers on bonfire night; although the light source is moving we can see where it has been. Clearly there is some kind of fleeting memory store that can retain visual information for further processing. Perhaps this memory is that used to retain information between saccades. For information encoded during a saccade to be useful for further processing it must be held in some sort of memory store or buffer. This would be similar to the sensory buffer in Broadbent's (1958) model, and would be the memory on which selective attention operates.

Sperling's experiments

How much can people attend to, perceive and remember from these brief intakes of information? Sperling (1960) investigated people's ability to selectively report items from very brief visual displays. These experiments are different from those just discussed. Posner's (1980) experiments only asked the participant to detect a stimulus and press a button as fast as possible. In Treisman and Gelade's (1980) tasks, the participant searched for a target with particular properties, but only from a small set of possibilities. These relatively simple tasks are called 'selective set' experiments (Kahneman and Treisman, 1984). In contrast, the kind of experiments done by early researchers on auditory attention asked the listener to shadow, or report back, much more complex material, for example a passage from a novel. In these *filtering* tasks the material to be selected and the response to it involves many more possibilities. Sperling's experiments on selective report from brief visual displays are much more like these auditory filtering experiments. Perhaps this is not surprising, because they were conducted at around the same time.

Sperling presented his participants with a very brief visual display using a tachistoscope, which is a light-proof box fitted with lamps that can be rapidly switched on and off. When a visual display of 12 letters was displayed for 50 ms, observers were only able to report about four or five items. However, subjects reported that they could 'see' the whole display for a short time after the light went off. The data suggested that although all items were initially represented in a brief visual memory, there was some limit on the rate at which items could be retrieved from this store before they had decayed. Sperling believed the pattern of results was evidence for a high-capacity, fast decay visual memory store that faded over a short time. Unless this rapidly fading memory for visual information was transformed into another more permanent state, it was lost. Neisser (1967) called this brief visual information store *iconic memory*.

Next, Sperling tried another experiment. Instead of asking for report of the whole display, observers were given a cue immediately after display offset, indicating which row to report (see Figure 5.6).

When the cue was a tone, subjects could report virtually all the items from the cued row although they had no idea beforehand which row would be asked for. This showed that they must have perceived all 12 items in the display. To try to discover how long this memory lasted, Sperling investigated what happened if he delayed

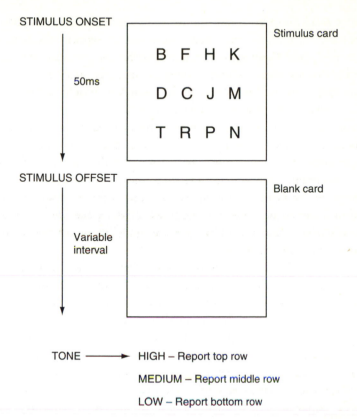

STIMULUS ONSET

50ms

Stimulus card

B F H K

D C J M

T R P N

STIMULUS OFFSET

Variable
interval

Blank card

TONE ⟶ HIGH – Report top row

MEDIUM – Report middle row

LOW – Report bottom row

FIGURE 5.6 The sequence of events and typical display in Sperling's partial report experiment. From Styles (1997).

presenting the tone. He found that the longer he delayed the tone, the less could be reported, until after a delay of 500 ms subjects' performance was no better than in the whole report (WR) condition, so the iconic memory must have completely decayed. The advantage that cueing gives is called the partial report (PR) superiority effect and suggests that the cue, in this case a tone, can be used to allow a subset of items to be selectively transferred to a later stage of processing. These results are important in understanding selective attention, because they reveal which cues are, or are not, effective for guiding selective attention in a complex display of visual stimuli. In the partial report condition the stimuli indicated by the cue can be selectively reported. As the tone indicated which row to report, this suggests that the spatial locations of the items in the display must have been represented in iconic memory. Subsequent experiments have shown that other cues such as colour (Dick, 1969; Von Wright, 1969, 1970), size or shape (Turvey and Kravetz, 1970) will also allow selective processing. At the short presentation times used in iconic memory experiments there is no time for any eye movements to be made, so in these cases, attention is able to 'search' the display for letters on the basis of information that is tagged to them in some way. Unless the information indicated by the cue is associated with the rows of letters, selection cannot be made. On the basis of which cues do, or do not, allow selective report, assumptions are made about the information available in iconic memory.

Rather like auditory filtering experiments, it seems as if physical cues are effective in allowing selective report. Another potential cue for selection is the category of the item, for example whether the target is a letter or a digit. However, Sperling found that if item category was given as the post-exposure cue there was no PR advantage, and hence argued that the representation from which selection was made was pre-categorical, i.e., before category membership had been determined. If category membership was not represented in iconic memory, then of course it could not act as a basis for selection. This is the same assumption made by Broadbent (1958) in his auditory selection experiments. However, as in auditory filtering experiments, it appears that stimuli may be processed to higher levels before selective attention operates (see auditory attention, Chapter 8.)

Mewhort (1967) presented participants with two rows of letters and used a post-exposure tone to indicate which row to report. Sometimes the information in the irrelevant row was just a string of letters, like YRULPZOC, and sometimes the row was more like a word, for example VERNALIT. Mewhort found that the content of the irrelevant row affected the number of letters reported from the cued row. When the irrelevant row was VERNALIT, more letters were reported from the cued row than when the irrelevant row was just letters. It seems that participants were processing the uncued row, otherwise it could not have affected performance. Just as listeners are affected by information on the ignored, or unattended channel in dichotic listening experiments, Mewhort's data suggests that the meaning of unattended items can 'break through' to influence processing of attended information.

These results suggest that iconic memory is not a purely visual store containing only the visual properties of colour and location, for if it was, semantics should have no effect. This result has implications for any theories of memory or attention that propose all information must pass through the conscious short-term store to reach long-term memory (see, for example, Broadbent, 1958, and Atkinson and Shiffrin, 1968).

Later experiments by Merikle (1980) showed that if the letters to be reported from amongst digits were formed into a perceptual group, either by the spatial arrangement of the display or by a colour difference, then there was an added advantage of having the category difference that was larger than the physical difference on its own. Merikle argued that the reason a category cue (e.g., 'Report the letters not the digits') does not easily produce a PR superiority effect was because a category difference does not form a perceptual group. We have seen already that experimenters are now convinced that perceptual grouping is an important factor in selective attention in attentional engagement theory (Duncan and Humphreys, 1992).

Change blindness

Change blindness is an intriguing but robust effect that demonstrates the fragility of visual memory. Normally our attention is drawn to changes in the environment, and we make an eye movement to the novel stimulus to encode the new information. However, if the scene we are looking at before attention is drawn away is quickly substituted for a different one, people do not notice the change. Rensink, O'Regan and Clarke (1997) found in laboratory experiments that detecting a change in a scene could take many seconds or even minutes. In a 'real world' situation, Simons and Levin (1998) engaged a participant in conversation with a stooge. Then, using a carefully planned distraction, they swapped one stooge for another, who continued the conversation. Results showed that, in about 50% of trials, people did not notice that the person they were holding a conversation with had been swapped. This is rather like forming an illusory conjunction between the person and what they are saying. Similarly, Rensink (2000), in his 'coherence theory', suggests that focused attention is necessary to bind the sensory features into a coherent object representation and to maintain this representation in visual short-term memory (VSTM). VSTM maintains information across saccades. However, when attention is withdrawn from the object it becomes 'unglued' and the sensory features come apart again. This is why a change of object may not be detected when attention is diverted. Hollingworth and Henderson (2002) have tested change blindness in a number of experiments where they monitored eye movements and have found evidence that participants can successfully detect changes if the changed object is refixated. They suggest that relatively accurate memory for scenes is retained in long-term memory. We shall discuss this issue further when we consider *episodic memory* in Chapter 12.

Summary

As the eyes fixate, positions in visual space make saccades from location to location to take in information. However, where we fixate and where we attend are not necessarily the same. Attention can be oriented covertly without making an eye movement. Visual attention to a location enhances processing of information at that location and can be exogenously controlled by a peripheral cue, or endogenously controlled by the intention of the observer. Cues for endogenous shifts of orientation can be voluntarily ignored, but peripheral cues cannot be ignored as they summon attention automatically. Patients with unilateral neglect have difficulty orienting attention to neglected space. Feature integration theory proposes that search for a visual target defined by a conjunction of features requires serial search with focal attention. Features are encoded automatically in parallel and serial search is unnecessary. Attentional engagement theory proposes that targets and non-targets can be segregated from each other on the basis of similarity; the more similar targets are to distractors the more difficult search will be. Iconic memory is a transient store of visual information on which selective attention can operate to transfer information to a more durable, reportable form. Change blindness can arise when attention is diverted from the current focus of attention and suggests that attention must be maintained on an object for an episodic memory to be laid down.

Self-assessment questions (Solutions on p. 321)

1 Differentiate between endogenous and exogenous orienting of attention.
2 Give four different examples of unilateral neglect.
3 What is the difference between feature search and conjunction search?
4 What does the partial report superiority effect demonstrate?

Further reading

Pashler, H. (Ed.) (1998) *Attention*. Hove, UK: Psychology Press. For more advanced readings on varieties of attention and neuropsychological studies.

Styles, E. A. (1997) *The psychology of attention*. Hove, UK: Psychology Press. For more detail on theories and experiments on visual attention.

Chapter 6

The world of objects and people

Recognising objects in a complex world

YOU ARE WALKING DOWN a busy street. There are shop fronts
displaying their goods; there are buses, cars and people walking
their dogs; there are some people we recognise and others we have
never seen before. All these objects are made up from different colours,
shapes and sizes, in different places. Yet we 'see' buses, cars, people
and dogs, signs and goods in the shop windows; we experience the
visual world as a unified whole with unified objects within it. We can
recognise a bus, a car or a person from many different angles, as they
move with respect to us. The signs on the shops are all in different
designs of writing, but we read them effortlessly. As we saw in the
previous chapters, there is good evidence that different parts of the
brain are concerned with processing information about shape, movement, depth and colour while other pathways code where an object
is and what it is, or how to act on it. One of the ways in which this
combination of attributes or features can be achieved is by focusing
attention on them (Treisman, 1988); we discussed feature integration
theory in the previous chapter.

All the sensory properties of objects we know about are stored in memory and, when we perceive a familiar object, the sensory information from the senses is acted on by perceptual processes, attentional processes and object recognition processes. Together these processes interact with stored knowledge to give rise to conscious recognition of an object; we 'see' it—it is recognised. Together with memories for the sensory properties of objects, we also have memory representations of other, functional properties that specify what we do with objects, such as how to peel a banana and that hammers are for hitting nails. One problem for object recognition is 'what is an object'? Take the example of looking at a plate of fruit. Is the object the plate with the fruit on it, the plate itself, or each piece of fruit? Most objects are made from parts, which together specify the overall shape and features of the whole object. See the 'fruit face' picture in Figure 6.1. In this figure the first impression is of a face, although not a real one. However, the whole object, or face, can be decomposed into the component parts of the other objects that are configured into a 'face' object.

FIGURE 6.1 The arrangement of the bananas, grapes and apple give the impression of a face on the plate.

To see but not to see

Recognising fruit is easy for us, but there are some people who have suffered from brain damage and who are unfortunately no longer able to do this 'simple' task. For example, HJA, investigated by Riddoch and Humphreys (1987), is a patient suffering from a neurological problem called integrative *visual agnosia*. Although HJA is able to describe many of the sensory properties of an object he is looking at, such as its size, shape and texture, he is unable to integrate that information into a unified percept. He cannot tell that what he is looking at is a piece of fruit, or what kind of fruit it is. Sometimes he may be able to make an educated guess on the basis of the features he has analysed. Something about the form of the object will suggest to him that it is a natural object, not an animal, maybe fruit? As a raspberry or a bunch of grapes is made up from lots of smaller pieces, HJA uses this information to help reduce the number of possible fruits. However, he may then confuse a raspberry with a bunch of grapes. HJA knows that fruit is sweet and juicy and has seeds inside, so he has stored knowledge about sensory properties. The difficulty seems to be in making contact between the knowledge stored in his memory and what he 'sees'. HJA can understand and produce speech, and perform many other psychological tasks perfectly well, but he does also have difficulty in recognising people's faces, a neuropsychological problem called prosopagnosia. He cannot even recognise his wife by her face. He knows her by her voice, the way she moves and the clothes she wears. So although HJA has deficits in some aspects of processing, other aspects remain intact. This selective breakdown of psychological functions illustrates the fact that different areas of the brain are specialised to perform particular functions. One of the most important assumptions underlying neuropsychology is that the brain is modular.

In people with no damage, many of the processes of perception and object recognition are so fast, accurate and automatic that it is not easy to do experiments that highlight or can separate out the components at work in the fully functioning information processing system. We shall now cover some of the main aspects of perception of the visual environment. Vision is usually the dominant sense, which means that if there is a conflict between information coming to the brain from vision and a different sense, it is often the visual information that takes precedence. However, when we come to the chapter on cross-modal effects in attention and perception it will be evident that vision, hearing and touch influence each other in constructing our interpretation of the world around us.

Recognising patterns: Templates and features

Before we approach the problem of recognising three-dimensional objects, can we explain how two-dimensional patterns are recognised? Although this would appear to be a simple problem, it has, in fact, proved rather difficult. Let's take the example of letters. How do you recognise an 'A'? One possible approach would be to suggest that there are templates for different letters stored in memory and that the letter in mapped onto that template. The problem with this theory is immediately apparent if I ask you to recognise 'a'. Now the letter is the same in terms of its name, but the template must be different. Given the wide variety of 'A's that we encounter, it seems improbable that there could be a template for all of them. What is more, we can recognise all different kinds of handwriting, and letters that are at different orientations. Clearly a *template theory* is not workable.

An alternative suggestion might be that letters are defined by critical features, for example an 'A' has a point at the top where two lines meet and a horizontal line joining the two uprights. An 'H' is similar, but the uprights do not meet at the top. Initially this feature detection account seems more economical than template theory, and would fit in with evidence that the visual cortex has cells responsive to lines of different orientations, or feature detectors, as discovered by Hubel and Wiesel (1959). This evidence led to the development of a number of models that provide a feature-based account of pattern recognition. The most important of these is 'pandemonium' proposed by Selfridge (1959).

In the pandemonium model, each letter or digit is represented by a 'cognitive demon', which holds a list of the features that define its shape. The cognitive demons listen for evidence that matches their description, which comes from 'feature demons' that detect individual lines, such as a horizontal or a vertical, and shout out if they are activated. When a cognitive demon starts to detect features consistent with its shape, it too begins to shout. So, if a letter such as 'A' is presented to the image demon, the feature demons will start providing evidence for it. Some of this will be consistent with both an 'A' and a 'H', and the A demon will start shouting, but so too will the H demon. As more evidence comes in from the feature demons, the evidence for 'A' will be greater than for 'H' and the A demon will be shouting the loudest. The decision demon then makes a decision on which is the most likely letter by seeing which voice dominates the noise (see Figure 6.2).

When information from the features is ambiguous, for example in handwriting, cognitive demons can take account of word knowledge and context to disambiguate the letter. Of course Selfridge did not propose that there really were demons in the brain, but the principles of parallel processing for all features, and levels of excitation in the nervous system, are consistent with what is known. However, the problem of who listens to the demons and the arrangement of features relative to each other within a shape are crucially important. Two vertical lines and a horizontal line do not define 'H'; it is the relation between them that does so, for example ll-, is not an H. A theory of pattern or object recognition must be able to specify the relation between parts of an object. However, pandemonium can be considered a precursor for parallel distributed processing (PDP) models, of which one very influential contribution is the interactive activation model.

Properties of parallel distributed processing architectures

In essence, PDP and connectionist models are richly interconnected systems that represent knowledge at a number of levels; features, letters, words, semantics or concepts. Information is processed in parallel and distributed across all units in the system at once, and there are connections within and between levels that are either excitatory or inhibitory. The activation of one part of the system feeds backwards to lower levels of analysis and upward to higher levels of analysis. Through the processes of activation and inhibition interacting, the system will eventually 'relax' to a stable state where the best fit to the

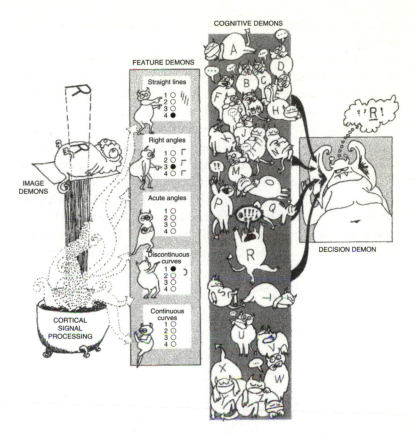

FIGURE 6.2 The pandemonium model. From Lindsay and Norman (1972).

data is found. In many ways this is how the brain works, and such models are sometimes said to be 'neuronally plausible'. PDP models are implemented on computers to discover how effective they are, and can even be experimentally 'lesioned' by damaging part of the network to see if performance on the task breaks down in the same way as human performance. Such models are too complex an issue for this book, and here we shall only consider some early simple models. To illustrate the power of PDP, let us consider one of the first and most influential models, the Interactive Activation Model (IAM) of letter recognition constructed by McClelland and Rumelhart (1981). See Figure 6.3.

There are three levels in the architecture: the feature level, the letter level and the word level. Within each level there are inhibitory links, and between levels there are excitatory links. Lines ending in arrows indicate excitatory links, where as lines with blobs on the end indicate inhibitory links. When a letter is activated—let's say it is a T—any features consistent with T are activated and immediately begin to activate words at the word level that have T in the first position. At the same time the letter T begins to inhibit any neighbouring letter that might be partially activated, in this example, because it shares any features with T, but if I was shown it, too, would be activated by the central upright line feature. As words that have T in the first position become activated, they feed excitation down to the letter level to

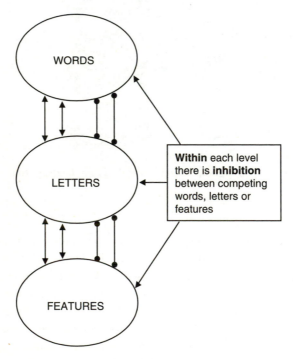

FIGURE 6.3 Basic framework of the interactive activation model proposed by McClelland and Rumelhart (1981).

activate T and inhibit inconsistent letters. At the same time they send inhibition to neighbouring words. As the cycles of excitation and inhibition are gone through, and information coming from letters from other positions feeds into the system, one candidate letter or word becomes more and more active, while the other letters and words become more and more inhibited. Eventually one candidate will 'win' at each level, and then it is recognised.

This model can account for a number of findings, including our ability to read letters that are incomplete, that letters in words are recognised faster than a letter on its own (this is called the 'word superiority effect'), and that letters in words that are similar to real words, such as 'MAVE', are read more quickly than letters in words that are not like any words, such as 'VMEA'. This is called the 'pseudoword superiority effect'. Pseudowords have many neighbours that are similar to them, for example MAVE shares letters with CAVE, HAVE, MAKE, MARE, which all contribute activation to letters in MAVE. VMEA has no helpful neighbours. Imagine reading a newspaper that has been rained on; your stored knowledge, like that contained in the word level of IAM, can work out what the letters are most likely to be because of the influence of top-down word context. However, if the newspaper was in a foreign language, making out the missing letters would be much more difficult, as there would be no word knowledge to act top-down to aid your interpretation of missing or obscured letters.

Marr's computational theory of vision

Marr (1982) proposed a theory concerned with the construction of a description of an object from analysis of its component parts that explains how the early stages of visual processing produce a description of the way that surfaces, contours, textures and shading relate to each other. Marr (1982) described a computational theory of vision, which has been extremely influential in the way psychologists think about the problems of visual processing. It also gets round some of the difficulties with earlier theories of pattern recognition. It is to those theories that we now turn.

Objects are even more complicated than letters or words, because they are three-dimensional, and have a different appearance depending on the angle from which they are viewed. Perhaps the most influential theory of vision was proposed by David Marr (1945–80). Unfortunately he died aged 35, but his book *Vision* was published posthumously (Marr, 1982). Not only did Marr propose a theory of visual processing based on computer vision, but he also discussed the nature and purpose of psychological explanation. A computational theory does not necessarily have anything to do with computers, although it is usually the case that such models are tested out by actually trying them on a computer to see if they provide a good description of the task that the theory is about. One very good thing about having to write a computer program to simulate a task, such as visual processing, is that it requires very careful and logical analysis of what the computer would have to be able to do in order to perform the task effectively. Marr's main question was: How can our processing system derive a conscious percept of three-dimensional representations of the world from the patterns of light intensity that stimulate the retina? Marr also asked: What is the purpose of vision? He felt that the images of the external world produced should be useful to the viewer and not cluttered with irrelevant information.

So, how do we get from the hardware of the retinal and neural pathways to a conscious three-dimensional representation of the world, and is there evidence from neuropsychological patients to help us understand the stages or modules involved? Marr proposed that processing proceeds in a series of stages. At each stage a representation is computed and algorithms operate on each representation to produce the next, new representation. Gradually the pattern of light intensity on the retina is transformed into a three-dimensional representation of an object. Marr distinguishes three stages involved in the computation of the visual representation: the primal sketch, the 2.5D sketch and the 3D sketch.

Stage 1: Computing image descriptions — the primal sketch

This computation is in two parts. First the raw *primal sketch* is computed and then the full primal sketch. The raw primal sketch consists of a 'grey level description' of information on the retina, based on the light intensity changes over the image. This image is viewpoint-dependent, because if it were viewed from a different angle the intensity changes would be different. One important thing to detect are 'zero-crossings', where there is a sudden intensity change that usually means an edge or a boundary. The primitives derived in the raw sketch are represented as tokens and go to make up the full primal sketch, where small local changes in the image are grouped together according to *Gestalt principles* of proximity, good continuation or closure into larger-scale blobs, boundaries or lines to produce contours and tokens that represent areas of importance in the image.

Stage 2: The 2.5D sketch

At the level of analysis called the 2.5D sketch, representations are formed that provide descriptions of visual properties like slant, boundaries, overlaps and intensity of illumination of the surfaces. Some depth information is represented but not all, and the representation of the image is still viewpoint-dependent. If we only derived 2.5D sketches we would have difficulty in recognising objects from various orientations. Marr suggested that the contours of shapes could be derived from the 2.5D image and mapped onto stored knowledge about the shapes of three-dimensional objects.

Stage 3: The 3D object representation

The 3D representation of a shape is *object-centred* rather than *viewer-centred* and allows us to map an object viewed from almost any angle onto its representation in memory. So we can recognise a bucket whether we view it from above, below or from the side. The basic idea behind deriving the 3D representation from the 2.5D representation is that the major axis of orientation is worked out and the parts of the object arranged around it. Marr and Nishihara proposed that the 'primitives' for describing objects are cylinders with major axes. The major axes of a human, a dog and a gorilla are shown in Figure 6.4.

To derive the major axis the system has to detect concavities: a concavity is a place where the contour points into the object. The concavities allow the visual image to be divided into segments and, from this, the major axis can be determined. The proportional lengths of segments help in object identification. For example, the differences in the proportional length of the arms and legs can easily allow us to tell the difference between a human and a gorilla (Humphreys and

HUMAN   GORILLA   QUADRUPED

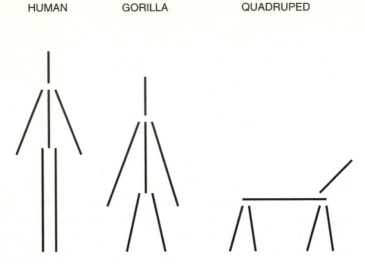

FIGURE 6.4 The principal axes of the human body, a gorilla and a quadruped.

Bruce, 1989). Complex shapes will be made up of a number of axes that articulate in a known way. So the human body, arm, hand etc. will each have their own major axis but those axes will articulate differently from those of a quadruped, like a dog. Of course to be able to 'know' we are seeing a dog, a gorilla or a man, the correct object description must be accessed from memory and made available to conscious experience.

Beiderman's theory of recognition by components

Rather than cylinders, Biederman proposed that objects can be considered as comprising 'geons', which are basic shapes such as cylinder, sphere, wedge, etc. Although there are only about 36 types of geon, in multiple combinations they provide a powerful way of describing object shape. To determine which geons make up the object's shape, there is an early stage of analysis in which the edges in the visual image are detected on the basis of texture, colour and brightness differences. The object is then segmented on the basis of concavities, in a similar way to that proposed by Marr and Nishihara (1978). Then it is necessary to discover those edges that remain invariant over different viewpoints. Biederman proposed that the invariant properties of edges are that they derive from a set of points which are collinear on a straight line, points set on a curve or points on parallel, or are coterminous, i.e., end at the same point. These invariant properties do not change over different orientations and are what Biederman called 'non-accidental properties', that is, they remain the same when the viewpoint changes, so indicating the real shape of the object as a basis for recognition. Biederman's theory can help explain how we can recognise objects from parts, when information is incomplete because objects are overlapping or in poor viewing conditions. This is because invariant properties of edges can be detected even when only part of the edge can be seen. Also, provided the concavities can be seen, the missing parts can be filled in by top-down knowledge from memory and identified on the basis of a 'best fit' between the data and known objects. Imagine trying to differentiate a cylinder from a brick; even when they are partly hidden, sufficient information remains to allow you to tell one from the other, because you know what bricks and cylinders look like (see Figure 6.5).

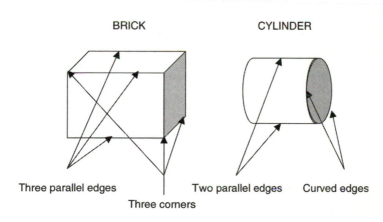

FIGURE 6.5 Some of the non-variant properties of a brick and a cylinder.

Does object recognition depend on a familiar viewpoint?
Canonical views

The brick and cylinder in Figure 6.5 are shown as if they are viewed from a slight angle, in a three-quarters view. When people are asked to imagine or draw an object from memory, they typically recall or draw this three-quarters view, which is called the *canonical view*. They do the same when asked to select which of a variety of views of an object represents the 'best' view (Palmer, Rosch and Chase, 1981). Thus although Marr and Nishihara (1978) and Biederman (1995) propose theories of object recognition that involve analysing the object into its component parts and that allow recognition from any viewpoints, it appears that people actually have a preference for some views over others and that perhaps the canonical viewpoint may have a privileged role in recognising and remembering objects because it is familiar or does not obscure any crucial visual information. So, an alternative theory of object recognition suggests that, rather than compute the 3D shape of an object, you recognise it by matching it to a close match stored in memory. There is a variety of experimental evidence to support this alternative. For example, Tarr (1995) created a small set of 'canonical' viewpoints for a set of three-dimensional nonsense objects and trained participants to recognise them. After practice the participants became progressively faster at responding to the more familiar views than to unfamiliar views. This suggests that we are quicker to recognise an object on the basis of our familiar experience of it than on the basis of the object's three-dimensional geometry. Blanz, Tarr and Bulthoff (1999) investigated the factors contributing to preferred or canonical views of objects in two experiments using computer graphics that allowed a subject to manipulate an object's image. The images were familiar everyday things such as furniture, cars and animals. In the first experiment, participants adjusted the rotation of each object to the viewpoint they would use to take a photograph; in the second experiment they were given the name of an object, asked to imagine it and then to adjust the object on the screen to the viewpoint they had imagined it from. Surprisingly consistent results were found across participants, and the canonical view was not the same for both tasks. For the photography task people preferred a three-quarters view; for the imagery task they tended to prefer front or side views. It was also evident that the three-dimensional geometry of the objects also played a part in recognition. The authors concluded that preferred or canonical views are produced by an interaction between experience, the task and geometry and that all these factors contribute to the way that the object is represented. Evidence from some patients with the disability of visual object agnosia shows that recognition of an object from the canonical viewpoint is preserved while recognition from more unusual viewpoints is impaired. This suggests that different abilities underpin these different forms of object recognition.

Deficits in visual object recognition

Warrington and Taylor (1973, 1978) argued that normal object recognition requires the ability to assign equivalent stimuli to the same perceptual category so that an object can be recognised as the same in different lighting conditions, from different orientations, at different distances, etc. Patients with right-hemisphere posterior parietal lesions were tested on a number of object recognition tasks in which they were asked to recognise 20 common objects such as a bucket or an iron, photographed from a variety of viewpoints. The patients had no real difficulty with the canonical views, but were markedly impaired in recognising objects taken from more 'unusual' views. As the objects could be correctly identified in the canonical view, the 2.5D object-centred representation and object recognition units must be functional. This pattern of results suggests that the patients were having difficulty in constructing an object-centred description to match to the unusual view of the object onto the correct object recognition units in memory. There are other varieties of visual object agnosia, which we met in Chapters 4 and 5.

Perceiving and recognising faces

Objects such as buckets and irons do not usually change shape and move themselves around while we are looking at them. However, when we identify a face, we can do so even when the person is moving their mouth while talking, as well as when they are smiling, frowning or shaking their head. Another problem for face perception and recognition is that most faces are structurally very similar in terms of their component features: they all have two eyes, a nose and a mouth, yet we are able to differentiate one face from another quite easily. It is one thing to recognise a visual stimulus as 'a face'; it is quite a different problem to recognise a particular face and retrieve knowledge about that person. This can be particularly difficult if you meet a person out of their normal context. For example, you may have a feeling of familiarity about a face, but if you meet this person in a different place to usual it may be some time before you realise 'That is the man who works in the bank', if you see him at the swimming pool. Context can have powerful effects on retrieval from memory because it activates likely candidates by a process of spreading activation, making retrieval of an associated memory easier and therefore more likely.

Discriminating between faces is a case of within-category discrimination. Another example of this would be telling one make of car from another, but generally faces are more similar to each other than cars. So, are faces identified in the same way as other objects, as we described in the section above? Well, first of all there is something special about faces; they are socially significant and psychologists have found specialised cells in monkey brain that respond selectively not only to any face, but also to familiar faces, (Hasselmo, Rolls and Bayliss, 1989). This kind of neural specialisation does not exist for other objects.

Bruce *et al.* (1996) review evidence on face recognition, and suggest that face recognition is not very successful if it is only based on 'edge' features, and that faces are poorly discriminated when only outlines are shown. It seems that information about surface features such as skin and hair colour are also needed to differentiate one face from another. Difficult within-category discrimination also requires colour and texture information. For example, you could imagine that trying to discriminate, within the category 'fruit', between an apple, a nectarine and a peach on the basis of outline alone would be more difficult without information on colour and surface texture. You could quite easily reach the conclusion that you are viewing 'fruit', but beyond that finer discrimination would be difficult.

Further, unlike basic object recognition, priming between faces is affected by changes in the image, for example a photograph versus a sketch, even when viewpoint and facial expression remain the same. This is not the case for other basic objects. For example, Biederman and Cooper (1991) found priming between objects despite changes in properties of the image features. Another difference between the sorts of objects considered by Marr and Nishihara (1978) and Biederman (1995) and discussed above, is that in their theories the object's shape is decomposed into its parts in order to work out the axes of the object. When we recognise a face we need to know the spatial relationship between the facial features, as these are essential to discriminate one face from another.

Experimental evidence supports the idea that faces are processed more holistically than some other objects. As an example, an experiment carried out by Young, Hellawell and Hay (1987) shows that when people are shown the upper or lower half of the face of a famous person, they can still identify it reasonably well. However, when the upper half of one face was combined with the lower half of a different face, people reported seeing a new, unfamiliar face. Further evidence shows that an individual's facial features, such as the nose, are recognised better in the context of a properly organised whole face than in a face where all the features were present but not organised as a proper face (Tanaka and Farah, 1993). The importance of the configural properties of a face for its recognition is supported by the inversion effect. This is demonstrated by the fact that normal people have more difficulty in remembering faces when they are inverted than when they are shown the right way up (Leder and Bruce, 2000). Bruce *et al.* (1996) suggest that the present evidence supports the view that there may be a difference between the relative importance of component parts and their configuration in recognising faces in comparison to recognising the basic kinds of objects we discussed when we looked at object recognition theory.

Disorders of face recognition

Some people who have suffered brain damage are left with the disorder called 'prosopagnosia', or the inability to recognise faces. While they know that they are looking at a face, they are unable to identify it, even if it is their own reflection, or someone with whom they are very familiar, such as their spouse or mother. Bodamer (1947) reports a patient who had suffered a bullet wound in the head. The patient could pick out individual features of a face, but sensed no feeling of familiarity from the face as a whole. He could see the features, but not 'see' them as a face. Another patient reported by Pallis (1955) could also identify eyes, nose, mouth, etc. but said they did not 'add up'. In order to identify people, prosopagnosics rely on information from other sensory systems, such as voice, or on other visual information, such as distinctive gait or mannerisms. Patient HJA, reported by Riddoch and Humphreys (1987b), who suffers from visual agnosia, is also prosopagnosic. He cannot recognise his wife; he knows she has a face, but it is just a face—he cannot tell it is her. The only way he knows her is by her voice and movements. He tells men from women by their hair and clothes and voices.

Whilst it is often the case that a prosopagnosic patient has also lost the ability to recognise objects, i.e., they also have visual object agnosia, this is not always the case. If visual object agnosia and prosopagnosia can be dissociated, that is be lost separately, this would suggest that recognising objects and recognising faces depend on different processes and, therefore, different brain areas. Recent evidence from fMRI studies by Farah and Aguirre (1999) have revealed distinct brain areas particularly involved in face recognition. If face and object recognition processes were exactly the same, there should not be dissociation between agnosia and prosopagnosia, or the involvement of different brain regions. This evidence supports the view that faces are more than a special kind of object. Farah *et al.* (1998) review the evidence in an appropriately named paper *What is 'special' about face perception?*

Perception of facial expression

Of course, apart from recognising who someone is, we also need to know if they are looking at us, are threatening or happy. We need to be able to analyse facial expression and direction of gaze. There is some evidence for the inherited ability to distinguish the facial expressions that express emotion and this could be important for survival. These non-verbal communications we interpret as anger, fear, surprise, disgust and happiness. Ekman and colleagues have done most work in this area (for a review see Ekman, 1982) and have shown that there is close agreement across different cultures on the classification of these emotions on the basis of facial expression. Whist some facial expressions may be universal and 'hard-wired' in our genetic make-up, we are also able to distinguish a far wider range of expressions that indicate, for example, someone is interested or bored, or whether the smile they are wearing is, in fact, genuine. Evidence shows that we can distinguish between a true and an acted expression. The difference between genuine, spontaneous expressions and posed expressions lies in subtle difference between the timing and extent of the movements of the facial muscles (Ekman, 1992). Bruce *et al.* (1996, pp 355), suggest 'A particular emotion or group of related emotional states might be characterised by the relative dispositions of and shapes of the face, perhaps in respect to the axis of symmetry.' Here we can see there could be a some parallel between extracting major axes in object recognition around which the parts are distributed, and recognising the arrangement of features in facial expression.

Knowing who we are looking at: Memory for person knowledge

We don't only recognise a face as a familiar or that it may be friendly or unfriendly; we also know about the person to whom the face belongs. In the same way that we need to know the semantic properties of objects (as in the fruit bowl example), we have semantic knowledge about people. When we see a picture of Robbie Williams, we know he is a pop-star, is very rich, and has tattoos. When we meet someone familiar in the street we know they are a member of our seminar group, or work in the bar, and so forth. Often, however, we see a face, know we know it, but cannot place where from. More embarrassing, perhaps, we meet someone we recognise, know all about them, but cannot remember their name. It is evident that information about people can dissociate. Retrieval of the name does not automatically generate where we know them from, their occupation, etc. and knowing their occupation does not necessarily give access to their name.

A diary study of errors in recognising people

Young, Hay and Ellis (1985) asked people to keep a diary for eight weeks in which they were to record errors or difficulties they had had in recognising people. Bruce and Young explain that the errors were classified into four major categories as follows (from Bruce and Young, 1998, p. 177):

1 Where a familiar person went unrecognised. One example was 'I was going through the doors . . . of the library when a friend said "hello". I at first ignored him, thinking that he must have been talking to the person behind me.'

2 Where a person was misidentified; sometimes an unfamiliar person was misidentified as a familiar one, or one familiar person misidentified as the other. An example of the first kind of error was 'I was waiting for the phone. A lot of people were walking past. I thought one of them was my boyfriend.'

3 Where a person seemed familiar, but the diarist did not know why. An example of this kind of error was 'I was in the back waiting to be served. I saw a person and I knew there was something familiar immediately. After a few seconds I realised she was from the shop on campus, or a secretary in one of the departments. I eventually remembered by a process of elimination.'

4 Where only partial details about a familiar person could be retrieved. For example, 'I saw another student walking past, but I couldn't remember his name, even though I'd been talking about him only a few days ago. Someone had to tell me.'

These examples show that face recognition can fail in a number of ways and for different reasons. However, amongst all the errors, no one ever reported knowing a person's name without also knowing who they were. Other evidences from reaction time studies of judging faces for familiarity, occupations or names. Familiarity decisions were always fastest, and name decisions were always slowest. Bruce (1996) explains that this data, together with studies from neuropsychological patients, favours the view that face are recognised in a three-stage process of familiarity–identity–names.

Bruce and Young's model of face recognition

Bruce and Young (1986) developed a functional model for the components involved in face perception and recognition that could account for everyday failures in recognising faces, and for the breakdown of abilities in patients with prosopagnosia. The model comprises nine processing components (see Figure 6.6).

Down the right-hand side of the model are the processes that allow the generation of a person's name and these processes interact with other specific face-relevant processes and the rest of the cognitive system.

Taking the right-hand side of the model first, the generation of a viewer-centred description of the face is based on similar principles to Marr's model for object recognition. However, unlike other objects, faces can change their shape according to expression, so we have to be able to derive a description of the face irrespective of whether it is laughing or crying. This is the expression-independent description. Following structural encoding, the description of the face can be mapped onto face recognition units. Bruce and Young suggest that the face recognition system must be highly differentiated because we are capable of recognising hundreds of different faces, but this is not usually true for other kind of objects. Therefore, they suggest the existence of 'face recognition units' rather than *prototype* memory representations used for other categories of objects. (see Chapter 12). Face recognition units feed onto the 'person identity nodes', which represent knowledge about the person with that face, such as their occupation, whether they are married, their age group, their interests and so on. From the person identity nodes, names can be generated.

The processes on the left-hand side of the model are interconnected with the processes on the right-hand side. The process of expression analysis is used to infer a person's mood from the arrangement of the facial features. Facial speech analysis is used to support speech perception by lip-reading. We shall see how this is important in Chapter 9 when we consider cross-modal effects in speech perception. Directed visual processing allows specific aspects of the face to be attended to selectively, for example to discover the colour of someone's eyes. Finally, all processes are in interactive contact with the cognitive

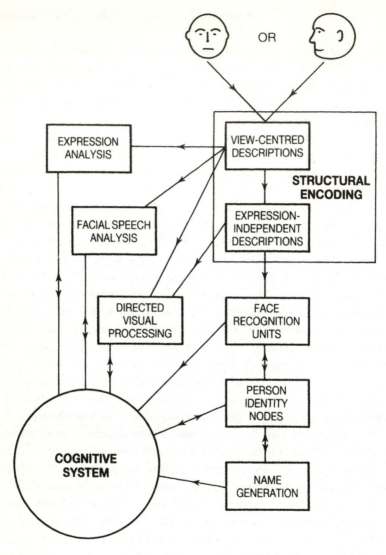

FIGURE 6.6 Bruce and Young's (1986) model for face recognition. From Humphreys and Bruce (1989).

system, which involves all other cognitive processes apart from face perception.

Recognition of familiar and unfamiliar faces is achieved slightly differently. Familiar faces are recognised mainly via structural encoding, face recognition units, person identity nodes and name generation, However, unfamiliar faces or new faces will not have a face recognition unit or person identity node, and so processing of unfamiliar faces mainly involves structural encoding, expression analysis, facial speech analysis and directed visual processing. Presumably, new faces are learnt via the cognitive system and the setting up of person identity nodes. This model can account for most, but not all, data, and has subsequently been developed by Burton and Bruce (1993) into an interactive activation and competition model, IAC (see Figure 6.7).

The interactive activation and competition model for face recognition is an example of the kind of model that has become popular since the mid 1980s, with the increasing acceptance of the connectionist approach to modelling cognition. In many ways this model is similar to the 'Jets and Sharks' model we shall discuss in the final chapter, which represents general and specific knowledge in long-term memory. Burton and Bruce's (1993) model incorporates units specialised for representing different types of information, and these units have interconnections that can vary in strength, so that some units can activate other units more than others. Face recognition units (FRUs) store information about faces, and name recognition units (NRUs) store names. The person identity nodes (PINs) allow access to semantic information about individuals and can be activated by their name as well as their face. This knowledge is stored in the semantic information units (SIUs) and enables the system to know if the face is familiar or not. This model accounts quite well for the data on face recognition errors (prosopagnosia) and can explain the priming effect of one face by a previously seen semantically related face. For example, recognising the face of Prince Philip spreads activation to SIUs for the royal family, and so primes the response to the face of the Queen.

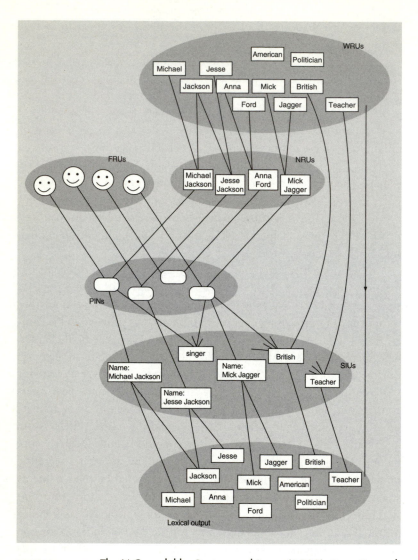

FIGURE 6.7 The IAC model by Burton and Bruce (1993). From Eysenck and Keane (2000).

What is 'special' about face perception?

Farah *et al.* (1998) proposed the hypothesis that the difference between face and object recognition is the degree to which each depends on decomposing the visual image into parts. Most theories of object recognition, including those we have discussed of Marr (1982) and Biederman and Gerhandstein (1993), propose that the shapes of objects are represented in terms of parts, and that the parts are themselves represented as separate shapes. Farah *et al.* suggest that face recognition involves more holistic representations than other types of object. This hypothesis was tested in a series of experiments in which 'masking' was used to test interference with stimulus recognition. A mask is a stimulus presented soon after the test stimulus and depending on the type of processing it interrupts, it will affect the participant's ability to identify the target. Farah argued that if a picture of an object, such as a house, is identified by part analysis, then a mask made up from muddled parts of a house would interfere with target identification, but a mask which was a picture of a whole house would not. On the contrary, if faces are processed holistically, then a whole face would produce more interference than a mask made from muddled face features. As predicted by the theory, recognition of faces was less disrupted by the part masks, and recognition of houses was less disrupted by whole masks. So, the data are consistent with the hypothesis that faces are processed more holistically than other objects. Take together with the dissociation between face and object recognition in neuropsychological patients, and the specialised neurons which are responsive to faces found in monkeys, it would appear that face perception is indeed special.

Is face processing really special?

Some researchers believe that faces are only special inasmuch as we have become experts at identifying them. If this is the case, then face recognition is dependent on the same perceptual and cognitive properties that are involved in any fine discrimination task at which we have become expert. Recently evidence gathered from brain scanning techniques such as fMRI has added to the debate. Kanwisher,

McDermott and Chun (1997) and Kanwisher (2000) found that the right fusiform area in the brain becomes strongly activated during face recognition. This evidence suggests that this brain area *is* specific to face processing. However, Gautier, Behrmann and Tarr (1999) were interested to test if face recognition was really special, or if it was just a special kind of object recognition involving fine discrimination. They trained people to distinguish between families of strange little characters called 'greebles'. At first greebles are very difficult to differentiate, but with practice recognition improves. Importantly, as people became more expert in recognising greebles their brain activity showed more activation in the fusiform face areas. In further studies Gautier *et al.* (2000) have also shown that people who are experts in differentiating between cars and birds also show activation of brain areas involved in face recognition when making their judgements. So, it could be argued that face processing is treated in a special way by the brain because we have extensive experience of differentiating between different faces, that is, we are expert at it. However, some cells in the right fusiform area that are sensitive to face inversion are not sensitive to the inversion of greebles, so there may still be some difference between face and object recognition. Kanwisher (2000) provides a fuller explanation of this debate.

Summary

For us to be able to recognise patterns and three-dimensional objects, their descriptions must be derived and matched to memory. Early theories included matching features of objects onto templates, but this was proved to be difficult as there are too many variables in the shapes and patterns for features to map onto, and with only partial informa-tion a match could not be made. The interactive information model could account for the effect of top-down activation in letter and word recognition better than previous models such as Pandemonium. To be able to recognise objects from different viewpoints, an object descrip-tion that is centred on the object is necessary. Marr and Nishihara (1978) developed a computational theory that derives object descrip-tions in three phases from the retinal image. The 3D sketch is object-centred and is based on the derivation of the major axis of the object. Marr and Nishihara suggested that an object could be analysed into generalised cones, but Biederman (1993) proposed that component parts of objects are better described by geons and other non-accidental properties of objects. There is also evidence that canonical views are important for object recognition, but the view that is chosen to be canonical may depend on the current task. Faces seem to be recognised differently from other objects because they are processed more holistically rather than being constructed from component parts. However, recent studies by researchers such as Gautier suggest that faces may only be special because we are expert at differentiating between them. Recognising a face provides access to other information about a person, but studies have shown that information about a person can dissociate and we are prone to errors in face recognition and person identification. Models such as IAC can account for the breakdown of face recognition ability.

Self-assessment questions (Solutions on p. 321)

1 Can you explain some of the observations in the scenario at the start of the chapter?
2 What are the problems for theories of pattern recognition based on features?
3 Why is a viewer-centred description of an object important?
4 How can we explain the dissociation of knowledge about a person?

Further reading

Bruce, V., Green, P. R. and Georgeson, M. A. (1996) *Visual perception: Physiology, psychology and ecology*. Hove, UK: Psychology Press. For more detailed coverage.

Bruce, V. and Young, A. (1998) *In the eye of the beholder: The science of face recognition*. New York: Oxford University Press. A very readable, well illustrated book on face recognition.

Eysenck, M. W. and Keane, M. T. (2000) *Cognitive psychology: A student's handbook*. Hove, UK: Psychology Press. Includes a very good chapter on face and object recognition.

Kanwisher, N. (2000) Domain specificity in face perception. *Nature Neuroscience*, 3(8), 759–763. For a summary on the face versus object recognition debate.

Chapter 7

Auditory perception and memory

The world of sound

YOU ARE OUT IN THE GARDEN AGAIN. You can hear many distinct sounds coming from different locations around you. The traffic in the street is a buzz, punctuated by the noise of particular cars approaching and passing. Then the sound of the siren of a police car rises in the distance; it comes closer, then the sound of the siren falls as it, too, passes by. The wind rustles in the trees. Your next door neighbours are having a conversation, but you can only make out some of what they are saying. Sometimes you can follow what they say, but then you cannot make out the words when they start talking about their work on atmospheric physics. You hear a dog bark, and recognise it as the little dog belonging to a friend whose footsteps are crunching up the front path, so you go to meet them.

The complexity of the auditory environment

Although there are many sound sources in the auditory environment, we are able to hear these sounds separately. The sounds are correctly categorised and matched to memory to allow us to recognise what the object is or the source that produced them. We usually think of visual objects, but we can hear auditory objects too. The sound we recognise as barking indicates a dog; another sound may be recognised as an engine. Particular properties of the nature of the sound will allow us to recognise if we are listening to a small dog—we may call this sound 'yapping' as opposed to the sound of a larger dog, which we may categorise as 'woofing'. Likewise, depending on the properties of the engine sound, we may identify the engine as belonging to a car or a lorry. Clearly, in the same way that visual object descriptions can access memory representations of visual objects, auditory descriptions can also be matched to the memory representations that include the auditory properties of objects, including the sounds that make up speech.

What is really quite remarkable is that although incoming sounds are superimposed upon each other, the auditory system is able to analyse them into their individual components, and segregate auditory streams into sounds sourced from objects. The physical properties of light and sound are rather different, and the sense organs are therefore designed rather differently. If you miss something in the visual environment you can look again to check, as most objects, apart from things like a flash of lightning or rapid movements, persist in time. A pattern of light from a visual scene stimulates the light-sensitive cells in the retina all at once, in parallel, to produce the retinal image. On the other hand, the patterns of acoustic vibrations that produce the sounds we recognise in speech, such as a cat meowing, or the characteristic sound of a particular car or musical instrument, are distributed over time. If we miss them we cannot go back and listen to them again.

Audition: The sense of hearing

Although the majority of work on the psychology of sensation, perception and attention has been concerned with visual information processing, we obviously rely on information from all the other senses as well. Objects in the world are defined not only by what they look like, but also how they feel, the sounds they make, and what they smell or taste like. It is also the case that, although the sense modalities are often considered in isolation, there is a good deal of evidence that information from the senses works together in allowing us to form a more full and reliable interpretation and representation of the environment. Although a great deal is known about visual perception, somewhat less is known about the other senses. In many books of attention, perception and memory the senses other than vision are largely ignored. However, there is an increasing literature on cross-modal effects in cognition, which we shall visit in Chapter 8. After vision, we probably know most about hearing, or audition.

Physical properties of sound: Frequency and amplitude

Sound is produced by vibrations in the air, which are pressure changes over time. *Frequency* of the sound vibration is measured in cycles per second, or Hertz (Hz). *Amplitude* is measured as sound pressure level, or decibels (dB). To aid your understanding of frequency and amplitude, you could think of pushing someone on a swing. The rate at which you have to push the swing to make it go properly is the frequency, which will depend upon the length of the chains that suspend the seat. A swing with long chains will need to be pushed at a slower rate than a swing with short chains. How hard you push the swing determines the amplitude, or how high the swing goes. With sound, the frequency determines the pitch you hear and the amplitude determines the loudness. The most simple sound is a sine wave, which is heard as a very pure tone, like that of a tuning fork. Tuning forks come in different sizes that determine the frequency and hence the pitch of the tone they produce. Short-pronged forks vibrate more frequently, i.e., have a higher frequency, and produce a higher-pitched sound than long-pronged forks. In the same way a short vibrating string makes a higher pitched sound than a longer string. This is why violin players stop the strings with their fingers to alter the pitch produced by the instrument. Depending on how hard you strike the tuning fork, or how much pressure the violin player puts on the string, the sound made will be louder or softer. Musical instruments produce complex tones and a sound property called timbre, which characterise the different instruments. We shall consider timbre and complex tones a little later.

Loudness is an important perceptual property and is involved in locating and identifying sounds. Note that the amplitude changes, which produce the air pressure changes that stimulate the ear, are a physical property of sound; loudness is the psychological experience of that sound. Usually we hear sounds, but very loud sounds may be felt rather than heard, with the threshold for feeling being at around 120 dB. However, the relationship between amplitude and loudness is not one to one, and at the same time, loudness also depends on pitch. Large increases in sound pressure produce small changes in loudness, and different frequencies have different absolute thresholds (see Chapter 2), and are perceived as equally loud at different sound pressures.

You can notice the relationship between different frequencies and loudness by turning the volume on your audio system up or down. At moderate loudness, say 80 dB, you will be able to hear all the frequencies from 30 to 15,000 Hz, as they all are above threshold. But as you turn the volume down, the lower frequencies will become inaudible, as they fall below threshold. This is why music systems often have a 'loudness' button that you can press at low volumes to boost the low-frequency range so it can be heard.

Basics of the auditory system

Given that sound vibrations have frequency and amplitude, these are the most important properties of sound that the auditory system needs to be able to detect. This is achieved by a combination of mechanical and neural activity in the ear. Sound is picked up by the pinna (the part we normally call the ear), and travels down the auditory canal where the sound vibrations in the air cause the tympanic membrane, or ear drum, to vibrate. These vibrations are transmitted via the little bones, or ossicles, in the middle ear to another membrane called the oval window, which is at the entrance to the inner ear, or *cochlea*. Cochlea means shell, and reflects the spiral, shell-like shape of this part of the inner ear. The cochlea has a membrane running along its length, called the *basilar membrane*, and as the vibration at the oval window transmits its energy into the cochlea, the basilar membrane is set in motion. The motion of the basilar membrane is similar to that made when you shake a ribbon to make a wave travel along it, except the basilar membrane is fixed at both ends. Along the length of the basilar membrane are rows of hair cells, which touch against the moving membrane and translate the mechanical movement of the membrane into neural activity. This neural information is sent to the auditory nerve and then via the ventral and dorsal cochlea nuclei, the superior olive, lateral lemniscus, inferior colliculus, medial geniculate, and the cortical hemispheres. As in vision, information from both ears goes to both hemispheres. Cortical neurons are sensitive to preferred frequencies and direction of frequency change, and about 20% of cortical neurons are sensitive to complex stimuli such as clicks and hisses.

The peak of vibration that occurs on the basilar membrane is related to the frequency of the sound source stimulating the ear. This means that different sound frequencies activate different places along the basilar membrane, allowing coding for pitch. The greater the amplitude of the vibration stimulating the ear, the more neurons will fire, producing the perception of loudness. However, the perception of loudness to some extent depends on pitch, (Moore, 1995).

For a simple sine wave there will be only one peak reflecting frequency and amplitude, but most sounds are complex, or composed of a number of sine waves that are added together. In the case of these complex sounds a number of peaks will be produced on the basilar membrane that correspond to the frequency and amplitude of the component sine waves. The fact that the basilar membrane can respond to all these components means it is performing what is known as *Fourier analysis*. In the 19th century, Fourier demonstrated mathematically that any complex tone can be analysed into its component frequencies and amplitudes. When, for example, a violin string of the same length, and hence the same frequency, is vibrated by the bow, or is plucked by the finger, the tone produced sounds different. This is because of the way in which the string is set into motion. Plucking produces high amplitude early in the sound, whereas bowing starts with low amplitude and increases as the bow gets more grip on the string. These differences lead to a different pattern of loudness over time, or power spectrum, for the two tones. Therefore, although we can tell they have the same pitch, they sound characteristically different. If the violin player played two notes at once, we would also be able to analyse out the pitches of those notes. A violin produces a characteristic sound that is different from a trumpet or a piano. This is because not only the string is vibrating, but also the body of the instrument. These vibrations add in many more frequencies and produce the perceptual property called *timbre*. Different violins, because they are built slightly differently, will have their own differences in timbre, but be more similar to each other than, say, a trumpet or piano, which also vibrate characteristically giving them their individual timbre or sound qualities. The fact that we can identify these differences is evidence of the astonishing capability of the auditory analysis system. The characteristic auditory attributes of objects will be stored in long-term auditory memory.

Segregating the auditory world: Gestalt principles

The Gestalt school of psychology was active during the early part of the last century. Proponents such as Wertheimer (1923) and Kofka (1935) identified a number of what they believed to be innate and fundamental principles of grouping and organisation in perception. Whilst these principles are most often applied to vision, and incorporated into the derivation of object descriptions in Marr's theories for vision, they can be applied equally well to auditory perceptions. No individual rule will always work, but one or other will usually allow us to sort out the problem of which aspects of the auditory environment belong together and which do not. I shall mention only some Gestalt principles of perceptual organisation here; see Moore (1995) for a detailed account.

Similarity

The Gestalt principle of similarity is that elements that are similar will tend to be grouped together. In a book, which relies on the visual medium, this is difficult to show auditorily, so we shall start with a visual example. In Figure 7.1 we can see that although all items are equally spaced, those that have a similar shape are grouped together. In audition, sounds that are similar in timbre, pitch or loudness, will, likewise, tend to be grouped together.

Proximity

This principle says that elements that are close together belong together. Now observe Figure 7.2. Here the separations between the horizontal rows have increased; a different grouping is observed. Rather than the stars and circles belonging together, the spatially separated rows are grouped together, irrespective of their local structure. In audition a series of sounds coming from the same location is likely to be coming from the same sound source.

Common fate and continuity

This principle says that elements that move together, go on and off together, or follow on from each other, belong together. In vision, an

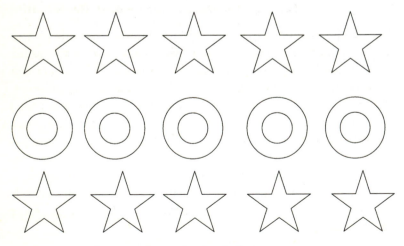

FIGURE 7.1   Perceptual grouping by similarity.

FIGURE 7.2   Perceptual grouping by proximity.

example would be the neon lights around a sign, which, although switching on and off, do so alternately, giving the visual impression of the lights forming one perceptual stream, moving around the hoarding. With sound sources, those that have properties that change frequency, intensity or location smoothly and continuously are likely to be perceived as coming from a single sound source. Patterns of sound that are regular, for example a repeating series of tones, are likely to be coming from the same source object, perhaps a bird singing.

Sloboda (1999) argues that 'these natural mechanisms for visual grouping are motivated by "action" requirements. They help the organism to move about the environment effectively, to locate and track objects in the environment and so on. We should expect auditory grouping mechanisms to have their roots in similar requirements' (p.155). (Selection for action is a topic in Chapter 9.) He goes on to explain that Deutsch (1982) has proposed that such mechanisms have the primary function of allowing us to detect environmentally significant sound-producing objects. Deutsch has suggested that similar sounds are likely to be arising from the same source, and different sounds from separate sources. If we think of the example of stepping into a garden, you can hear the wind in the trees, a bird singing, or several birds singing in different places, and the buzz of insects. As the bird flies overhead, its sound moves with it, smoothly. These separate sources of sound can be grouped and segregated on the basis of Gestalt principles. A number of these principles rely on the ability of the auditory system to locate where sounds come from.

Locating the origin of sounds

In the same way that the two eyes receive slightly different views of an image, enabling stereoscopic vision, the two ears receive slightly different messages about surrounding sound sources. In visual perception, cues involving both eyes are called binocular; in auditory perception, cues involving both ears are called binaural.

Binaural cues

These cues provide important information about where sounds are coming from. The first binaural cue is the time difference between the arrival of a signal at each ear, or the *interaural time difference*. If a sound is located to your right, then the sound will reach your right ear fractionally sooner than it will reach your left ear. Thus by detecting the difference in arrival time it is possible to locate the direction from which the sound is coming. A sound directly in front or behind you will arrive at each ear at the same time. When you listen to reproduced stereophonic sound, the illusion of being in front of the band or orchestra is achieved by delivering the sounds to the ears from the direction they would really be from if you were there in person. They may also have been synthesised to mimic the way sound is modified by the pinna of the outer ear.

The second binaural cue is *intensity*. Because one ear is usually nearer the sound than the other, the intensity of the sound will be greater at the nearest ear. Intensity differences between the sounds arriving at each ear are most useful at high frequencies, because the head casts a sound shadow on the more distant ear. At low frequencies, the wavelength of sound is longer than at high frequencies, and if its length is greater than the distance between the ears then the shadow is less noticeable, because the sound waves pass over and around the head, resulting in less difference in intensity of the sound. However, at low frequencies the auditory system is highly sensitive to the interaural time difference. Differences as small as 10 microseconds, which are equivalent to a 1 or 2 degree movement of the sound source, can be detected (Moore, 1995). As interaural intensity is most useful for locating high-frequency sounds and interaural time difference is most useful for locating low-frequency sounds, it might be expected that we use intensity difference to locate high pitches and time differences to locate low pitches. However, most sounds in the environment are complex, with a combination of frequencies whose cycle repeats regularly. Even if the overall frequency is high, provided the repeat of the cycle is below about 600 Hz, interaural time difference is a cue to localisation (Neutzel and Hafter, 1981).

When a sound source is located directly in front or behind, interaural differences in intensity or time of arrival will be of no use. However, we are quite capable of making this judgement. One obvious property of the part of the ear we can see, the pinna, is that it faces forward. This means that a sound will be affected by whether it arrives from behind or from in front of the pinna, and this difference in sound quality also provides information about the position of the sound. To tell if a sound source is moving rapidly towards or away from you, the change in frequency called the *Doppler shift* can be used. Think of the sound of the siren on a police car as it approaches from behind and goes past into the distance. Not only does the sound get louder as the car approaches, but also the pitch appears to rise. As the car goes past the loudness decreases and there is a rapid lowering in pitch. This is because as the car moves forward, the sound waves become pushed together, or compressed, in front and stretched out behind. As pitch is determined by the frequency of the air waves, those at the front have a higher frequency than those behind the moving vehicle. The rate of change of loudness and pitch are cues to the speed of movement.

Auditory scene analysis and attention

The properties of sound we have discussed above provide the basis for creating a representation of the auditory environment, and there is general agreement that Gestalt principles are applied to such aspects as frequency, location and timbre. This process is called auditory scene analysis or auditory streaming (see, for example, Bregman, 1990;

Handel, 1989). The phenomenon of streaming by pitch illustrates how grouping can change depending on the frequency difference in a series of tones. When a series of tones that alternate in frequency is presented in a sequence, one or two auditory streams will be perceived depending on the frequency difference. When the frequency difference is small, or presentation rate is slow, a single stream is heard, which has a 'galloping' rhythm. As the frequency difference increases, a point will be reached when the single stream separates into two (see Figure 7.3).

The segregation into streams can take a short while to 'build up'; a stream may sound like a single stream to start with and only segregate after several seconds. An important question about auditory streaming is whether or not this perceptual analysis requires focal attention, or takes place pre-attentively. This has only recently been addressed. Carlyon *et al.* (2001) engaged participants in a divided attention experiment. The two tasks were presented one to each ear. One task involved making a judgement on the number of streams heard; the other was to discriminate between bursts of sound that were either increasing or decreasing in frequency. For the first 10 seconds of each trial participants were to attend to the frequency discrimination task, and then, after another 10 seconds, make the stream judgement. In comparison to a control condition that only involved stream judgements, the build-up of stream segregation was reduced.

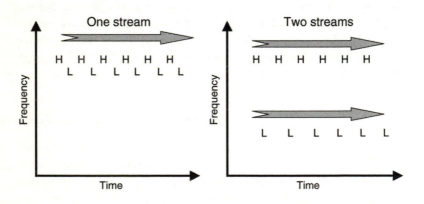

FIGURE 7.3 Perceptual grouping in auditory streaming.

This was taken to indicate that attention is necessary for auditory streaming. To test this, the authors conducted another experiment in which the secondary attentional task was carried out on the same tone sequence as the stream judgement. In this case there was no difference between conditions, presumably because attention had to be directed to the stimulus for the primary task.

While these experiments suggest that attention is important for segregating acoustic attributes into streams, Macken *et al.* (2003) argue that it is important to establish whether auditory streaming happens without attention. In Carylon *et al.*'s experiment the auditory stimuli were always the object of focal attention at some stage of the study. To discover if unattended auditory information is analysed into streams, they devised a test for the effect of streaming without directly asking participants to attend to it. One way to do this was to utilise the irrelevant sound effect. This is the interference caused by task-irrelevant sound on recall for visually presented items (e.g., Salame and Baddeley, 1987). Sounds differ in their ability to interfere; in particular, sounds that are constant do not have a disrupting effect, but sounds that have what is called 'changing state' do. Using this critical difference between stimuli that do or do not cause disruption, Macken *et al.* devised a very clever experiment. They reasoned that if auditory streaming can happen pre-attentively, without focal attention, then by manipulating the frequency difference between successive tones in the unattended stimulus, they could influence whether it should form one or two streams. One stream would be producing a changing state, and so interfere with recall of visually presented items. However, if the unattended stimulus became segregated it would become two steady streams, cease changing, and so would be less disruptive. This is what the results showed. Participants had been instructed that the sounds were irrelevant and that they should ignore them and would never be asked about them. Despite this, as the rate of presentation of the tones increased, they interfered more and more with the letter recall task up to the point where the streams segregated, and then the interference dropped to the same levels as no sound. Therefore, it would appear that despite being outside focal attention, the auditory stimulus was analysed into streams. For a review of auditory distraction effects, see Jones (1999).

Speech perception

We listen to and interpret speech effortlessly, at least for our native language or one we know well. Possession of language is arguably the most important distinguishing feature of the human race. Yet an analysis of what needs to be done to decode the acoustic signals into the components that differentiate one speech sound from another shows that even deciding that a 'd' is a 'd' is difficult. To understand some of the problems that need to be solved in speech perception, we must first know a little about speech production. A primary distinction between the sounds of any language is between vowels and consonants. When a consonant is pronounced, the vocal tract is constricted somewhere to cause a build-up of air pressure. This may be achieved by closing the lips, or placing the tongue on the roof of the mouth—if you repeat the word 'butter' several times, you will be aware of doing this. In the word 'butter' there are two places in the word where you produce an explosive burst of air, and the sound produced depends on whether constriction is made by the lips or the tongue. These aspects of consonant production can be described in terms of a) place of articulation and the b) manner of articulation. If you try another word, this time 'figure', and say it a few times, you will discover different places where the constriction can be made. To produce /f/ you place your bottom lip against your upper front teeth and then push air between the lips and teeth. To produce /g/ you close the airway by pushing the back of the tongue up against the roof the mouth, or upper palate. You will also notice that the vowels in these words are voiced. That is, the vocal cords are made to resonate. All vowels are voiced but only some consonants, for example /b/ is voiced but /p/ is not. When saying /b/ the vocal cords begin to resonate as soon as the lips are parted, but with /p/ the voicing comes a little later. A *phoneme* is defined as the smallest unit of sound that can alter the meaning of a word. So /b/ and /p/ are phonemes because *but* and *put* have different meanings. A phoneme is not necessarily equivalent to a letter, as some phonemes are composed of two letters, for example the letters 'oa' in boat. There are many possible phonemes that can be assigned distinctiveness in a language, but different languages have chosen a different selection. For example, in English we distinguish between

/r/ and /l/, but in Japanese there is no such distinction. Hence the confusion for Japanese learners of English: 'We had flied lice for runch and frapjack for tea.'

Speech spectrograms and the invariance problem

Phonemes stand for specific sounds, and these sounds are different because they are made up from a particular pattern of frequencies and amplitudes called the *acoustic signal*. A speech spectrogram can be plotted to show the pattern of frequencies over the time course of a phoneme, a word or several words. The spectrogram for even a single phoneme looks rather complex, but it would be convenient to expect that provided a listener were able to learn to identify the acoustic signal corresponding to each phoneme in the language, the problem of speech perception would be solved. Unfortunately there is a problem, because the acoustic signal corresponding to a phoneme is not always the same, i.e., it is not invariant. The acoustic signal of one phoneme is greatly modified by the presence of other phonemes. An example of this is shown in Figure 7.4, which shows idealised spectra for /di/ and /du/.

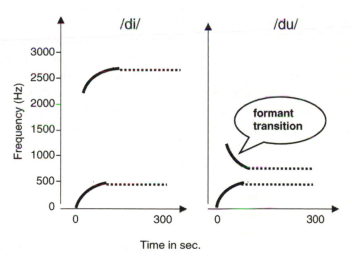

FIGURE 7.4 Illustration of formant shapes for /di/ and /du/.

Here we can see that the phoneme /d/ has a different spectrogram depending on the vowel that follows it. There are two characteristics evident here; the 'formant' and the 'formant transition'. The formants in the spectrogram are the horizontal bands of energy at 200 Hz and 2500 Hz for /di/ and 200 Hz and 600 Hz for /du/. The formant transition is the shift in frequency leading into each formant. In this figure you can see that the formant transition for the first formant at 200 Hz is the same for both /di/ and /du/. However, the formant transition for the second formant is different; for /di/ it rises and for /du/ it falls, even though in both cases we hear the same /d/ sound. So, here is the puzzle—the characteristics of the acoustic signal for /d/ change according to the context of the other sounds it is put with, yet we hear the same sound. How can we hear an invariant sound when the signal varies? One attempt to get round this problem is the motor theory of speech perception.

The motor theory of speech perception

Liberman *et al.* (1967) produced a classic paper called *Perception of the Speech Code*. After outlining the problems we have just considered with /di/ and /du/, they concluded that the invariance in our perception of consonants cannot be explained by looking at their acoustic signal because the acoustic signal varies with the context in which the consonant is found. What we must do, they argued, is look for some other property of the phoneme that does remain invariant even when context changes. According to Liberman *et al.*, it is the way we pronounce a consonant that remains the same. We have already seen that the different consonants are produced by different patterns of articulation, in that each consonant has a place of articulation, a manner of articulation and voicing that make it different from all other consonants. For the phoneme /d/ the place of articulation is always made by placing the tongue against the alveolar ridge behind the top teeth, so the place of articulation is called alveolar. /d/ is always voiced, in that the vocal cords are made to resonate, and it involves closing off the air to produce a small rush, called a 'stop'. So, the consonant /d/ can be described as a voiced, alveolar stop, and this method of production remains the same, even in different contexts. Liberman *et al.* pointed out that as both our perception of a phoneme and the way we produce it remain the same, there must be a link between perception and production that explains how we perceive speech.

The phonemic category boundary and categorical perception

Liberman suggested that the phenomenon called *categorical perception* provided further evidence for this theory. Let us look at this phenomenon. The only difference between these phonemes is that /d/ is voiced and /t/ is unvoiced. This difference causes another acoustic characteristic called the 'voice onset time', which is the delay between the beginning of the sound and the beginning of the voicing, so that /da/ has a shorter voice onset time than /ta/ and therefore sounds different. If I ask you to pronounce a sound that is halfway between a /d/ and a /t/ you will not be able to do so. However it is possible to produce a graded set of acoustic signals that gradually move from /da/ to /ta/ using a speech synthesiser. When participants are asked to categorise the artificial sounds, you might expect that they hear /da/ at first, then hear something like a mixture in between and then a /ta/ at the other end of the sequence. Eimas and Corbit (1973) did such an experiment and discovered that listeners never heard an in-between sound at all—they only heard /da/ or /ta/. Although the sequence of sounds was constructed in such a way that the voice onset time increased in very small steps between 0 and 80 milliseconds, listeners heard only /da/ between 0 and 35 milliseconds delay. Around this point listeners suddenly begin to report hearing /ta/, although they may still hear /da/ sometimes. After 40 milliseconds delay in voice onset, /ta/ is always reported. This is the phenomenon of 'categorical perception'. Participants categorise the acoustic signal as either /da/ or /ta/; there is no perception of a mixture. What is quite extraordinary is that listeners cannot perceive the difference between sounds over the range 0 to 35 milliseconds, but they do, quite suddenly, hear a change somewhere between a voice onset time of 30 and 50 milliseconds. The point where we hear the change is called the phonemic category boundary. Liberman felt this invariance in perception, linked with the invariance in production, was evidence that we perceive speech according to the way we produce it.

In their experiment, Eimas and Corbit were also able to provide evidence for feature detectors for speech. Taking the /da/–/t/ example again, where if you remember the difference is that /d/ is voiced and /t/ is unvoiced, Eimas and Corbit showed that by repeating /d/ many times and then asking listeners to make a discrimination between artificially generated /d/ and /t/, the boundary for perceptual categorisation had moved. They argued that the feature detector for voicing had become fatigued, or less responsive, making listeners less likely to hear /d/ than /t/. Other category boundary effects have been found by Mann and Repp (1980) and Massaro and Cohen (1983).

Some problems for the motor theory of speech perception

Not the least of these problems is that there are examples of neuro-psychological patients with Wernicke's aphasia who are able to produce speech but not understand it, and others with Broca's aphasia who can understand speech but not produce it. Ellis and Young (1996) provide an overview of these disorders. Other problems arise because categorical perception can be demonstrated in circumstances where the ability to produce speech cannot be the explanation for categorical perception. Eimas *et al.* (1971) tested babies using a selective sucking technique and demonstrated that infants will suck a dummy in order to hear repetitions of a syllable. To start with, infants like repetition but soon habituate to the sound, and will suck more slowly. If the infant is then presented with a slightly different sound, the sucking rate will increase again. Eimas *et al.* were able to show that the infants could perceive very small changes in the acoustic signal and demonstrate fatigue of feature detectors and categorical perception in the same way as adults. Whilst these findings might suggest innate ability for detecting features of speech, Cutting and Rosner (1974) have found categorical perception for bowed and plucked notes and Kuhl and Miller (1978) were able to show the same effects in the chinchilla. As bowing and plucking are not units of speech and chinchillas cannot speak at all, it is likely that the mechanisms underlying these abilities are not directly evolved or related to speech perception, but are more general underlying abilities, which are nevertheless important in analysing acoustic signals.

The importance of phonetic memory

Given the wealth of evidence for categorical perception, there can be no doubt over its existence and importance. However, when a listener makes a categorical judgement, they are ignoring a large amount of detail in the acoustic signal. We are simply not aware of the differences between relatively large changes in voice onset time. What we perceive is due to phonetic memory, not the raw percept. Miyawake *et al.* (1975) tested Japanese and American listeners on a phonemic categorisation task where the phonemes /l/ and /r/ were graded as in Eimas and Corbet's (1973) experiment. The American listeners showed categorical perception for these phonemes, but the Japanese were unable to make a discrimination. This result suggests that phonetic memory is important in perception. If particular acoustic signals have different names, we can put those signals into the categories with those names. When there is no name for such a distinction stored in phonetic memory then categorisation is not possible. In Japanese there is no phonetic contrast between /l/ and /r/; they are not labelled as different phonemes, and are therefore not discriminated as being different. We are all familiar with the difficulties involved in pronouncing and understanding foreign languages. Part of this problem is at the level of long-term phonetic memory.

High level auditory analysis

Perception of a word we can recognise indicates that the knowledge about that word has been activated. This is called *lexical access*. Psychologists call the place where information is stored about the words we hear, the *auditory input lexicon*. The auditory input lexicon holds information about pronunciation, spelling, grammatical category, i.e., whether a word is a noun, an adjective, a pronoun, an adverb and so forth, and the word's meaning. Auditory information has to interact with other cognitive and linguistic processes and information stored in long-tem memory in order for us to be able to assign the right meaning or pronunciation to words that sound the same. For example 'see', 'sea' and 'won', 'one' sound the same (known as homophones), but have different meanings. Ellis and Young (1996) proposed that the results of early analysis of the acoustic signals are transmitted to the auditory input lexicon. If there is a match between the input and the stored characteristics of a known word then the recognition unit for that word is activated. This leads to activation of the meaning of that word in semantic memory, where word meanings are stored. There is two-way activation between the semantic system and the auditory input lexicon, which means that currently active meanings can raise the activation level of units in the auditory input lexicon. In this way, the meaning of what we are listening to, or semantic context, can bias our responsiveness to words that are related to the ones that are currently or recently active. We shall see the importance of this in the next section. Of course we can also hear words that are new to us; for example, if I say the word 'glurk' to you, you are perfectly able to decode it into its phonemes. However, if you heard that word for the first time in a noisy environment you would probably ask me to say it again. However, I now tell you that a glurk is a small furry animal from South America, and that I have recently acquired one as a pet. You carry on listening to my story about glurks but now if someone else coughs during my tale at the point I am saying the word 'glurk', you will probably not have the same difficulty. This is because you will now know that glurk is a noun and you have some semantic knowledge and context to help you.

The perception of continuous speech

The work we have reviewed so far has concerned isolated phonemes, but in continuous speech the sounds are not usually isolated. A speech spectrogram of someone talking in a normal conversation is a continuous 'smear' of acoustic signals, with no apparent breaks between the phonemes, let alone the words. Beyond the sounds themselves, language is for communication, and the words represented by the sounds form meaningful passages that obey the rules of grammar. And of course, when people are talking the signal is often noisy and incomplete. All these factors mean that when listening to someone talking there is a great deal to do. So how do we do it? Part of this problem is solved by auditory attention being directed to a location or particular voice property, and we shall cover this in Chapter 8.

Redundancy in speech

Acoustic signals from the environment are extremely complex, because they carry not only information about what is being spoken, but also all the other noises that are going on at the same time. However, we are experts in our own language; we are familiar with its grammar, words and syntax. We also know what kinds of sounds can be attributed to speech, cars, telephones and so on. Because we know so much, we are able to understand what people are saying even when some information is missing. We can, for example, use context to fill in what we would have expected someone to say if a noise masks a word. When there is more information available than is actually needed, we say that there is redundant information. It is largely this *redundancy* in language that enables us to interpret speech.

Some classic experiments on speech perception

A number of important experiments have involved asking people to identify speech sounds obscured by noise. These have given us insights into some of the factors that help us understand speech.

Miller and Nicely (1955) asked participants to identify phonemes embedded in noise. They discovered that there was a systematic pattern of *phonemic confusability*. Phonemes with only one difference were confused first, and as the signal became weaker and the noise got louder there were more confusions. Miller and Nicely proposed five articulatory channels that could be used to distinguish phonemes; voicing, nasality, duration, stridency and place of articulation. As each phoneme has a number of channels, some of them are redundant and this allows for the loss of some information before identification becomes impossible.

Miller, Heise and Lichten (1951) looked at people's ability to hear words in noise. When the words were presented in isolation, for example 'green', listeners identified the word on about 40% of trials. However, if the word was embedded in a sentence, for example 'The grass is green', then accuracy rose to 70%. This experiment shows that word perception is aided by the context of a sentence. Miller and Isard (1963) took this experiment further and embedded the words to be tested into different kinds of sentences; some were grammatical, some ungrammatical and others were anomalous, that is, they obeyed the rules of grammar but did not make sense. Results showed that the more predictable a sentence is, the better the listeners' ability to identify the test word. So, how does predictability help in understanding words? It might be that a listener simply guesses the most likely word, but Neisser (1967) proposed 'that linguistic constraints act on the perception of the sentence' using *analysis by synthesis*. The same principle was put forward for explanations of visual perception by the *constructivists*, who proposed that perception involved hypothesis testing. This means that knowledge stored in memory provides candidates that might match the perceptual input, and using whatever evidence is available, the best candidate is chosen for synthesis. It is a prime example of top-down processing interacting with bottom-up processing. Evidence for Neisser's view comes from an experiment by Pollack and Pickett (1964). First, they edited out isolated words from tape-recordings of different kinds of speech to present to their listeners: 47% of words from spontaneous speech were correctly identified, 55% from normal reading and 41% from fast reading. Next they took the same words but, rather than the words being isolated, they were followed by sections of the rest of the tape. Pollack and Picket found that accuracy of word identification improved as more information followed the word and, importantly, there was a critical point where perception of the word became perfectly clear. Therefore, as the section of tape that enabled the listener to hear the word clearly came after the target word, they must have been hearing the word they had synthesised, not the word that was presented. This experiment shows that the clarity of speech is an illusion; we make it clear by hearing what we expect to hear! Another example of filling in missing information by synthesising what we expect was found by Warren (1970) and is called the phonemic restoration effect. Warren removed a phoneme from a word and replaced it with a cough or a noise. Listeners in the experiment heard the word quite clearly, despite the fact that part of it was not there. Again, the listener fills in top-down what is missing in the bottom-up information.

Change deafness

We have discussed the effect called change blindness with respect to visual attention. It is the apparently unlikely phenomenon in which people may fail to detect quite gross changes in the visual environment, not even noticing if the person they are talking to has changed whilst their attention was distracted. The inability to detect obvious changes in the environment has also been demonstrated for voices. Vitevitch (2003) proposed that as the acoustic signal contains two kinds of information, one, the word and what it refers to, and the other, the voice in which it is spoken, when participants are attending to what the words are, they will not be paying full attention to the speaker's voice. Vitevitch asked participants to repeat aloud, as quickly and as accurately as possible, lists of isolated words that were spoken over headphones. Half-way through the experiment participants were given a 1-minute rest, and then continued. When the experiment resumed, half the participants heard the same speaker presenting the word, while the other half heard a different speaker. At the end of the experiment participants were asked three questions: (1) 'Did you notice anything unusual about the experiment?', (2) 'Was the first half of the experiment the same as the second half?' and (3) 'Was the voice in the first half the same voice that said the words in the second half of the experiment?'. The results showed that all the participants who had heard the same voice throughout the experiments replied 'yes' to the third question, indicating they had heard the same voice throughout the experiment. In contrast, 5 out of 12 participants who had heard different voices in the first and second half of the experiment also replied 'yes' to the third question, indicating they had failed to detect a change in voice. It appears, then, that when participants are paying attention to the meaning of the word in order to repeat it back, they are failing to attend to other characteristics of the acoustic signal, in this case, the properties of the speaker's voice. They demonstrate 'change deafness'.

Memory for sound

Whenever a sound stimulus is detected by the auditory system, it must be retained in some memory form while further processing is performed on it. Sounds can vary in complexity and duration: they may be bursts of noise, tones, phonemes, words, sentences, or passages of speech or music. The brief memory for sound is called 'echoic memory'. We have all had the experience of asking someone to repeat what they just said, but before they have had a chance to do so we have been able to answer on the basis of a kind of 'echo', which allows us to retrieve what they had said. Studies of the duration of echoic memory have used four main techniques: masking, e.g., Massaro (1970), periodicity, e.g., Guttman and Julesz (1963), partial report, e.g., Darwin, Turvey and Crowder (1972), and divided attention, e.g., Glucksberg and Cowan (1970). From these experiments various estimates of the duration of echoic memory have arisen; the first two methods suggest 250 ms and the second two, 4–5 seconds. These differences may reflect different memories. Crowder and Morton (1969) suggested that initial auditory information is held briefly in a memory store for pre-categorical acoustic information, which is a store for auditory information that had not been recoded into a more durable verbal form. Pre-categorical acoustic storage could account for the *modality effect* and the *suffix effect*. The modality effect refers to the finding that in serial recall visually presented lists show little recency, but spoken lists show marked recency. The *recency effect* is the finding that the last three or four words in a list are recalled better than earlier words (see Chapter 10 for the serial position curve). If there were a persisting echoic memory aiding recall of auditory lists, this could improve final recall. The suffix effect refers to the fact that the presentation of a suffix, or extra irrelevant spoken word at the end of a to-be-remembered list, reduces recency. If the spoken word interferes with echoic memory, this could produce the suffix effect. However, later discoveries showed this cannot be the full answer, as Campbell and Dodd (1980) and Gathercole, Gregg and Gardiner (1983) have shown that a lip-read suffix can have the same effect as a spoken one. This suggests that the suffix effect is produced at a later stage of language processing.

The phonological loop in working memory

For the perceptual input to interact with long-term memory it must be stored for as long as it is being processed. There is a large body of evidence for the use of speech-based codes in short-term memory, which we shall discuss in more detail in Chapter 10. Baddeley and Hitch (1974) proposed a model of working memory (WM) in which there are separable components of short-term storage. The component of WM responsible for holding acoustic and speech-based information is the *phonological loop*. Baddeley (1997) summarises the assumed characteristics of the phonological loop as being made up from two interacting parts; the phonological store, which holds speech-based information, and an articulatory control, or rehearsal process, that is based on inner-speech. Cohen, Eysenck and Le Voi (1986) liken the phonological store to the 'inner ear', and the articulatory rehearsal process to the 'inner voice'. If you read the words on this page aloud, you have to overtly articulate the spoken words; however, if you continue to read silently, you can become aware of a subvocal articulation process. Usually you may not notice this, but it is certainly true that you can rehearse a list of items using subvocal rehearsal. Try repeating this list of digits to yourself while you look away for a few seconds: 2, 6, 9, 3, 7, 1, 4. So, overt articulation is not essential for the operation of the phonological loop. Information in the phonological store fades in 1 or 2 seconds unless it is refreshed by being read out into the articulatory rehearsal process, which can then feed the information back into the store. Subjectively, it is as if the 'inner ear' can hear the 'inner voice'. Baddeley (1997) argues that this phonological loop can provide a coherent account of the phonological similarity effect, i.e., items that are acoustically or phonemically similar in their articulation are easily confused in STM. This was part of the evidence for a distinction between STS and LTS that we shall discuss in Chapter 10. As the code in the phonological store is phonological, and rehearsal is in an articulatory code, any ambiguity in either of these components is likely to produce errors that are phonologically similar.

The phonological loop is also able to account for the 'unattended speech effect'. This effect was found by Colle and Welsh (1976) and extended by Salame and Baddeley (1987). Unattended speech interferes with immediate serial recall for visually presented digits, even when participants are told to ignore the speech and it is in a language they do not understand or even in nonsense words. Salame and Baddeley concluded that speech-based stimuli automatically gain access to the phonological loop and so interfere with other phonemic processing going on within it. The code cannot be semantic, as there was no difference between the interference effect of nonsense and meaningful words. The unattended speech effect is also found with music as the unattended distractor. If the piece of music has vocals, it interferes, but if it is purely instrumental then there is no effect (Salame and Baddeley, 1989). With auditory presentations, words have direct access to the phonological store whether or not any articulatory control processes are used.

Another pattern of data to be explained is the *word-length effect*. A number of experiments have shown that rather than the number of 'chunks', the limit on the number of items that can be held in STM depends upon how long it takes for the item to be pronounced. Miller (1956) found that seven items plus or minus two could be held in STS; however, the phonological loop can hold information for about 2 seconds, and the number of items that can be held there is influenced by a number of factors apart from 'chunking'. Baddeley, Thompson and Buchanan (1975) asked people to remember a sequence of five monosyllabic words such as wit, top, bag, or five polysyllabic words such as aluminium, university, constitutional. Rather than the number of chunks, the number of words that can be remembered is directly proportional to the number of words that can be spoken in about 2 seconds. Furthermore, a person's 'span' length depends on their rate of speech. A number of studies have shown that memory span for digits varies according to language. In Chinese, digits are articulated very rapidly, but in Welsh, for example, they are articulated more slowly, consequently in Chinese speakers digit span is, on average, higher than for Welsh speakers. See Baddeley (1997) for a full review of word length effects.

Further evidence on the phonological loop comes from experiments on *articulatory suppression*. Articulatory suppression involves repeating some irrelevant words, such as 'the', 'the', 'the', over and over again. Presumably, if a participant engages in a digit-span task, their span will be reduced because the irrelevant articulatory task will fully occupy the phonological loop, suppressing articulation of the digits. Baddeley, Lewis and Vallar (1984b) conducted a number of experiments showing that articulatory suppression specifically interfered with phonological and articulatory coding. However, a different secondary task, such as tapping a rhythm with the fingers, does not have the same effect, so the results are not simply reflecting a dual-task decrement. Under conditions of articulatory suppression the word-length effect disappears, as does the phonological similarity effect. Taken together, this seems good evidence for the use of a phonological loop for speech-based processing, but also indicates that when the phonological loop is occupied or unavailable, processing is still possible, and therefore there must be other components of WM capable of dealing with the information in another form. In Chapter 11 we shall consider Baddeley and Hitch's (1974) model of WM as a whole.

Long-term auditory memory

Although much of the auditory material stored in memory will have been interpreted and stored in terms of its meaning, or semantics, there are other auditory memories that must be stored in an auditory form. For example, we are able to recall and recognise familiar tunes, and identify different mechanical noises such as cars and aeroplanes, and the voices of people we know. Pollack, Pickett and Sumby (1954) showed that at normal speech levels, people were 95% correct at recognising familiar voices. White (1960) showed that people were able to recognise familiar tunes 90% correctly. By manipulating the pitch and melodic contour of the pieces he was able to show that both these factors contribute to recognition. Expert musicians can memorise large passages of music and reproduce them accurately later. See Sloboda (1999) for more on the cognitive psychology of music.

Summary

Auditory perception involves the analysis of the sounds superimposed in the environment. The physical properties of sound are frequency, which determines pitch, and amplitude, which determines loudness.

These properties are initially analysed by the basilar membrane. To segregate sound sources, natural mechanisms of grouping are used along the principles put forward by the Gestalt movement. Sounds can be located using the binaural cues of interaural time difference and intensity difference. The most important sets of sounds we perceive belong to speech. The phonemes that comprise the speech sound are perceived categorically and rely on phonetic memory. The formant for a phoneme differs depending on which phonemes are combined together. This is the invariance problem. The motor theory of speech perception suggests that we hear speech according to the way we produce it. However, as there are neuropsychological patients who can understand speech but not produce it, this theory cannot be entirely correct. In a noisy environment auditory perception is supported by the redundancy in language that allows us to fill in missing information using top-down processes from memory. These same processes allow the segregation of words from continuous speech. The phonological loop of working memory is responsible for holding phonological information, which fades unless recirculated by articulatory contol processes that are used to maintain it.

Self-assessment questions (Solutions on p. 322)

1 Can you explain the events in the scenario at the start of the chapter in terms of what you have learnt in this chapter?
2 What are the major differences between the visual and the auditory environment?
3 What is the invariance problem?
4 How does the phonological loop account for phonemic confusability?

Further reading

Baddeley, A. D. (1997) *Human Memory: Theory and practice*. Hove, UK: Psychology Press. A useful source for auditory memory.

Harley, T. A. (1995) *The Psychology of Language: From data to theory*. Hove, UK: Psychology Press. For the psychology of language.

Moore, B. C. J. (1994) Hearing. In: R. L. Gregory and A. M. Colman (Eds) *Sensation and Perception*. Harlow, UK: Longman. For a short overview of hearing.

Moore, B. C. J. (1989) *An Introduction to the Psychology of Hearing*. London: Academic Press. For full coverage of the psychology of hearing.

Sloboda, J. A. (1999) *The Musical Mind*. Oxford: Oxford University Press. If the psychology of music is your interest.

Chapter 8

Touch and pain

The world at your fingertips

IF YOU CLOSE YOUR EYES and move your hands to explore your immediate environment you are able to feel the textures and shape of objects around you. You may not think of your skin as a sensory organ, but in fact the ability to sense what is happening on the skin surface is essential for survival, and sometimes just useful. For example, to check if the bath is really clean, you can run your fingers around the surface to check if it is as clean as it looks. We use the expression 'squeaky clean', which implies that vision is not adequate to detect cleanliness; only touch and audition give the true answer!

Imagine what it would be like if you were unable to sense pressure, temperature or pain. Sensors in the skin are used when we explore the tactile properties of objects to see if they are rough or smooth, slippery or wet, soft or hard, warm or cold. Although vision is usually the dominant sense, we may need to touch a surface to discover, for example, if it is actually wet or simply very shiny. Wetness will give a different sensation to shiny, as the water evaporation will produce coldness on the skin in addition to smoothness. The shiny surface will only be very smooth. The gripping force needed to lift an object will depend on an object's surface texture. Pain is a warning that the skin is in danger of damage, or is being damaged, and a signal for the brain to instigate an action to avoid further harm.

The skin

The skin is the largest organ of the human body. It not only provides a protective layer, but also provides information that enables us to respond to potentially harmful stimuli. We need to know if the object we are touching is so hot that it is damaging our tissues, or if we are being touched by something that might be about to attack or damage us in some way. Stimulation of the skin gives rise to the cutaneous sensations of pressure (touch), temperature and pain. There are a variety of receptors embedded in the layers of the skin, and it has been proposed that different receptors are specialised for encoding different sensory properties. For example, *basket cells*, which are wrapped around the base of hairs embedded in the skin surface, detect movement of the hair so that when the hair is touched by, say, brushing against a twig, a message is sent to the brain indicating possible contact with an environmental stimulus. Not all the skin surface is equally hairy, and where hair is sparse or on hairless regions such as the palm of the hand, soles of the feet, lips and mouth, there are other structures specialised for sensation called *encapsulated end organs*. The majority of these are *Pacinian corpuscles*, which also provide information about pressure on the skin surface, and give rise to the sensation of being touched. All regions of skin contain *free nerve endings*, which are also sensitive to contact or pressure and produce the sensation of being touched. The skin also has receptors for temperature, although the absolute sensing of temperature is relative. We saw in Chapter 2 that water will feel hot or cold to your hand depending on whether your hand had previously been in cold or hot water.

Sensitivity: Localisation of the touch sensation

Sensitivity to being touched varies over the surface of the body. Some parts, such as the fingertips, are highly sensitive and can detect a displacement of less than 0.001 mm. Although only a very small indentation of the skin will be detected by the finger, other parts of the body are less sensitive, for example the back or the sole of the foot. Not only does the body surface differ in sensitivity to pressure, but our ability to detect the separation between points of stimulation also varies. This can easily be demonstrated with the help of a friend and two cocktail sticks. You ask them to tell you whether they feel one or two sticks touching them. Then you either take two cocktail sticks, and making sure you touch their finger with both sticks at exactly the same time, touch the two points of the sticks on the fingertip, or take one stick and touch the fingertip. Try comparing one-point stimulation with two-point stimulation at different separations. You will find that, even at very small separations, your friend can tell whether you are touching them with one or two sticks. Repeat the experiment on their back, their forearm, the back of their hand, etc. and it will become clear that your friend's ability to tell the difference between being touched in one or two places is vastly different depending on where on the body surface they are touched. The smallest separation between two points of stimulation that give rise to a sensation of two discrete impressions of touch is called the *two-point threshold*. Thresholds were discussed in Chapter 3. The *receptive fields* for the more sensitive areas are smaller than those for the less sensitive regions. Within a receptive field only one stimulus can be encoded. When the 'receptive field' is large, two points may be touched but cannot be discriminated. As the receptive fields become smaller, so the distance between points that can be discriminated decreases. This difference in sensitivity means that surface texture can easily be detected, or felt, with the fingertips. For example, we can feel the difference between velvet and fur, glass or polished wood if we run our finger across the surface, but such differences are not easily detected by other areas on the skin. In general the parts of the body such as fingers, hands, lips and mouth, which are used to explore the environment, are more sensitive than areas not used for this purpose. For details of the structure of the skin and its specialised receptors see Schiffman (1994).

The sensory homunculus

As we have seen, the sensitivity of the skin varies over its surface, and this difference is mirrored by the representation of body parts in the *somatosensory cortex*. Soma means body, and this part of the cortex represents information from the body surface in the brain. The more sensitive the area of skin, the more somatosensory cortex is needed to represent that information. Penfield and Rassmussen (1950) reported studies of patients about to undergo brain surgery under local anaesthetic. (The brain has no receptors for pain, so this process is less brutal than you might imagine.) While the brain was exposed, specific regions were electrically stimulated and the patients asked to report their sensations. All sorts of images, memories and sensations were experienced as a result, but of interest here are reports such as 'you are touching my face, now you are touching my hand, now my leg'. Penfield was able to map what he called the *'sensory homunculus'*. The homunculus shows that the more sensitive areas of the body occupy far larger regions of the sensory cortex than the less sensitive regions (see Figure 8.1).

So, the sensory cortex has the body mapped onto it in an organised way: it has a *somatotopic map*. This is similar to the representation of information from the retina as a retinotopic map in visual cortex.

Knowing about and acting on being touched

If we are touched by something, for example a mosquito landing on the skin, it is important to know exactly where the touch sensation is located on the body surface, so that we can react to it. Like the sensitivity demonstrated by the two-point thresholds, our ability to point accurately to the location of a stimulus (*point localisation*) is most precise on the hands, fingers, mouth and lips. However, if we are touched anywhere on the body, provided the threshold is reached, we 'know' about it and can respond. We know where to scratch, or where to try to brush off the offending insect. We also know that when we are scratching ourselves, the stimulation on the skin is generated by our own action rather than from some other environmental source. The surface of our bodies is constantly bombarded with sensory stimuli; we voluntarily touch some things and are involuntarily touched by other things. At the same time parts of the body are under continuous stimulation, for example, as you sit in the chair reading this book you can, if you wish, attend to or become aware of the pressure of the seat or the floor under your feet. Your hand may be resting on the desk, but

Genitals
Toes
Foot
Leg
Hip
Trunk
Neck
Head
Shoulder
Arm
Elbow
Forearm
Wrist
Hand
Little finger
Ring finger
Middle finger
Index finger
Thumb
Eyes
Nose
Face
Upper lip
Lips
Lower lip
Teeth, gums, jaw
Tongue
Pharynx
Intra-abdominal

FIGURE 8.1   The sensory homunculus.
The list above shows the ordered arrangement of body parts in the sensory cortex.
The size of the writing shows the relative size of the area of sensory cortex dedicated to processing information from the different body parts.
(Information from Penfield and Rassmussen, 1950).

until you direct your attention to it that information goes unnoticed. Unless there is a change in stimulation indicating novelty, this information is unimportant. How do we do know which changes in touch are important to act on and which ones we can ignore?

We have seen that there are receptive fields on the skin surface that map onto somatosensory cortex in a somatotopic organisation. They provide the 'afferent' input to the brain from the skin. In turn, the somatosensory cortex maps onto the motor cortex, which is also organised in the same somatotopic way and, when activated, produces an 'efferent' output that is involved in the production and control of motor actions back to the point of stimulation. In this way the localisation of stimulation on the body surface can be used to guide the direction of the action or response—we know where to scratch. However, there is an important difference between making an action in response to a sensory input and intentionally initiating an action ourselves that of itself results in a sensation.

Why can't you tickle yourself?

An interesting area of study has been opened up by Blakemore and her colleagues. Blakemore, Wolpert and Frith (2000) asked the question 'Why can't you tickle yourself?'. They point out the importance of being able to distinguish the difference between sensations that are a consequence of our own actions and those that result from possibly important environmental changes. It has been suggested that the information about motor commands is used to differentiate the sensory consequences of our own actions from those produced by external agents. We have already met one example where this need arises, when we considered how we are able to distinguish whether it is the eye that is moving past an object, or an object is moving past the eye (see Chapter 4). The answer to this problem in vision was that the brain receives an *efference copy* of the motor command that is moving the eye muscles. This lets the brain know that the eye is moving. In the absence of an efference copy of a motor command the brain does not 'know' that the eye is moving and assumes that an object is moving across the visual field rather than the eye moving across the environment. A similar proposal is made to account for the difference between knowing we are being touched as a consequence of our own action and knowing we are being touched by an external agent. When you touch yourself, the brain knows it because it receives an efference copy of the motor command that generates a prediction of the sensory consequences of the action to be made. For example, if you move your hand to scratch the place on the skin surface where you have just felt something touch you, your brain is expecting to receive a sensory signal that matches the timing of your hand movement to the stimulated location, and the frequency of your scratching action. The sensory signal from whatever it was that led you to scratch was not accompanied by an efference copy and was therefore unexpected by the brain. It is this difference between intentional, self-inflicted sensations and externally generated sensations that allows us to know whether we are actively touching ourselves or are being passively touched. Usually the actions we are making ourselves are not threatening and can be ignored, allowing unpredicted sensations to capture attention and action. Blakemore *et al.* (2000) suggest that we cannot tickle ourselves because self-produced tactile stimulation is attenuated, or suppressed in comparison to externally generated stimulation. So, if you try to tickle yourself, there is no unexpectedness about the sensation and ticklishness does not result. If someone else tickles you, the brain does not have any expectations about the location or frequency of the tactile sensation and ticklishness results.

Evidence in support of these ideas was found by Blakemore *et al.* (1999). In an experiment it was arranged for people to tickle themselves with a piece of foam attached to a robotic arm. There were two conditions, the only difference between them being the causal nature of the stimulus. In the externally produced tactile stimulation condition the robot generated the stimulus, whereas in the self-produced tactile stimulation condition the subject controlled the robot, and the movement of the stimulus corresponded exactly to the subject's movements of the left hand.

It was found the subjects were less tickled by the movements they controlled themselves than by those produced by the robot. Subjects reported that when the tactile sensation was self-produced it was less tickly, less intense and less pleasant.

Using the same apparatus, Blakemore *et al.* (2000) were able to introduce two new variables. First, they introduced a delay between the movement of the left hand and the delivery of the stimulus to the right hand. Second, they were able to rotate the direction of movement of the stimulus in relation to the subject's movement. Subjects reported a progressive increase in the tickle sensation as the delay between their movement and the delivery of the stimulus increased between 0 ms and 200 ms, and as the rotation was increased between 0 and 90 degrees. The authors argue that these data suggest that the attenuation of self-produced tactile sensations is due to precise predictions of the expected outcome of the motor commands controlling the delivery of the stimulus. When the time and place of the stimulus is predicted, no tickling occurs, but when the stimulus arrives at a different time and/or place to that predicted by the efference copy of movements made by the subject, then ticklishness increases with increased uncertainty.

These results are also relevant to the need for us to monitor the consequences of our own actions. Frith (1992) proposed the need for a central monitor that can allow us to distinguish the consequences of our own actions and intentions from externally produced sensory stimuli. fMRI studies have shown that whilst the somatosensory cortex shows increased activity during externally produced sensations, the cerebellum seems to be important for predicting the sensory consequences of movements and provides a signal that attenuates the sensory response to self-generated tactile stimulation (Blakemore, Wolpert and Frith, 1999). We shall see the importance of self-monitoring again when we consider selection and control of action in Chapter 9.

Pain

One of the most important roles of the sensory receptors in the skin is to warn us that our body is suffering injury. The Latin word *nocere* means 'to injure' and from this we derive the term for a pain receptor, which is *nociceptor*. As there are many potentially damaging stimuli, pain is not associated with any particular type of stimulation. Pain may result from being burnt, either by extreme heat or cold, or from being cut, grazed or bruised. It may result from a trapped nerve or appendicitis, from the labour of childbirth, or from toothache. The perception of pain is influenced not only by the pain receptors but also by emotional, motivational, social, cultural and cognitive factors. As we saw in the introductory chapter, Neisser (1967) suggested that everything we can consider to be psychological is fundamentally cognitive. Any theory of pain has to be able to account not only for the encoding of noxious stimuli but also for how these stimuli are interpreted differently depending on cognitive factors. Melzak and Dennis (1978, p. 92), put this point aptly: 'Stimulation of receptors does not mark the beginning of the pain process. Rather stimulation produces neural signals that enter an active nervous system that, in the adult, is already the substrate of past experience, culture, anxiety and so forth . . . Pain, then, is not simply the end product of a linear sensory transmission system. Rather it is a dynamic process which involves continuous interactions among other complex systems.'

Variability of pain perception

Beecher (1956) noted that during wartime, soldiers who had suffered severe wounds seemed to feel little pain, while the less seriously injured were demonstrably suffering extreme pain. It appeared as if there was no relationship between the severity of the wound and the severity of the experienced pain. What appeared to be more important was the consequence of the injury, rather than the severity of injury itself. The consequence of a very severe injury was that the soldier would probably have to be sent home, and despite their terrible injuries, these soldiers knew they had (probably) survived and that the war was over for them. Less severely injured soldiers knew they could soon be better and when they had recovered would be sent back to the front to fight again. This knowledge and the associated emotions of relief on one hand, and fear and anxiety on the other, modified the response to pain in the two groups. Studies of patients about to undergo surgery indicate that counselling in what will be happening and what to expect can not only reduce anxiety levels but also reduce perceived pain levels after the surgery. Clearly the emotional state of an individual can affect the perception of pain. Other examples can be found in cultural traditions where individuals undergo painful but socially important and rewarding ceremonial rites without any apparent suffering. Closer to our own experience, a player injured in a sports match may not notice the pain until after the match has finished. For information from the senses to be useful for survival and selection for action it needs to capture attention.

Pain and attention

Eccleston and Crombez (1999) have developed a cognitive-affective model as an attempt to account for how pain interrupts and demands attention. They argue that pain captures central processing mechanisms to allow selection for the action of escaping the pain. The perception of pain would have no evolutionary function if it were not able to interrupt ongoing activity and allow escape from noxious stimuli. However, if you automatically responded to pain irrespective of ongoing activity, that in itself could be dangerous. For example, if, as you lift a pan of boiling fat, the handle burns your hand, simply dropping the pan may result in greater injury by allowing its contents to pour down your body, or catch fire. Likewise, you may be prepared to hold your hand in freezing water longer than you normally would, enduring considerable pain, if you are trying to reach your car keys from a ditch. Clearly any action plan must take account not only of the current pain experience but also of the consequences of making or not making an action. Eccleston and Crombez invoke the concept of attention as a 'dynamic mechanism of selection for action' (p. 357) (see 'Selection for action', Chapter 10). Following Allport (1989), they argue that 'The problem for any model of attention is that it must account for the two potentially contradictory requirements of an attentional mechanism: "the need for continuity of attentional engagement against the need for interruptibility" (p. 652).'

Whilst pain can interrupt ongoing activity, our response to it can be affected by cognitive, emotional and motivational factors.

Eccleston and Crombez review experimental evidence that demonstrates that pain interferes with and interrupts performance on another attention demanding task. In one study, Eccleston (1994) compared the performance of chronic-pain patients with pain-free controls on an easy and a difficult attention task. He found that patients with high-intensity chronic pain showed significantly worse performance than low-intensity chronic pain patients and pain-free controls. Therefore, it appears that pain demands attentional engagement. However, as in the earlier example of dealing with the pan of hot fat, responding to pain is only one of the demands for action that the environment makes on us. Pain may or may not be prioritised as the focus of attention. A number of studies, e.g., Fernandez and Turk (1989), have looked at the effect of distraction on pain perception to discover if diverting attention from pain can be used as a method for relieving chronic pain. In general it appears that a distraction task must be sufficiently difficult, or demanding of attentional processing, for there to be an effect. Emotions such as fear or motivation to succeed can be attentionally demanding, and some of the variation in the pain experience reported, for example by Beecher (1956), may be due to the distracting effect of emotions demanding attention.

Eccleston (1995) argued that environments in which pain emerges often provide numerous demands and possible interruptions. When a task is interrupted, the cognitive system appears to need to return to it and complete it if at all possible (Gillie and Broadbent, 1989). To maintain coherence of ongoing behaviour in the face of these interruptions, attention must be switched between tasks and demands. Using a modification of the intentional, executive switching task used on normal subjects by Allport, Styles and Hsieh (1994), Eccleston tested the performance of chronic pain patients. He discovered that the ability to switch between tasks in people suffering high-intensity chronic pain is significantly impaired. It appears that chronic pain acts as constant interruption to other ongoing activities, and the maintenance of coherent behaviour requires intentional switching between pain and other tasks.

A functional model of pain and attention

Eccleston and Crombez (1999) propose a functional model for the interruption of pain and attention.

The model incorporates seven interrelating components: the environment, stimuli arising from the environment, the sensory system, action programmes, a focal task, threat mediation and moderating factors. Before the introduction of a noxious stimulus the system is engaged in a focal task; the example they use is listening to an interesting story being told by a friend. The priority for attentional engagement is focused on the sensory information related to listening to the story. Other information will be being received by the senses, for example background noise or colours of the walls, but these are not the focus of attention. Then you bite into a hot sausage roll that burns your tongue. Attention to listening to the story is interrupted by the pain. The novel, threatening sensory information has broken through the filter and captured control of action. At the same time, other activities you were previously unaware of, such as maintaining posture and normal breathing, are also interrupted. You suddenly take a sharp intake of breath and start moving your head about. Listening to the story has ceased to be the focus of attention; attention has switched to escaping the damage of the hot food in your mouth. There are now two demands: carry on listening to the story, and continue to cool the food in your mouth. It is possible to continue with both tasks, but only by rapidly switching attention between them. The amount of attention demanded by the burning in your mouth compromises your ability to maintain a sensible conversation, but moderating factors such as who you are having the conversation with may influence the priority of the two demands. For example, with a good friend you may feel able to stop listening, spit the offending food into your hand and so avoid further pain. In this case the action program to escape the noxious stimulus and remove the food from your mouth could be implemented. However, if you are in a more formal situation where you are trying to give a good impression of yourself, it would be to your advantage to bear the pain and the damage it is signalling by suppressing the escape actions. Your appraisal of the situation is that it would be more to your advantage to suffer pain rather than social embarrassment. The pain may still continue to interrupt your attention to the conversation, but the action you take is moderated by different factors.

Gate control theory and the sensation of pain

The free nerve endings are assumed to be the major nociceptor and, as mentioned previously, are distributed all over the skin surface. However, as evident from the quote from Melzak and Dennis (1978) and the examples above, this is just a part of the process of sensing and perceiving pain. To account for the variability observed in pain perception, Melzak and Wall (1965, 1982) proposed the *spinal gate control theory*. In essence, this theory suggests there is a 'gate' in the spinal cord that opens and closes to allow or inhibit the activity of specific cells—T-cells—that transmit pain. When T-cells are strongly stimulated by nociceptors, they open the 'gate'. However, when a nociceptor or pain stimulation is accompanied by another less powerful stimulus, the lighter touch inhibits the T-cell activity, and the gate is closed. This is the reason we rub our shin after we have hit it on the table—the pain transmission is inhibited by the gentle rubbing. In addition, and important for explaining cognitive effects on pain perception, central cognitive mechanisms can also regulate the gate mechanism. Central control is transmitted via large diameter or 'L-fibres', which can close the gate and result in inhibition of T-cell activity. The reasons that, amongst other things, stress, emotion and attention can moderate pain is because of the action of this cognitive mechanism.

When we are in pain a doctor may prescribe an analgesic, or pain killer. One such substance, used for extreme pain, is morphine, which is an opiate. Opiates are related to one of the important sets of *neurotransmitter substances* called the *endorphins*. Endorphin means 'endogenous morphine' and this neurotransmitter interacts with special neurons called 'opiate receptors'. The spinal cord is rich in opiate receptors and the action of the endorphins is to close the spinal 'gate' and so reduce pain. Thus the brain seems to have its own pain killer. When morphine is administered by the doctor, its action mimics that of natural endorphins and suppresses pain.

The phantom limb

People who have had a part of their body removed by amputation quite often experience a mysterious condition in which they are aware of sensations arising from the missing body part. The patient may have a powerful feeling that the missing limb is still there. They may even come round from the anaesthetic and not believe the operation has taken place because they can still 'feel' the limb. Mitchell (1871) first coined the term 'phantom limb' to describe this peculiar phenomenon, which has generated much speculation but remained a mystery until recently.

Ramachandran and Blakeslee (1998) describe the case of a young man, Tom, who lost his left arm just below the elbow following a motorcycle accident. Even though Tom knew the arm had been amputated, he still felt a 'ghostly presence below the elbow'. He felt he could move the fingers on the missing hand, reach with it, and do anything with the phantom that the real arm would have done automatically, such as using it break a fall or ward off oncoming objects. In some amputees the sensations from the phantom are of pain, and this pain can be extreme and continuous. But how can this be? How can something that is not there feel any sensation, let alone pain? Various explanations have been put forward. One is that the patient effectively denies that there has been a loss, and is indulging in a sort of wishful thinking. Alternatively, it has been suggested that the pain results from damage to the nerve endings in the remaining stump. Irritation of these could send information that is interpreted by the brain as evidence that the limb is still there. Ramachandran and Blakeslee believe that neither of these explanations is plausible and put forward an intriguing and convincing alternative view.

Let us return to the sensory homunculus we discussed earlier. Remember that Penfield discovered, using electrical stimulation in patients about to undergo surgery, that the entire body is mapped in an orderly way in the *somatosensory cortex*. More detailed experiments on monkey have extended Penfield's work. In these experiments a fine electrode is inserted into the somatosensory cortex of an alert monkey and the activity of neurons displayed on an oscilloscope. As we saw previously, each area of the skin has a receptive field in which neural activity is generated in response to touch. When the monkey's hand or arm was touched, the activity corresponding to that area could be recorded. In this way the entire map of the body surface can be seen to exist in the brain of the monkey, which is closely similar to that in humans. When the somatosensory cortex of monkeys who had been experimentally paralysed was studied, a startling result was found. To produce paralysis the operation had severed all the neural connections between the arm and the brain, so like the amputees, there could be no sensory input from the paralysed arm to the brain, and so there should have been no activity in area of somatosensory cortex corresponding to that arm. The result was as expected. When the paralysed hand was stroked, there was no activity in the expected area. However, when the monkey's face was stroked there was strong neural activity in the cells corresponding to the paralysed hand, as well as the cells corresponding to the face. This astonishing result gave Ramachandran an idea about the causes of phantom limbs, which he tested on his patient Tom.

Tom was seated, blindfolded, in Ramachandran's laboratory, completely ignorant of the purpose of the study. Ramachandran took a Q-tip and stroked Tom's cheek. What did Tom feel?

> 'You are touching my cheek.'
> 'Anything else?'
> 'Hey, you know, it's funny', said Tom. 'You're touching my missing thumb.'
> I moved the Q-tip to his upper lip. 'How about here?'
> 'You're touching my index finger. And my upper lip.'
> 'Really, are you sure?'
> 'Yes, I can feel it in both places.'
>
> (Ramachandran, 1998, p. 29)

Tom had a complete map of his missing phantom hand on his face. Ramachandran explored Tom's body with the Q-tip and found a second 'map' of Tom's missing hand on his left upper arm, just above the amputation line (see Figure 8.2).

If you look at the sensory homunculus, you will see that the face is represented on one side of the hand area and the shoulder on the other. These results show that not only can the brain reorganise itself, but also the regions of somatosensory cortex either side of where the 'hand' information is usually represented, have taken over the vacancy left by the missing hand. This re-mapping could help to explain the ghostly presence of the phantom. Whenever Tom moves or touches his face, some activation will arise in the area corresponding to the missing hand, and give the sensation it is still there. However, Ramachandran argues that this cannot explain why amputees like Tom have the impression that they can move their phantoms. Following consideration of other patients with phantom limbs who, unlike Tom, had the impression of a paralysed phantom, Ramachandran concluded that the relation between sensation, motor control and visual feedback also plays an important role.

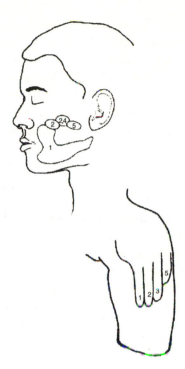

FIGURE 8.2 The distribution of the phantom hand on the face and shoulder of an amputee. From Ramachandran and Blakeslee (1998).

Normally, when we make an intentional movement, the *primary motor cortex*, which maps the body in the same way as the somato-sensory cortex and lies alongside it, sends signals to the target muscles to make the movement. Intentional movement is initially triggered by activity in the frontal lobe; we shall consider intentional behaviour in detail in Chapter 9. Primary motor cortex controls simple movements, but another region, the *supplementary motor area*, or SMA, co-ordinates the complex sequences of motor commands from the primary motor cortex. Each time the SMA sends a command to the primary motor cortex, an *efference copy* (see 'Why can't you tickle yourself') informs the cerebellum and parietal lobe of the intended action. As we have seen before, the brain needs to 'know' which sensory-motor effects are a consequence of its own messages and

175

which are a consequence of outside stimulation. It needs to monitor what it is doing and what is being done to it.

Returning to the problem of the phantom limbs, in normal movements there is a feedback system that monitors the outcome of the motor commands. The muscles execute the motor command, proprioceptive information from the muscles and joints feeds back to the brain, via the spinal cord, that the command is being executed and allows the brain to compare the intended action with the actual performance. In addition, of course, we can usually see what we are doing and this visual information is also important in providing feedback for visually guided movement, such as picking up an object. Fine adjustments can then be made, using the feedback to allow smooth coordination of the action.

Ramachandran discovered that most patients with 'paralysed' phantom limbs had, prior to amputation, suffered paralysis, and had learnt that although motor commands were going to the limb, proprioceptive and visual feedback constantly reinforced the fact that there was no movement. Eventually, the brain learns that the arm does not move in response to its commands and paralysis is learnt. Once the limb is amputated the paralysis remains.

Curing phantom pain

Paralysed phantom limbs often cause their owners extreme pain. They have the sensation that their nails are digging into their palm, or that the limb is in an awkward position from which it cannot be moved. Ramachandran reasoned that if paralysis could be learnt, it could also be unlearnt. Using a box with mirrors, he was able to give his patients the visual impression that they had two 'good' arms. The patient can see the good arm together with its reflection in the position of the missing one. One amputee, Philip, was suffering terrible pain in his phantom elbow, wrist and fingers. He was asked to place his right hand on the right side of the mirror and imagine his missing left arm was placed on the other side. Ramachandran instructed Philip to move his right and left arms simultaneously. Despite his protestation that his left arm did not move, Philip agreed to try. Looking at the mirror Philip experienced the unbelievable. He felt his phantom wrist and elbow move. However, when he closed his eyes, and the visual feedback was absent, Philip could no longer move his phantom arm. On re-opening his eyes the movement returned. After several weeks of practice, Philip's phantom, which he had had for 10 years, had gone, and the pain from the wrist and elbow with it. All that remained was a phantom hand, which he felt at the shoulder. Ramachandran is not sure why the hand remains, but suggests it might be because it occupies such a large area of somatosensory cortex.

Another patient, Robert, suffered the pain of his phantom fingernails digging into his phantom palm. Using the same mirror technique, Robert was immediately able to open his phantom hand and the pain was relieved. It is interesting to observe that the pain of fingernails digging into the palm must have been retrieved from memory, based on occasions when this had actually happened. Ramachandran claims that these occasions have left a memory link between the motor command to clench the fist and the sensation of 'nails digging in', which we are easily able to imagine. However, although we can summon up this sensory image we do not actually feel the pain, because we have feedback from our hand which tells us that, in fact, the hand is not clenched—and reality wins.

Other aspects of touch

The surface–weight illusion

We mentioned at the start of this chapter that receptors in the skin are sensitive to surface texture. Information about surface texture is less to do with the localisation of sensation in terms of where on the body the sensation arises, and more to do with the fine discriminations of skin displacement, which we saw can be as small as 0.001 mm. When we go to pick up an object we need to know if it is smooth or rough, as a smooth object may slip as we grip it. If it likely to slip, we grip it harder. The fact that we grip smooth objects more tightly than rough objects has been suggested to underlie another illusion called the 'surface–weight illusion'. The perceived heaviness of a lifted object is influenced by its surface texture, such that when an object is gripped between the thumb and forefinger (known as a precision grip) the perceived weight increases with the smoothness of the surface texture (Rinkenauer, Mattes and Ulrich, 1999). It seems as if the harder we grip the object the heavier it seems to be. Using the psychophysical method of *just-noticeable differences* for weight discrimination, which was described in Chapter 3, Flanagan *et al.* (1995) asked their subjects to lift small test canisters, using the precision grip. The test canister could vary in weight and also in surface texture (rough/smooth). On each trial the subject compared the test canister to a reference canister, which was either the same or a different surface texture. Subjects judged which of the two canisters was the heavier. When the test canister was smooth and the reference canister rough, subjects over-estimated the test canister's weight. Conversely, when the test canister was rough and the reference smooth, subjects underestimated the test canister's weight. So, if an object is smooth and slippery, it is judged to be heavier than an identical rough canister. To ensure that the effect was due to increased grip rather than some effect of surface texture independent of grip, Flanagan *et al.* did another experiment, where they showed that the surface weight illusion disappeared when subjects used a horizontal grip in which the canister was rested on the thumb below and held by the forefinger at the top of the object. As most of the weight was carried on the thumb, with the object steadied by the forefinger above, there was little difference in the grip necessary for the different canisters. Flanagan *et al.* suggested that the illusion arises from the adjustment of gripping force determined by the surface texture and the inability of people to differentiate the neural signals feeding back about weight from those feeding back from the grip.

Rinkenauer *et al.* (1999) carried out further psychophysical experiments on the surface–weight illusion. As the grip force necessary to hold a smooth object increases more steeply than that required to hold a rough object of the same weight, they predicted that the subject's confusion between the weight of an object and the grip used to hold it would lead to the illusion increasing with object weight. Contrary to expectation, the surface–weight illusion does not increase with object weight. Rinkenauer *et al.* suggest that the brain does dis-criminate between the neuronal activity resulting from grip and from lifted weight, but uses both sources of information in arriving at an estimate of weight. It is as if computing grip force increases the sensitivity of weight judgements.

Reading Braille

The density of receptors on the fingers useful for determining texture has been exploited in the development of the Braille system. In this system the letters of the alphabet and some commonly used whole words are represented by a pattern of embossed dots. Each pattern is based on a matrix of 2 × 3 dots separated by 2.3 mm, and each 'bump' is raised above the paper surface by approximately 1 mm. The skin of the fingertips is able to discriminate the pattern of bumps, and with practice it is possible to 'read' the letters and words at some speed (Kennedy, 1984). Experienced Braille readers typically use both sets of fingers, one hand leading the other, to provide the sort of preview of upcoming words available to sighted readers. This preview provides context that helps to disambiguate sentences and increases reading speed. If you imagine, or even try, reading a sentence one letter or even one word at a time, you will see how this preview is useful.

Tactile memory

To be able to read the Braille system, it is evident that there must be at least a short-term working memory for tactile information. This memory needs to be able to encode and retain the tactile information whilst it is transformed into another more permanent code. Clearly, once a word has been 'read' by the fingertips it can be verbally labelled with its word name, but prior to full analysis some memory for the pattern of tactile stimulation will be needed. Bliss *et al.* (1966) studied tactile memory. If you look at your hand palm upward, you will be able to count three areas on each finger, separated by the joints, on each hand. With four fingers on each hand and two hands, this gives 24 locations on the underside of the hand that are readily distinguishable. Using a special device that could deliver a brief puff of air to each of these finger areas, and presenting a sequence of puffs, Bliss *et al.* attempted to measure tactile span. Span is the maximum number of items that can be reliably recalled in the correct order; for verbal information this is usually seven plus or minus two (Miller, 1956). For the sequence of tactile stimulation, Bliss *et al.* found that span was four or five stimuli. In the experiment, the subjects were unpractised; it might be expected that with experience and with meaningful stimuli, this span could improve. Either way this is certainly sufficient to support reading in Braille readers.

In comparison to the vast literature on the other senses, particulary vision, relatively little work has been done in the areas of touch and much more is still needed.

Summary

The skin is not only a protective layer but also the largest sense organ. Information from skin receptors is represented in somatosensory cortex and is arranged somatotopically. Different areas of the skin surface occupy smaller or larger areas of cortex depending on the number of receptors on the skin for that area. Sensitivity of the skin is measured by two-point thresholds for touch and localisation. When we are touched, the brain is not expecting the stimulus, but when we touch ourselves an efference copy from the motor command informs the brain that the skin will be touched at a specific place and time. The ability to tickle yourself is reduced by this lack of surprise. Pain is the warning signal that the body is being damaged, but emotional factors can affect the sensation. Gate control theory includes the role of cognitive processes in moderating the pain response. Pain can be reduced by an attentionally demanding task, suggesting that pain is an interrupt mechanism essential for survival. Phantom limbs are sensed despite no sensation coming from the amputated limb. Ramachandran has shown that the phantom is represented in another part of somatosensory cortex neighbouring the region normally innervated by the amputated limb. Phantom pain can be alleviated by leading the brain to believe it is moving the phantom by providing the illusion of a real limb in the place of the missing limb. Information from the skin is used in gripping objects and reading Braille, for which a tactile memory is necessary.

Self-assessment questions (Solutions on p. 322)

1 What is the two-point threshold and how could you measure it?
2 What makes you ticklish?
3 How can an injured player finish a football match before feeling the pain?
4 What has happened to allow an amputated limb to be sensed on another part of the body?

Further reading

Ramachandran, V. S, and Blakeslee, S. (1998) *Phantoms in the Brain*. London: Fourth Estate. This is a fascinating book about sensation, perception, phantom limbs and conscious experience.

Shiffrin, R. (1994) The skin, body and chemical senses. In: R. L. Gregory and A. M. Colman (Eds) *Sensation and Perception*. Harlow, UK: Longman. For an overview of touch and pain.

Chapter 9

Auditory and cross-modal attention

At the cinema

A S YOU WATCH THE FILM you look from one actor to the other as they speak to each other. The individual voices appear to belong to the different actors speaking on the screen, and at the same time the theme music fills the auditorium. Behind you a couple are having a disagreement, and now and again you listen in to find out what they are arguing about. However, while you listen to them you miss what is being said on screen.

We all know that we cannot listen to what two people are saying, or to any other two auditory signals at once. Although we can detect the location of a variety of auditory objects in the environment, it is not possible to listen to them all at the same time. The separate sounds are analysed from the auditory input, and we considered some of the problems of auditory analysis in Chapter 7. However, attentional processes are also involved in allowing us to selectively listen to one source of sound rather than other. Walking in the garden you can intentionally control what you listen to. You may listen to the birds, then switch attention to listening to the wind in the trees, then back to your friend's chatter. Most of the time one sound source is the focus of attention, and is in the foreground, which other sources merge into the background. As you switch between the sounds, what appears to be in the background or foreground changes places. However, if there is a sudden noise, for example an apple falling to the ground, this will automatically capture your attention. We have already looked at endogenous and exogenous control of attention in Chapter 5, concerning visual attention. While there are some important differences between hearing and vision, these modalities interact in some interesting ways. For example, if you are trying to hear what someone is saying to you in a noisy environment it helps if you can see their lips moving, so attending to sounds can be improved if we also attend to visual properties of the same object.

Auditory attention

When we search a visual scene, we can move our eyes and head to bring the fovea to focus on the part of the environment that we wish to attend to. If we want to ignore a visual stimulus we can shut our eyes, or look away. However, this is not the case with the auditory environment. The *cochlea* has no equivalent of the *fovea*, and we cannot shut our ears or move them around. So how are we able to selectively attend to objects or locations in the auditory environment?

Scharf (1998) suggests that the auditory system is 'an excellent early warning system, one that is ready to receive and process stimuli from all directions regardless of an organism's current orientation'. However, he goes on to point out that 'this openness to all the vagaries of the environment makes it especially important that the organism be able to select for devoted processing one among two or more simultaneous sources of sound' (p. 75).

Attention to acoustic properties

Scharf (1998) reviews a range of experimental data that demonstrates our ability to selectively attend to frequency, spatial locus and intensity. Attention can be focused on a particular frequency region. Tanner and Norman (1954) measured a listener's ability to detect a 1,000 Hz tone presented over headphones. The tone could arrive within any of four time periods, and the listener had to indicate when in which time period the signal occurred. The sound level was set so that detection rates were 65%. After a few hundred trials the frequency of the signal was changed to 1,300 Hz, and immediately detection accuracy fell to 25%. This result was interpreted as showing that the listeners had focused on the original frequency, and so when it changed they were listening in the wrong frequency range and missed the signal. The spatial locus of auditory attention was studied by Scharf (1988). He hypothesised that listeners would be better at detecting sounds coming from an expected direction rather than an unexpected direction. However, detection was found to be no better for the attended than the unattended direction. In general, there is little evidence for directional sensitivity for weak sounds, but Rhodes (1987) showed that clear, loud sounds do show an effect of attended location on speed of response to sound. Other experiments reviewed by Scharf have produce a complex literature of evidence, with some contradictory results. In all it seems that subjects can focus attention on a narrow band of frequencies, but the advantage of exogenous cueing to a location has little effect. However, endogenous orienting speeds the detection and discrimination of spatial and frequency information. Orienting of visual attention was discussed in Chapter 5.

Selective listening : Dichotic listening experiments

Most of the fundamental work on auditory attention was conducted nearly 50 years ago. A classic series of experiments on hearing and attention set out to discover how we are able to selectively listen to one auditory message amongst other simultaneous messages. As we shall see, these experiments culminated in some of the first influential theories of attention in cognitive psychology. Some of the earliest work carried out on auditory selective attention was done by Cherry (1953), who investigated the *cocktail party effect*. For those of you unfamiliar with cocktail parties, imagine being in a crowded bar, engaged in conversation with someone. Despite all the conversations going on around you, it is possible to select one speaker to listen to. This may be the person you are with, or the person speaking behind you, who may be saying something rather more interesting! In this example, we can see there is a voluntary decision that controls where auditory attention is directed. There are no associated movements of the ears or head that aid the direction of your attention. It must, therefore, be directed by some internal mechanism that can allow one message to be selected in preference to another.

Cherry used a technique called *dichotic listening* to experimentally investigate our ability to attend to one source of auditory information. In a dichotic listening task the participant is presented with two simultaneous messages using headphones. One message is delivered to the right ear, the other to the left ear. The listener is told to attend to one message and ignore the other (see Figure 9.1).

eight, two, one

seven, four, nine

"eight, two, one"

FIGURE 9.1 A person in a dichotic listening task reporting sequences of number recalls by ear.

187

To check the accuracy of the listener in selecting the attended message, they were asked to repeat it aloud; this is called '*shadowing*'. Cherry manipulated the differences between the messages and found that physical properties of the auditory input such as the voice (male female) or location (left or right ear) could be used to select one auditory stream, but semantic properties, or the meaning of the passages, could not be used as a basis for selection when there were no physical differences. The studies seemed to confirm that whether asked to select just one auditory message or divide attention between two messages, subjects were able to utilise physical, acoustic differences between voices, and physical separation of locations, but not other properties of the auditory information. In addition, Cherry found it was no good telling the listener which message to recall after the experiment; they needed to know before the messages started. Furthermore, listeners had virtually no memory for the information that had not been attended. However, listeners were able to notice if the language of the unattended message had changed.

Split-span studies

Broadbent (1954) experimented on the division of attention using simultaneous, dichotic presentation, in what became known as the '*split-span*' *technique*. The listener is presented with six digits, arranged into three successive pairs. In each pair, one digit is heard through a headphone to the right ear, with the other digit presented simultaneously to the left ear. When all three pairs, i.e. six digits, have been presented the subject is asked to recall as many digits as they can. The interesting finding here is that when all digits are reported correctly, it is usually the case that the subject reports the three items from one ear before the three items from the other ear. Thus, Broadbent argued, selection is ear by ear, and the second set of digits is waiting in a buffer store, to be output when attention is switched. Even in this simple task it seemed that people could not simultaneously attend to both ears.

Studies such as these led to the development of Broadbent's (1958) model, mentioned in Chapter 2, which was put forward as a model of human information processing. It not only includes attentional processes, but also other processes involved in perception and memory. According to this model, the sensory system analyses the input for its physical properties, and this information passes to a short-term buffer memory store. The next processing stage is the perceptual system, where information can be identified, and becomes conscious. This stage is protected by a selective filter, which allows information selected on the basis of the desired physical property, such as female voice, to pass through for further processing by the limited capacity perceptual system. Other information is blocked from entry and remains in the short-term storage buffer for a short time before it decays. The filter may, when the limited capacity channel system has sufficient processing space again, switch back and allow more information from the buffer to pass, provided the information has not decayed away. This model is an example of an *early selection* model, in that selection is made on the basis of stimulus properties available from early stages of analysis. Stimulus properties derived by later processing, i.e., the meaning of the stimulus or its semantics, are not able to guide selection and so are assumed to be unavailable.

How do we set the filter?

Reflect for a moment on the nature of the selective listening tasks just described. You are the listener and you have been told to attend to one message rather than another. The experiment begins and you are able to do it. The question that we must ask is: how were you able to prepare your nervous system for the task at hand? As we said before, you cannot shut an ear in the same way as you can shut an eye, in order to block out the message to be ignored. Further, unlike some other animals, we cannot move the ear to focus attention at the location of the to-be-attended message. In vision, we can move the fovea to focus on the area of visual space we are interested in. Therefore, when we selectively listen, some internal changes must take place. Although we seem to select an auditory message on the basis of early sensory features, the processes necessary to prepare the auditory system to do this must be initiated at a much higher cognitive level. This difference between the processes that control attention and those processes that actually result in the selection of one stimulus in preference to another highlights the difference between attention for perception and attentional control.

Scharf (1999) provides a possible explanation for how the filter at the sensory level could be controlled by other cortical structures. So far, we have concentrated on the bottom-up aspects of auditory processing, starting with the stimulus and working toward 'later' central cortical processes. However, not only do messages from the receptors feed afferent signals into more specialised auditory areas and the auditory cortex, but these higher brain centres have efferent pathways that feed back to other systems and the muscles. The importance of efferent and afferent information was discussed in the previous chapter. Scharf explains that the *olivocochlear bundle* (OCB) is a bundle of 1,400 efferent nerve fibres that transmit neural information that has originated from the auditory centres in the temporal lobe to the cochlea. This top-down neural information may be able to prepare the hair cells on the basilar membrane of the cochlea to be more responsive to one sound rather than another. So, although auditory selection may be implemented at the receptors, the message that determines the basis of that selectivity has been generated internally. There is evidence that the OCB is involved in interaction between in the senses, in that responses to auditory stimuli can be suppressed while an animal attends to another modality. When we must select from within the stream of auditory information, other mechanisms are required.

To discover if the OCB does play a part in selective attention to frequency, Scharf, Magnan and Chays (1997) tested patients who had their vestibular nerve, which incorporates the OCB, severed to relieve the symptoms of Mernier's disease. Normally, people can selectively attend to a narrow frequency band. Greenberg and Larkin (1968) used a probe-signal procedure to show that people can focus their selective auditory attention down to a range of frequencies centred on a target frequency. Within this range targets were detected accurately, but outside that range signals were not responded to, or ignored. For most listeners expecting a target of 1,000 Hz, the range was between 1,000 and 1,200 Hz, with frequencies outside the range being detected at chance levels. Scharf *et al.* used a modification of Greenberg and Larkin's experiment on the patients. Before their operation, patients behaved like the normal listeners, and ignored frequencies outside the target frequency range. However, following the operation, this selectivity was lost, and responses were made to signals as far apart as 300 and 3,000 Hz.

Scharf (1999) suggests that this result can be explained if, in normal ears that have input from the OCB, the basilar membrane is tuned to the expected frequency range, and other signals are attenuated. He suggests that this selective tuning is 'achieved by the OCB's innervation of the outer hair cells, which are analogous to a miniature motor system; they contract and dilate when stimulated. Accordingly, auditory selectivity may also involve a kind of motor control remotely akin to that in vision where the oculomotor system directs the fovea toward the attended stimulus' (Scharf, 1999, p. 112). This ability of the OCB to bias the response of the auditory system might be one mechanism that allows us to selectively attend to a particular voice at the cocktail party.

The early–late debate

The difficulty of attending to information on the basis of its semantic content was one of the major reasons why Broadbent (1958) put the selective filter at an early stage of his model. However, evidence soon began to emerge that the meaning of 'unattended' messages was breaking through the filter. One challenge came from a series of studies by Moray (1959). Using shadowing experiments, Moray showed that when the same small set of words was repeated on the unattended ear, recognition memory for those words was very poor, even a few seconds after presentation. If the unshadowed words had received attention, they should have been easily recognisable. This result is predicted by filter theory and appears to support it. However, some of Moray's results were not consistent with the predictions of Broadbent's theory. For example, Moray found that listeners often recognised their own name when it was presented on the unattended ear. This result is inconsistent with a selective filter that only allowed input to the limited capacity channel on the basis of physical attributes. Moray's results suggest that there is more analysis of unattended information than Broadbent thought. In particular, there must be some semantic processing prior to conscious identification. However, in Moray's experiment subjects were not able to recognise all words from the unattended message; only particularly relevant words, like the subjects' name, were likely to *break through* the filter.

Following Moray's original studies, breakthrough of the unattended message was studied in more detail by Treisman (1960). She showed that even if a subject is attending to the stream of events on one channel, there may be information breakthrough from the unattended message, especially if there is a meaningful relation between what is currently being attended and what is coming in on the unattended channel. Subjects were told to shadow a story (story 1) on one ear and to ignore the other story (story 2) presented to the other ear. During the experiment, story 1 was switched to replace story 2 on the unattended ear and a new story (story 3) began on the attended ear. According to Broadbent's theory, subjects would have their select-ive filter set to the attended ear, and would have no knowledge about the meaning of information on the channel that was blocked off. So when the stories were switched, they should have immediately carried on shadowing the new story, story 3. However, Treisman found that as soon as the stories were switched, subjects shadowed a few words from story 1 from the unattended ear before picking up story 3 from what should have been the attended ear. This result shows that subjects did have some knowledge of the semantics of the unattended story.

Treisman (1964b) compared performance when the unattended message was a passage from the same novel with conditions where the unattended message was a technical passage, a foreign language or nonsense syllables. Shadowing the attended message was significantly affected by the content of the material in the unattended message, and the most difficult condition was when the same voice was reading two passages from the same novel. Experiments like these showed that a semantic difference could be used to aid selection, although this information is much less effective than a physical difference. Treisman put forward a modification of Broadbent's (1958) model, in which the unattended information was not completely blocked, but only attenuated, or 'turned down'. Words that are of high importance to the listener, like their name, will be triggered on the basis of less activation than words of low importance, and will break through the attenuator. Similarly, words that are primed by semantic association may also become sufficiently active to break through (see Figure 9.2). This attenuator model can account quite well for breakthrough of the unattended message at the same time as allowing almost perfect selection most of the time.

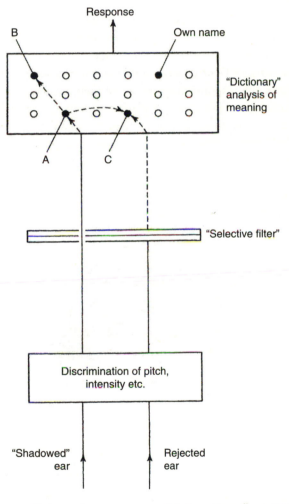

FIGURE 9.2 Treisman's attenuator model. From Broadbent (1971).

Additional evidence consistent with the idea that selection could proceed on the basis of meaning was supplied by a modification of the split-span experiment, done by Gray and Wedderburn (1960). They presented the following kind of stimulus pairs 'mice', 'one', 'cheese', to the right ear, while simultaneously presenting 'four', 'eat', 'two' to the left ear (see Figure 9.3). Subjects in this experiment did not preferentially report ear by ear, but grouped the information by meaning, so they reported 'mice, eat, cheese' and 'four, one, two'. Evidence such as this led Deutsch and Deutsch (1963) to propose a rather different view of selective attention that could account for semantic effects of the 'unattended' message.

Deutsch and Deutsch suggested that selective attention operates much nearer the response stage than the identification stage of processing and 'that a message will reach the same perceptual and discriminatory mechanisms whether attention is paid to it or not; and such information is then grouped or segregated by these mechanisms' (1963, p. 83). They suggested that incoming signals were weighted for importance and in some way compared to determine the currently most important signal. Clearly there are contradictions in the literature. Sometimes auditory attention appears to rely on properties of the

One, eat, three   Mice, two, cheese

"mice, eat, cheese"

FIGURE 9.3 A person in a dichotic listening task reporting according to semantic relationship.

stimulus that are extracted early in processing; sometimes attention appears to operate on semantic properties that should only be available after full analysis by later processing stages.

Where is the bottleneck in auditory processing?

Norman (1968) argued, rather like Deutsch and Deutsch, that sensory inputs are extensively processed automatically before we consciously 'know' about them. He believed that this processing relies heavily on information in long-term memory. He suggested that sensory features of the input automatically address their location in semantic memory so that if the input matches some stored representation, the meaning will be accessed. We discuss semantic memory in Chapter 11. If the input was a nonsense word, i.e., had no pre-existing representation, no meaning would be found, telling you that the input was not a word. In Norman's model, selection comes after semantic memory has been accessed, and both attended and unattended sources of information have automatic and effortless access to semantics. Once semantics have been activated, pertinence values are assigned to those activations according to current ongoing cognitive activities. Pertinence is determined by the context of the inputs and activates nodes, or locations in semantic memory. Selection is then based on the total activation in semantic memory from both sensory input and context. Norman allowed attention to be a matter of degree. Pertinence values are assigned at all levels of processing, and the pertinence value may change with further processing. A message that initially seems of low pertinence may be found to be more pertinent following further processing. Finally, most messages will have been rejected, leaving only the most pertinent to become most deeply processed. Norman's model can easily account for the effects of semantics that were troublesome for original filter theory. Highly probable words arriving at the unattended ear will be attended because of the effect of context-determined pertinence.

The effects of unattended semantic information

Corteen and Wood (1972) and Corteen and Dunn (1973) did some intriguing experiments on the effects of information that subjects were not asked to attend to. When subjects expect to get a small electric shock, their skin resistance changes and this can be measured as *galvanic skin response* (GSR). Corteen and colleagues conditioned subjects to expect a shock in association with a particular set of words to do with the city. The subjects then took part in a dichotic listening task. Every so often one of the shock-associated words was presented on the unattended channel, and despite not consciously hearing these words, the subjects showed a clear change in GSR. These subjects also showed a GSR to other city words that had not been included in the training set. This result suggests that not only was there semantic access of the unattended words, but there was also semantic generalisation. Other experimenters have found similar results, e.g., Lackner and Garrett (1972). MacKay (1973) presented ambiguous sentences in a dichotic listening task. Subjects shadowed sentences like 'They threw stones at the bank yesterday'. Here *bank* was ambiguous, because it could equally well refer to a riverbank or a bank where you keep money. MacKay found that if the word 'river' was presented on the unattended channel, subjects did not remember having heard 'bank', but interpreted the sentence in terms of riverbank rather than money bank. Experiments like these can be interpreted as providing more evidence that the selective processes in attention come after the meaning of words has been accessed. All these findings suggest that semantics are available at the time of selection, but physical characteristics of the stimulus are the most effective when it comes to selecting a stimulus source for constant monitoring. Semantics can 'break though' but are not very effective for selecting an input.

Modification of Broadbent's filter theory

Broadbent (1971) modified his original theory to account for new evidence. He expanded the role of the filter and added two new selection processes; pigeon-holing and categorising. Filtering was seen as grouping the input on the basis of simple characteristics and this information passes to higher levels. The results of filtering represent evidence for the stimulus, rather than the providing determinate evidence from the outside world. The evidence may suggest that one state of the environment, or stimulus, is more likely than another, but this is not certain. Although there may be uncertainty about the state of the outside world, the output of the limited capacity channel must be either one state or the other. Broadbent named this the 'category state'. To determine which category state is best fitted to the evidence, a decision is required, and rather than using information theory, which was the basis for the 1958 model, Broadbent (1971) frames his explanation in terms of statistical decision theory, which we looked at in Chapter 2. This view allows noise, or uncertainty, to be incorporated into decision making in the system. According to this account, selective filtering links the stimulus states to states of evidence. Rather than the all-or-nothing filter, Broadbent accepted Treisman's (1964b) modification of the original filter theory, which allowed some stimuli to be responded to on the basis of less evidence than others. Now, the filter was seen as a strategy to allow performance under conditions where interference would otherwise occur. Filtering did not block out everything about the unattended message; some features could break through and other features could trigger other later processes. The other concept introduced is *pigeon-holing*, which is a process that relates the evidence from the filter to a category state. Pigeon-holing alters the number of states of evidence that lead to any particular category state. Broadbent (1982) says pigeon-holing is rather like filtering, except instead of selecting on the basis of features, selection operates by biasing the threshold of a category state, which allows some categories to be triggered by less evidence than would normally be needed. So, for example, if you were asked to listen out for the name of an animal, then you would very rapidly respond to animal words irrespective of the voice in which they were spoken and you would be more responsive to animal words than, say, words to do with fruit. In this model we see a close interaction between activity related to memory and the selectivity of attentional processes. Whenever we recognise a word or a sound it is because we 'know it again'—that is what recognise means. The activity of semantics in memory lowers the threshold at which representations will be activated by sensory input, recognised and become consciously available to us. If activity is too low to allow conscious identification of the sensory input, the activation in memory can still produce a response, measured for example by GSR in Corteen and Wood's (1972) experiment, or can produce the priming effects found by MacKay (1973). Experimentation on selective attention in hearing dwindled with the rise of interest in visual attention. Today, vision is the most widely researched area in attention, although increasing interest in cross-modal attention and perception is bringing experiments on auditory attention back into the literature. We turn to this research next. However, these initial data and models set the scene for attention research and we still see their influence in the concepts used when discussing attention today.

Wood and Cowan (1995) have replicated Moray's original experiment and showed that participants who did notice changes on the unattended channel, or heard their name, also showed an increase in shadowing errors and latency following the change. So, noticing a change on the unattended channel correlates with disruption of performance on the attended channel. There are also interesting individual differences between people with respect to the likelihood of them experiencing breakthrough. Conway, Cowan and Bunting (2001) found that people with a low memory span were more likely to notice their names on the unattended channel than people with a high memory span. They also found that low memory span correlates with distractibility, and suggest that name intrusion may be a result of inability to ignore the unattended channel. Conway *et al.* reasoned that name intrusions may result from reduced ability to ignore the unattended channel. This result suggests a close link between selective auditory attention and working memory. Similar results have been found by de Fockert, Rees, Frith and Lavie (2001) when a working memory load is combined with a selective visual attention task. De Focket *et al.* demonstrated that when participants were engaged in a visual selective attention task they showed more interference from distractor faces when concurrently holding a difficult working memory load than when holding an easy working memory load. They argued that working memory plays an important role in maintaining the focus of attention on relevant, to-be-attended material. If this is the case, then the participants with low memory span in

Conway *et al.*'s experiment may have less working memory capacity available to maintain attention on the shadowed auditory channel, and therefore be more open to interference, or breakthough of the other, to-be-ignored material. Lavie *et al.* (2004) propose a load theory of selective attention which appears to resolve the early-late debate. Selection will take place at different levels depending on the overall load of the talk.

Cross-modal perception and attention

Information about the world around us is made available to perception and memory processes by selective attention. So far we have been thinking about information from each of the sensory modalities, more or less separately, although I have mentioned several times that for a full understanding of the environment we need to know about all the properties of stimuli. For this to be possible, not only must we integrate information across the sensory modalities, but we must also be able to select which sensory and perceptual information is the most appropriate for making the most accurate judgement about an object's properties. When one perceptual system is selected as the most appropriate it may become dominant, and completely over-ride information from the other sources. Usually, vision is considered as the dominant sense, but as we shall see, this may depend on the task or judgement to be made. Also, there is increasing evidence that one sense may not completely dominate the others, but rather it will modify the interpretation of incoming information. We shall now consider a range of experiments concerned with multidimensional and cross-modal processes.

Is vision the dominant sense?

If participants are asked to make a judgement of the perceptual properties of an object, but the information from the two modalities is in conflict, psychologists can determine which of the senses is dominant. For example, Hay, Pick and Ikeda (1965) did an experiment in which the observer views one hand though a prism that displaces the visual information about where the hand is actually located. The visual displacement has the effect of putting where the hand is seen to be in conflict with where it is felt to be. The observer cannot see his or her other hand. The observer's task is to point with the unseen hand to the place where the visible, but visually displaced, hand is either felt, or seen to be. The accuracy of pointing in these conditions was compared with accuracy when judgements were made only on vision, or only on *proprioception*. Proprioception is perception of where our limbs are, and is provided by sensors in the joints and muscles. In this experiment it was found that visual information dominates; the hand is felt to be where it is seen. Observers seemed to resolve the conflicting information from proprioception and vision by deciding to believe their eyes. In a classic study, Rock and Victor (1964) demonstrated that vision completely dominates touch in a conflicting form matching task. Other studies have shown complete or very strong visual dominance for perceptual judgements of size, length, depth and spatial location. In these cases there is said to be 'visual capture' of the perceptual event. On the other hand, other studies have found that observers sometimes make compromise judgements, where one modality does not completely dominate, but only biases the judgement in the other modality. Studies of attentional cueing have shown that cues presented in one modality can affect speed of processing in another modality, and that the phenomenon of *extinction* in visual attention, discussed in Chapter 5, can occur across the modalities. For example, Mattingley *et al.* (1997) reported a neuropsychological case where a visual stimulus could extinguish a tactile stimulus and vice versa.

Visual capture of touch — the rubber gloves illusion

The example of the phantom limb patients discussed in Chapter 8 demonstrates how the senses interact with each other and with memory in constructing an interpretation of sense data. Spence, Pavani and Driver (2000) argue that normally we use information from touch, proprioception and vision to enable us to know which body part is touched and where in space we are touched, and that when sense data conflict, vision dominates (visual capture). Spence *et al.* used an interference task to discover if a flash of light would interfere with where subjects felt a tactile vibration. The subjects held a small box between their thumb and forefinger, and the vibration was delivered to the thumb or finger. At the same time as the vibration was delivered, a light flashed beside either the thumb or finger and subjects had to judge which digit was touched and ignore the light. Results showed that the light flash interfered with the tactile judgements, but only when it was very close to the hand. Using the light interference effect as an indicator of where in space subjects feel a touch, Spence *et al.* set up an experiment in which subjects, wearing rubber gloves, could either see their own hands while the touch and light were delivered, or could see what appeared to be their own hands, but were in fact only a pair of rubber gloves, (their own hands were hidden directly beneath.) The question was, where would the touch be felt, on the real, hidden, hands or the visible rubber hands? Results showed that subjects start to feel as though the rubber gloves were their own, and that the vibrations came from where they saw the rubber hands. The interference effect of the lights moved toward the rubber hands, confirming that where the vibration was felt had moved toward the rubber hands. Although the subjects knew the false hands were not their own hands: they could not overcome the illusion. Spence *et al.* argued that where we feel touch is determined by what we see. Such illusions suggest that vision is the dominant sense, and that visual evidence takes precedence over other sensory evidence. It is the case that, in humans at least, vision is best represented in the brain, and so it is not surprising that we believe our eyes in preference to the other senses. Usually, they tell us the truth and this can lead to us believing them in preference to what is usually less reliable information. Importantly, this example demonstrates that our perceptions can provide a wrong interpretation of the physical world and our relation with it.

Illusory conjunctions between vision and touch

When we discussed Treisman and Gelade's (1980) feature integration theory (FIT) in Chapter 5, we discovered that people can sometimes mistakenly combine the visual features of objects to produce illusory conjunctions. According to FIT, this is likely to happen when focal attention has not been directed to the object, and has not conjoined the features with the 'glue' of focal attention. Cinel, Humphreys and Poli (2002) report a series of experiments showing that illusory conjunctions can arise across modalities. In the basic form of the experiments, participants faced a computer screen on which visual stimuli were displayed, and at the same time placed their hands on a table covered by a screen on which tactile stimuli were presented. So, the visual stimuli could be seen but not touched, while the tactile stimuli could be touched but not seen. The tactile stimuli were rectangles onto which different textures, such as beans, fur and carpet were glued. The visual stimuli had three possible shapes—triangle, square or circle—as well as the same surfaces as the tactile stimuli. Visual stimuli were presented only briefly so that accuracy for shape and texture was between 75% and 90%. The participant's first task was to name the orientation of the tactile stimulus: this was to make the participant attend to the tactile stimulus sufficiently to determine its orientation, without drawing attention to its texture. The second task was to report the shape and texture of the visual items. A cross-modality conjunction error was made when the participant reported the visual target as having the texture belonging to the tactile stimulus. Cinel *et al.* found that conjunction errors, or illusory conjunctions, were made not only within modality, but also across modality. In further experiments they show, amongst other things, that these illusory conjunctions are more likely when the same tactile and visual stimuli are on the same side of visual space. This evidence is interpreted in the context of sensory dominance that we have looked at in the previous section, and cross-modal biasing of attention. Cinel *et al.* suggest that there is tagging of information across modalities.

The ventriloquist effect

Another example of vision gaining dominance over audition is the ventriloquist effect. When the ventriloquist speaks without moving his mouth, and synchronises the movements of the dummy's mouth with the words, it appears that the speech sound is actually coming from the dummy. Again, we have an illusion, which is a wrong interpretation of the state of the world. It seems that the dummy, not the ventriloquist, is speaking. This is further evidence that when sensory data conflicts we resolve the mismatch between auditory and visual information in favour of vision. Vision dominates. Although auditory cues can be used to localise sound, we can also use visual cues to confirm or contradict the evidence arriving at our ears. When we hear speech coming from a particular direction we expect to see the person who is speaking move their lips. When a ventriloquist speaks without moving his lips, the dummy with the moving mouth appears to be the source of the sound. Although people with normal hearing may not think they do any lip reading, when the sound and vision on a film are desynchronised, we become very aware of the conflict between lip movements and the speech that is arriving 'out of sync'. In a similar vein, those of you who are short-sighted may have found it difficult to hear what people are saying when you are not wearing your glasses. 'I'm sorry, I can't hear you without my glasses on!' McGurk and MacDonald (1976) demonstrated the importance of lip reading in normal speech perception. They produced a video of someone repeatedly saying 'ba, ba, ba' and synchronised it with a voice saying 'ga, ga, ga'. Participants reported hearing 'da, da, da', which is a blend between the visual and auditory information. In this case, we have the interesting finding that the conflict resolution process has come up with an interpretation that is wrong on both counts; it is neither a true interpretation of the auditory input nor a true interpretation of the visual input.

The effect of task on dominance

Perhaps there are some perceptual judgements that are better made by other senses. For example, we cannot precisely discover what something feels like by looking at it or by listening to it. We may be able to reach some sort of judgement from vision—for example, an object may look hard or soft, smooth or rough. Auditory information may also help. If someone else scratches or taps their finger nails on the surface of an object, the sound properties produced can suggest surface texture. For example, carpet and sandpaper sound different when scratched. Sometimes vision provides no answer, and we may have to tap a plate to find out if it sounds like china or plastic. Object recognition is covered in Chapter 6. We must remember that not only the surface properties of objects but also whole objects can be recognised in the other modalities. With eyes closed, it is possible to identify objects by feeling them, and objects with distinctive sounds, such as my cat, which has just meowed, can be identified by auditory information. I can even tell which cat it was, in the same way as we can identify people by their voices. Here we shall just remind ourselves that when we identify perceptual properties or identify objects, this requires a match between the outcome of perceptual processes and stored memory representations of object properties.

The modality appropriateness interpretation

A number of researchers have proposed that the different sensory modalities are specialised to process different kinds of incoming information. So, as vision is especially good for spatial information, and audition is good for temporal resolution, then the most appropriate modality will be chosen depending on whether the current task requires spatial or temporal judgements. Lederman, Thorne and Jones (1986) found that vision or touch dominated perception depending on the name given to the judgement that was asked for in a sensory conflict experiment. They suggested that vision tends to focus on the spatial aspects of texture, as proposed by Gibson (1950) and discussed in Chapter 4, whereas touch uses texture to judge the surface properties of objects. Lederman *et al.* thought that this difference between what the senses are used for would affect the modality they relied on to make texture judgements. Participants were tested using the method of magnitude estimation (see Chapter 3). When asked to judge spatial density, vision would predominate, but when asked to judge roughness, touch would dominate. The results confirmed the prediction. There was not, however, complete domination in each case. The data was consistent with a model in which information from the senses is integrated across the modalities, but with the most appropriate modality for the current judgement being given more weight.

Selective attention between the senses

If we are able to select one modality in preference to another because it is most appropriate for the task we are expecting to do, there needs to be some mechanism that can allow one sense to dominate the others. Earlier, we discussed how selective auditory attention could be internally directed by biasing the response of the hair cells on the basilar membrane. Earlier we saw that Scharf (1999) proposed that the olivocochlear bundle (OCB) could prepare the auditory system to be more or less responsive to particular sounds. This mechanism acts top-down, with the initiation of activity in the frontal lobes. This same mechanism may allow auditory information to be selectively inhibited when we select another modality in preference to audition.

A number of experimental studies support the view that OCB can selectively inhibit response to auditory stimuli. Initially it was thought that the OCB could be involved in turning down, or gating, auditory inputs. This would be useful when an animal wants to focus attention on another sense, say sniffing the ground, or looking for prey. In this case it might be advantageous to temporarily suppress response to auditory signals, and Hernandez-Peon, Scherrer and Jouvet (1956) demonstrated that when a cat smelled fish or saw a mouse, the response to sounds in the auditory nerve was reduced. Other evidence suggests that the OCB is involved in the interaction between visual and auditory stimuli (Igarashi *et al.*, 1974). Cats who had an operation to sever the connections of the OCB were more distractible by noise in a visual task than cats with intact connections. However, we said earlier that the auditory system could be an important early warning system, and to shut it down while attending to other sense data would not necessarily be a good idea. Scharf (1999) suggests that not all auditory information is suppressed, rather that response to loud monotonous sounds is reduced, but response to quiet or novel sounds remains unaffected. It appears that, for audition at least, there are neural mechanisms that can operate according to intention that allow the other senses to be selected in preference.

Integration of the modalities: Listening and looking

Although we may sometimes wish to give priority, or selectively attend, to one sense modality rather than another, we would usually be better off if we were aware of as much sense data as possible. So, for example, we usually look in the direction of the sound we are listening to, and when a number of people are speaking at once, we are able to integrate visual and auditory information to attribute the right voice to the right speaker. In addition, the McGurk effect, and the ventriloquist illusion discussed above, suggest that when we look and listen there is an interaction between listening and looking. Moving lips, requiring visual attention, have an effect on how we interpret auditory information. Driver and Spence (1994) investigated how visual and auditory attention work together by manipulating the spatial relationship between the words we see and the words we hear. When a listener attends to one ear in a dichotic listening task, attention is directed, endogenously, to the relevant location in auditory space. Similarly, to attend to one side of visual space, attention is endogenously oriented to the intended location. (See Chapter 4 for endogenous and exogenous orienting.) Driver and Spence presented participants with visual and auditory information to either side of the midline of environmental space. The side to which participants were to attend could be either the same or different for the two modalities. So, participants might need to attend to the left for the visual task and to the right for the auditory task.

Using this method it is possible to see if endogenous attentional orienting can be controlled independently for the two modalities. Two video monitors, one to the left and one to the right, displayed visual information. Immediately below each monitor was a loudspeaker for presenting auditory information. A third loudspeaker was positioned on the midline, in the centre in front of the subject. The monitor could show a video of someone speaking a list of words accurately synchronised with the same words on the loudspeaker on same side of space, or on the opposite side of space. Alternatively, the monitor could show a person who was not speaking, but chewing; in this case lip movements could not be used for any lip reading. The task was to name the words coming from a loudspeaker that was either on the same side as the monitor being fixated (same, speaking lips), or name the words coming from the loudspeaker on the opposite side to the monitor being fixated (opposite, speaking lips). Similar conditions for same, chewing lips and opposite, chewing lips were included. Eye movements were monitored to check that the listener was looking to the correct side. When the lip-read and auditory words were at the same location (same, speaking lips), performance was better than when the visual and auditory information came from opposite sides (opposite, speaking lips). Some benefit was found for the speaking lips in the opposite condition, when compared to chewing lips. Driver and Spence suggested a 'spatial synergy' between visual and auditory attention and that endogenous attention does not operate independently in the two modalities tested. So, if attention is oriented to a location, selection of information about both modalities is enhanced. As attentional mechanisms must have evolved to help us interact with the environment, such an arrangement is obviously sensible, as stimuli at the same spatial location are usually concerned with the same object.

Driver (1996) used a version of the dichotic listening task used by Cherry (1953) described at the start of this chapter. (see Figure 9.4). Driver presented participants with two simultaneous auditory messages, each made up from three two-syllable words in random order. The task was to repeat the target triplet of words, e.g., 'sunset, tulip, headline' while ignoring the other triplet, e.g., 'music, flooring, pigment'. However, the messages were in the same voice, in synchrony, from the same sound source. Therefore, there were no auditory or semantic cues that could be used to segregate the messages. The cue given was visual. A screen showed the speaker's face with the to-be-reported auditory sequence accurately synchronised with the lip and tongue movements. It was expected that lip reading would allow the participant to select the target words. However, we have seen that people tend to locate sounds towards where they see the movements which synchronise with the speech, in the ventriloquist illusion. Driver wanted to see what would happen as he moved the loudspeaker away from the 'speaking' face. He found a quite remarkable result. Shadowing was better when the sound source was moved away from the speaking face. It was as if, like the ventriloquist illusion, the visual information draws the sound source towards it, allowing better separation of the two auditory messages. This illusory separation allowed auditory attention to select the shadowed message more easily. This effect has been suggested to indicate that the integration of sensory data takes place pre-attentively (Driver and Spence 1999).

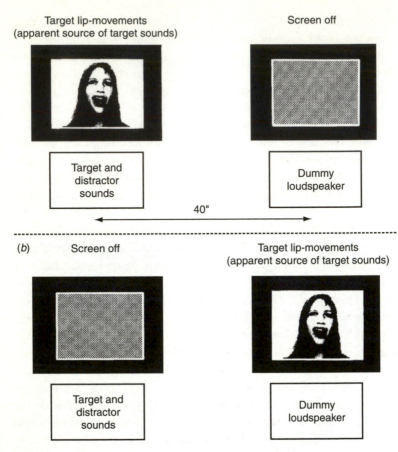

FIGURE 9.4 The arrangement of visual and auditory stimuli in Driver's 1996 experiment. From Driver and Spence (1999).

In another experiment, Spence and Driver (1996) used a version of Posner's cueing task (see Chapter 4), to examine cross-modal links between hearing and vision in endogenous orienting. Visual and auditory attention were centrally cued to either the same or opposite side of space. Results showed that participants could split auditory and visual attention under certain conditions, but when targets were expected on the same side of space for both modalities, the orienting effects were greater. It seems, therefore, that while attention can be oriented independently, to some extent, there are strong spatial links between auditory and visual attention. To find more examples of cross-modal effects see Driver and Spence (1999) for a review.

Summary

Early dichotic listening experiments demonstrated that an auditory message could be selected on physical properties of the message, but not on semantic properties. It was also found that there was very little memory for the unattended information. Broadbent proposed a selective filter that excluded any information not having the physical properties of the selected message. However, evidence for semantic processing of unattended information suggested that more processing was done on the unattended message than was first thought. This led to models of attention that place selection later in the processing system, or allowed for important information to break through the filter. Priming effects and physiological responses to words that could not be reported indicated that semantic properties could be activated without attention below the level of conscious awareness. Cross-modal effects on perception and attention have demonstrated that information from vision can modify attention to sounds and tactile stimuli. Although vision is usually the dominant sense, the modality that dominates in a task is affected by task demands. Sometimes information from the senses can give rise to misinterpretation of stimuli or illusory conjunctions between the senses.

Self-assessment questions (Solutions on p. 323)

1 Can you explain the listening activities described in the first paragraph of the chapter?
2 What is 'breakthrough' and why was it a problem for Broadbent's (1958) model?
3 Give an example of vision dominating the other senses.
4 What effect does the task we are doing have on dominance?

Further reading

Driver, J., and Spence, C. J. (1999). Cross-modal links in spatial attention. In: G. W. Humphreys, J. Duncan, and A. Treisman, (Eds) *Attention, Space and Action: Studies in cognitive neuroscience.* Oxford: Oxford University Press. For a review of cross-modal studies.

Styles, E. A. (1997) *The Psychology of Attention.* Hove, UK: Psychology Press. For more detail on auditory attention.

Chapter 10

Controlling attention: Selecting, planning and remembering actions

Cooking the Sunday lunch

YOU HAVE AGREED TO COOK LUNCH for your friends, something you do not do very often. They have all arrived just as you are coordinating the final stages that will ensure the vegetables, gravy and meat are all ready at once. Although you want to be a good host, you find it almost impossible to have a proper discussion at the same time, and you let the gravy boil over while you check the meat. At last all seems ready: then you discover you left the plates on the side, despite having intended to put them to warm. You all start lunch, and on tasting the sprouts you find they are extremely salty, while the carrots are unsalted. How, you wonder, does your mother manage to do this every week? Afterwards you drive some friends home and talk with them about the trials of cooking dinner.

We all know in some instances we cannot 'pay attention' to two things at once. For example, if someone interrupts us while we are reading, we have to stop reading to talk to them. However, if we are watching a television programme we can talk about what is happening to a fellow viewer. Why is it that we can combine some tasks easily, but not others? Why is it we sometimes find we are not doing what we intended to do or go to do something to find we have already done it? In this chapter we will try to understand how attention can be divided between tasks, and how it is involved in controlling sequences of actions for coherent behaviour.

The theories of attention discussed in the sections on auditory, visual and cross-modal attention were largely concerned with how we selectively process one stimulus rather than another. However, attention can also be divided, or shared, between concurrent tasks to enable us to do two things at once, or it can be used to control activities. Now we shall see that while selection is still important, so too is the allocation and maintenance of attention. Kahneman (1973) suggested that attention is a limited supply of mental processing capacity and that this capacity can be increased by mental effort and arousal.

If we try to do two attentionally demanding tasks at once, processing capacity can be shared, according to priority, between the tasks. However, if one task demands more resources, there will be less capacity left over for the other task. A good analogy of sharing a limited resource could be a domestic water supply. There is a finite water pressure arriving from the main supply. If you are running the bath, and someone else turns on the kitchen tap, the flow of water to the bath is reduced. When the kitchen tap is turned off, you see the flow rate to the bath go back to full power. With respect to combining mental activities, we are all familiar with the problem of trying to do two tasks at once and know that sometimes we have to stop doing one task because it somehow becomes impossible to do them both without making a mistake. A good example is driving a car. Usually, the driver can hold a conversation and control the car at the same time; changing gear and braking appropriately, as well as navigating obstacles and following the route. However, if something unexpected happens, the conversation stops. It is as if the new demand of dealing with the unexpected has suddenly drawn attention away from the conversation to allocate it to dealing with the increased demand on the driving task. Kahneman's view of attention being a limited pool of attentional capacity would be able to account for this example. A similar conception of attention was proposed by Norman and Bobrow (1975), who proposed the term 'resources'.

Data-limited and resource-limited processing

Kahneman's theory was solely concerned with attentional resources. Norman and Bobrow (1975) introduced another limitation, that of the quality of the data. Norman and Bobrow also introduced the idea of a performance-resource function. For a single task, resources can be invested up to a point where, no matter how much more resource is invested, performance will not improve. At this point, performance is said to be *data-limited*. There will be a data limitation if the data input is of poor quality, for example when conversations are noisy, or print is smudged. Data limitations could also arise in memory if we do not have previous knowledge to bring to the task. A data limitation cannot be overcome, no matter how much we try. However, if more resources are invested or withdrawn and performance changes accordingly, performance is said to be *resource-limited*.

When we try to combine two tasks, resources must be allocated between both of them. Depending on the priorities we set, more or less resource can be allocated to one or other of the tasks. If performance on one task is plotted against performance on the other, a *performance operating characteristic* (POC) is obtained. The curve of a POC represents the change in level of performance on one task when the level of performance on another concurrently performed task is changed. If the two tasks are resource-limited, there will be a complementary relationship between the two tasks, so that as performance on one task improves there will be a corresponding decline in performance on the other. If one task is data-limited, no matter how much resource is allocated to it, performance cannot improve.

Rather than a single resource of attentional capacity, Norman and Bobrow believed that there were a variety of resources such as processing effort, various forms of memory capacity and communication channels. This means that different tasks might require different kinds of resource and each kind of resource would have to be investigated separately to find out if tasks were competing for them. Allport (1980) criticises theories that suggest attention is a resource. The problem is that there is no independent way of measuring the resource demands made by any particular task or of discovering if these resources are from the same or different pools. If two tasks interfere they are said to be competing for the same resource; if they don't interfere, they can be said to be using separate resources. This is a circular argument. In addition, if a task is automatic, it does not draw on attentional capacity, and so may not be interfering for that reason. Again there is a problem of deciding how automatic a task is.

Dual task performance: How many resources?

Sometimes tasks interfere with each other, but sometimes they do not. Psychologists have tried combining tasks of various kinds in various ways to discover why this is. Posner and Boies (1971) did an experiment in which participants had to combine a visual matching task with a tone detection task. The visual task involved a warning signal, followed by the first letter and then a second letter. Participants had to press one or other of two response keys to indicate if the second letter matched the first one. Results showed that reaction time to detect a tone depended on when it was presented during a visual matching task. If the tone arrived while the warning signal was presented or while the participant was waiting for the first letter, there was no effect on tone detection. This suggested that processing the warning signal takes little attention. However, if the tone was presented at the same time as either of the letters, participants were slower to respond to it. The slowest response of all was when the tone was presented during the interval between letter presentation, that is, when the subject was attending to the first letter in preparation for response to the second. It appeared that both the auditory tone detection and the visual letter matching tasks were competing for the same resource. During waiting times of the visual task, attention is free to support the tone detection task, but when the visual task demands attention, these attentional resources are shared and there is less attention for detecting or responding to the tone.

However, in a modification of Posner and Boies' task, McLeod (1978) asked his participants to say 'bip' when they detected the tone. This response was completely different from the key press required in the visual matching task. With this combination of tasks there was no interference between the letter matching task and tone detection, no matter when the tone was presented. This important result shows that when the response systems for the two tasks are different, interference disappears, which is inconsistent with a general or shared attentional resource. Rather than a general resource limitation on attentional processing, the interference between tasks looks as if it depends on *stimulus–response compatibility*.

Shaffer (1975) showed that skilled typists could copy-type and simultaneously do a shadowing task, but could not audio-type and read aloud. Why should this be? When people are listening, the auditory words activate the motor programs for their pronunciation. If other words must be pronounced at the same time, the motor programs for the two competing pronunciations interfere. (See 'The motor theory of speech perception', Chapter 7.) In Schaffer's experiment, the copy-typing could be combined with shadowing, because the route from the shadowed input to speech output was using a route or channel that was independent of the route or channel used for mapping the visually presented words to the finger movements for typing. So, it appears that when there is no competition for specific processing resources or stimulus-response mappings, tasks can be combined more easily.

The psychological refractory period

Welford (1952) found that when people are asked to respond to two signals in rapid succession, and the second stimulus is presented before response has been made to the first, the second response is delayed. As two signals get closer and closer in time, the delay in the response to the second stimulus increases. This delay is called the *psychological refractory period* (PRP). Welford suggested that the PRP was evidence for a limited capacity mechanism that could only process one response decision at a time. So the difficulty with doing two things at once could be because there is a bottleneck at the point where decisions about response are made. This would mean that the second response has to 'queue' until the first response has been selected. Some studies have shown that the PRP, like the dual tasks we have seen here, is influenced by stimulus and response compatibility. Greenwald and Schulman (1973) showed that when stimulus and response are highly compatible, for example, hearing *one* and saying 'one', there is no PRP, but when the response to the second stimulus was incompatible, hearing *one*, but responding 'A', there was evidence for a refractory period. They suggested that when the response to a stimulus was *ideomotor compatible*, the feedback from the response resembled the stimulus to which the response was made, and tasks of this kind could be combined with other tasks without cost. However, by doing very carefully controlled experiments, Pashler (1990) demonstrated that even when the stimuli and responses required of the two successive signals in a PRP experiment were very different, for example, a spoken response to tone and a key-press response to a visually presented word, there was still a psychological refractory period. Of course, in a PRP task the stimuli and their responses are really quite simple and the time differences measured are very small. In general the effect would not be noticeable in tasks where the stimuli and the responses made to them are more complex. In a recent study Lien, Proctor and Allen (2002) have studied ideomotor compatibility and PRP, using a variety of task combinations with different stimulus response compatibilities, and have found a PRP effect in all cases. They suggest that there are delays in the decision of selecting a response even in ideomotor compatible tasks.

Automatic and controlled processing

Let us return to the example of driving a car while holding a conversation. Until something unusual happens, the conversation appears to be the focus of attention, and the driver does not seem to be thinking about driving the car at all. As we become skilled at a task, more and more aspects of the task become 'automatic', that is, they can proceed without demanding attention. This was not always the case. When we first begin driving it is very demanding, requiring a great deal of conscious effort. For the novice, driving is many tasks, not just one. There is the clutch to deal with, the gear lever, steering, using the indicators; all of these seem to be tasks in their own right. The expert driver is able to do all these tasks at once, and many actions will have become so automatic they are done without any awareness. If an expert driver changes to a different car, they may find that whenever they intend to indicate, they wash the back windscreen instead! To adapt to the new car, some concentration or effort is needed to re-learn the arrangements of the controls. What these examples illustrate is that learning can result in changes in the way we do tasks, and that there are differences between well-learned tasks and novel tasks. While we are learning a task attention and conscious control are needed, but with practice, less and less conscious control is required until the task becomes automatic. However, even when we do tasks automatically, they must be 'controlled' in some way to allow the appropriate actions to follow from the stimuli in the environment.

Two-process theory of attention

Posner and Snyder (1975) drew the distinction between automatic activation processes that are solely the result of past learning and processes that are under current conscious control. They proposed that mental processing can operate in two different modes. In 'automatic' mode, processing is a passive outcome of stimulation: it is parallel and does not draw on attentional capacity. In 'conscious control' mode, mental processing is consciously controlled by intentions and does draw on attentional capacity. Atkinson and Shiffrin (1968) had previously pointed out the importance of understanding not only the structure of the information processing system, but also how it was controlled. Although their model is about memory processes (see Chapter 11), it also involves attention because selection, rehearsal and recoding of information in short-term memory involve control processes. This 'working memory', as they called it, is used not only for storage but also for processing the information held in it. They argued that the more demanding the processing was, the less capacity would be available for storage and vice versa. If you try to multiply 23 by 14 in your head you not only have to store the original sum, but also use rules for multiplication, which are stored in long-term memory and will need to be retrieved, and keep track of the new numbers you are generating. Often you will find you get so far into the sum, and then you find you have lost track of where you were, or have forgotten what the sum was in the first place. Here we can see the close relationship between working memory and conscious attentional control. Later modifications of the working memory have all included these storage and control aspects, e.g., Baddeley (1986, 1993), Broadbent (1984). Chapter 12 discusses working memory.

Shiffrin and Schneider's theory

Shiffrin and Schneider (1977) investigated the factors that allowed automatic processing to develop or not. Subjects had to search brief visual displays for one letter from a set of letters they had memorised—the memory set. The critical manipulation was the mapping between stimuli and responses. In the *consistent mapping* condition, targets were always consonants and distractors were always digits, so there was a consistent mapping of target and distractors onto their responses. In this case, whenever the subject detected a letter in the display it had to be a target. In the *varied mapping* condition, both the memory set and the distractors were a mixture of letters and digits and the target and distractor sets changed from trial to trial. There was a clear difference between performance in the two conditions. With consistent mapping, search was virtually independent of both the number of items in the memory set and the number of items in the display, as if search is taking place in parallel. Shiffrin and Schneider said this indicated *automatic processing* of all display items. However, in the varied mapping condition responses to the target were slower and response times increased with the number of distractors in the display. Search seemed to be serial, requiring what they called *controlled processing*.

Letters and digits are very familiar stimuli and we have well-established learned responses to them. Shiffrin and Schneider went on to test how much practice was needed to produce automatic processing of items divided by a novel, arbitrary distinction. To do this they divided letters into two sets. In consistent mapping, only one set of consonants was used to make up the memory set and distractors were always selected from the other set. After over 2,100 trials performance began to resemble that of subjects in the letter/digit experiment. Search became fast and independent of the number of items in the memory set, or the number of items in the display. Next the same participants did the experiment again, but now the mapping between sets was reversed so that the previously learned targets were now distractors and vice versa. To start with, participants found the task very difficult; they were slow and made many errors. However, after 2,400 trials of reversal training, performance had returned to the same level as it had been after 1,500 trials of the original training. It was as if the subjects either had to 'unlearn' an automatic attentional response to the previous memory set or overcome some kind of learnt inhibition to the previous distractor set, or both, before the reversed set could become automatic.

Shiffrin and Schneider also showed that even after extended practice, varied mappings could easily be changed according to instructions, so the difficulty with changing target set in the consistent mapping condition was not simply due to changing from one set to another. Overall, two different processes do appear to be involved in controlling attention; one type can be quickly adapted by the subject's conscious intentions and another kind runs off automatically beyond conscious control. In another experiment, Shiffrin and Schneider found that when a target that had been a member of the consistent mapping set appeared in an irrelevant location there was an attentional *pop-out* effect rather like the pop-out effects we mentioned when we discussed the distinction between parallel and serial search in Treisman's theory of feature integration (see Chapter 5). In contrast, irrelevant targets from previous varied mapping, or controlled search conditions, did not capture attention by pop-out; participants were not aware of them and they did not interfere with target processing.

Selection for action

For us to be able to engage in coherent, goal-directed behaviour, we must be able to interrupt or over-ride automatic processing. This is necessary for us to be able to make the intended action to the right object at the right time on the basis of as much information as possible. According to this view, all stimuli are processed as far as response, but attention acts to select the most appropriate response according to the current goal of behaviour. Sometimes, or even often, a number of responses are possible, but only one meets the current behavioural goal. A well-known example where automatic processing has to be overcome to make the intended response is evident in the *Stroop effect* (Stroop, 1935). The typical Stroop task uses the words for colours written in an ink colour that conflicts with what the word says; for example, *red* written in green ink. Because we have spent many years learning and practising reading, there is an automatic response to the written word. However, if we want to say *green* in response to the ink colour, the response to the word must be stopped from controlling our behaviour. One response is selected for control of action in preference to the other according to the goal of the task. Allport (1980, 1987) and Neuman (1987) drew an important distinction between the role of attention in selection for perception and in selection for action. A typical environment provides multiple sources of information and stimuli, all provoking a possible response. Coherent behaviour demands we only respond to one source of information, although we may need to take other information into account. Allport (1987) gives the example of picking fruit.

> Many fruit are within reach, and clearly visible, yet for each individual reach of the hand, for each act of plucking, information about just one of them must govern the particular pattern and direction of movements. The disposition of the other apples, already encoded by the brain, must be in some way temporarily decoupled from the direct control of reaching, though it may of course still influence the action, for example as representing an obstacle to be reached around, not to be dislodged and so on. A predator, (a sparrow hawk, say) encounters a pack of similar prey animals, but she must direct her attack selectively towards just one of them; the fleeing prey must, with equal speed, select just one among the possible routes of escape (p. 396).

Although the senses are capable of encoding information about many objects simultaneously, there is a strict limit on action because our effector systems are limited. We can only move our eyes in one direction at a time or reach our hand to pick one apple at a time. Allport reasons that there is a biological necessity for 'selection for action', and there must be a fundamentally important mechanism that can select relevant information to have control over each effector system, and can selectively disconnect or '*decouple*' all other information. Allport (1989) suggests, 'Coherent, goal directed behaviour requires processes of selective priority, assignment and co-ordination at many different levels (motivational, cognitive, motor, sensory). Together this set of selective and coordinative processes can be said to make up the effective attentional engagement (or attentional set) of an organism at any moment' (p. 652). When we try to do the Stroop task, the goal could be either 'name the word' or 'name the colour of the ink'. Somehow attentional set must be intentionally changed depending on the current goal if we are to make the right response. Normally, this is (relatively) easily done. However, patients who have suffered damage to the frontal lobes find changing attentional set very difficult or impossible. Experiments on task-shifting in normal participants have shown that changing attentional set costs time (Allport *et al.*, 1994; see Monsell, 1996, for a review).

Disorders of control

Classical symptoms of frontal lobe damage are deficits in planning, controlling and coordinating sequences of actions. Bianchi (1985) first suggested that the frontal lobes were the seat of coordination of information coming in and out of the sensory and motor areas of the cortex. Luria (1966) introduced the term *frontal lobe syndrome* to describe patients who, following frontal lobe damage, showed similarly disorganised, incoherent, incomplete behaviour. A more recent example of the effects of bilateral frontal damage is patient EVR reported by Eslinger and Damasio (1985). EVR was unable to plan and make decisions. Even deciding what to buy at the shop or which restaurant to eat in was a major task involving in-depth consideration of brands and prices in the shop or menus, seating plan and management style in the restaurant.

The most typical problem patients have is called *behaviourial rigidity*, or difficulty in changing attentional set. Milner (1963) tested a variety of patients' performance on the Wisconsin Card-sorting Test. In this test the patient has to discover a rule, and is then told to change to a different rule. This requires changing attentional or mental set. Patients with frontal damage were unable to change from their original rule. They showed *perseveration*, in that despite being instructed to stop sorting on the old rule and look for another, they were unable to do so. It was not that they had forgotten the rule; they knew exactly what they should be doing, but were not able to do it. Milner suggested that her patients were unable to over-ride the activation of well-learned schema. This idea is supported by the fact that naming the ink colour of a Stroop colour word may be totally impossible in patients with frontal damage, and Perret (1974) found that patients with left frontal lesions were unable to inhibit word reading to name the ink colour. Clearly these patients have lost ability to intentionally control attentional set. Well-learned behaviour automatically captures control of attention and action.

Frontal lobe patients are also easily distracted. Shallice (1988) concludes that they have difficulty in both focusing and maintaining concentration. Although frontal patients have difficulty in shifting mental set, leading to inflexible behaviour, they also have difficulty in maintaining mental set or inhibiting unwanted actions. Baddeley (1986) reports a patient, RJ, with frontal lesions who was asked to measure out a length of string so that it could be cut later. RJ immediately picked up the scissors and cut the string. Although he knew the string was not to be cut, and said, 'Yes I know I'm not to cut it', he carried on cutting! This behaviour of RJ is similar to *utilisation behaviour*. Lhermitte (1983) reports a patient who, having had a glass and a jug of water placed in front of them, picks up the jug and pours water into the glass. Another difficulty frequently found in frontal lobe syndrome is the inability to maintain goal-directed behaviour.

Slips of action in everyday life

Reason (1979) conducted a diary study of everyday *slips of action*, and found that in normal everyday life, people without brain damage also make action slips reflecting loss of intentional control. Usually such errors are simply irritating or waste time, but if the person making the error is a pilot or a machine operator, the consequences of an action slip could be very serious. Reason argues that 'central to the notion of error is the failure of "planned actions" since not all failures to attain a goal can be classed as errors' (p. 69), and suggests that a plan is a mental representation of a goal, which may be broken down into component subgoals together with the possible actions required to achieve them. To try to find out about the nature of action slips, Reason conducted a study in which 35 volunteers kept diaries of their 'actions not as planned' for 2 weeks. Over this period 433 action slips were recorded by the group. The errors were classified into quite detailed categories. Here are just a few examples from the main categories.

1   Discrimination failures (11%) These involved confusion between the perceptual, functional, spatial or temporal features of the stimuli.

'I put my shaving cream on my toothbrush.'

'I turned on my electric fire instead of my transistor radio which was on the floor near to it.'

2   Program assembly failures (5%). These errors seemed to result from two ongoing plans changing places.

'I put the butter on the draining board and two dirty plates in the fridge.'

'My office phone rang. I picked up the receiver and bellowed "Come in" at it.'

3   Test failures (20%). These are due to failures to check the progress of actions at key points.

'I was about to step into the bath when I discovered I still had my underclothes on.'

4   Subroutine failures (18%). These errors result from components of the goal action being repeated, or omitted.

'I picked up my coat to go out when the phone rang. I answered it and then went out of the front door without my coat.'

5   Storage failures (40%). These result from forgetting or mis-remembering plans and actions.

'I had intended to post a letter while I was out shopping but when I got home the letter was still in my pocket.'

'I went upstairs to the bedroom but when I got there I couldn't remember what I came for.'

Reason's study provides us with evidence for many examples of failures to complete planned actions successfully, and we are all familiar with these sorts of failures. However, it is very difficult to be exactly sure what has gone wrong in each example, and to classify errors unambiguously. Nevertheless, some common themes do emerge. Most errors seem to occur during activities that are highly practised and routine. These tasks have been performed many times, for example, making a cup of tea. This familiar and often-repeated sequence had become largely automatic and can be done without demanding much attentional processing. This distinction was demonstrated in the experiments by Shiffin and Schneider that we discussed earlier. Reason and Mycielska (1982) proposed that actions that can be carried out according to a well-learned series of instructions are controlled by an *open-loop* system. In open-loop control the stimulus directly triggers the sequence of actions to control the task. Open-loop control is rigid and not very sensitive to feedback necessary for error correction. On the other hand, *closed-loop* performance is attention demanding and monitors ongoing activity to check actions are being made correctly and to determine if the behavioural goal is being moved towards. If activity does not appear to be likely to meet the goal, the actions can be modified. Earlier we discussed why an experienced driver would have to stop talking when an attentionally demanding situation arose. Whist driving a familiar route with no unusual demands from the driving environment, the skilled driver can operate the clutch and gearbox without needing to consciously monitor their actions; such activities are controlled in open-loop mode. However, when the traffic lights change, or a junction is approached, control will change to closed-loop, requiring moment-to-moment monitoring of actions using attentional processes. So, it appears that automatic responses are controlled in the open-loop mode, and controlled processing is necessary in the closed-loop mode. There are criticisms of this explanation, well explained by Matthews *et al.* (2000).

What is certainly true is that slips of action are more likely to happen in a well-learned, familiar situation, when attentional control is not closely monitoring ongoing activity. Norman (1981) and Reason (1984) explain the control, and failures, of action in terms of '*action schema*' stored in long-term memory. Norman proposed that schema are hierarchically organised, with 'parent schema' at the higher levels and 'child schema' at the lower levels. The parent schema represent goals—for example, 'make a cup of tea'—and the child schema represent the component actions that need to be recruited in order to meet that goal—for example, there will be a schema for boiling the kettle, getting out the tea bags and so on (see Figure 10.1).

Embedded in the schema for boiling the kettle will be other sub-schema for actions such as 'fill kettle with water', 'switch kettle on'. Each schema has a set of triggering conditions that must be met for

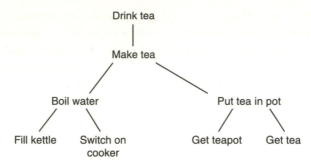

FIGURE 10.1 The schema hierarchy for making tea. From Cohen (1996).

it to be implemented, and when the activation of a schema reaches a sufficient level of activation, it will operate. In the example of making tea, the intention to have a cup of tea triggers the parent schema, which then sets into action all the schema related to the goal. When the kettle is full, that triggers the schema to switch it on. A slip of action occurs when the goal is not maintained—when there is faulty triggering of schema or inadequate activation. Schema theory will come up again in Chapter 12. The following model is an extension of Norman's model, and can account for accurate and inaccurate control of action and the difference between automatic and attentional, or 'willed', control.

Norman and Shallice's model of willed and automatic control

Shallice (1982), Norman and Shallice (1986), and Shallice and Burgess (1993) have put forward theoretical accounts for the control of action in both automatic and intentional *'willed' behaviour* (see Figure 10.2). Although each model is slightly different in essence, they all propose that stimuli enter the perceptual processing system and activate schema stored in long-term memory. The most active schema then captures control of the system that controls action. This process of schema activation and selection takes place below the level of conscious attention and is controlled by an automatic system, the *'contention scheduler'*. However, this automatic system must be interrupted if our behaviour is not to be entirely controlled 'bottom-up'. If

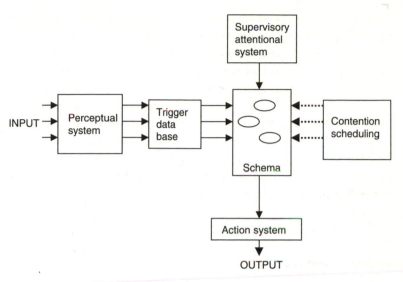

FIGURE 10.2 A simplified version of Norman and Shallice's (1986) model for willed and automatic control of behaviour.

the schema most strongly activated by an external environmental stimulus always captured control of behaviour, it would be impossible to pursue a goal-directed sequence of actions without performance being interrupted by stimuli strongly associated with a well-learned response; we would all behave like the patients with frontal damage. So, to explain goal-directed behaviour, Norman and Shallice propose the importance of a *supervisory attentional system* (SAS) that uses top-down attentional biasing to change the activation of the intended schema to take control of action. Baddeley (1986) has suggested that the SAS is similar to the central executive component of working memory and highlights the relation between attention and memory.

Norman and Shallice's model can account for everyday 'slips of action' (Reason, 1979) as well as the deficits in planning, goal-directed behaviour and attentional capture in patients with frontal lobe damage. It can also account for the fact that novel and poorly learned tasks require more attentional processing or resources than tasks that have become automatic through practice. Overlearned tasks have complex schema hierarchies stored in memory that are automatically activated by patterns of environmental stimuli, but novel tasks have no such schema and require attention to control each component of the overall task. Whilst this model acknowledges the importance of attentional control it does not address the problem of how the SAS is itself controlled. Duncan (1986) discusses the disorganisation of behaviour following frontal lobe damage and points out the importance of setting and maintaining goals for coherent behaviour. Goals must be set, maintained and then cancelled when the goal is achieved and failure at any of these stages produces incoherence of goal-directed activity. Frontal patients not only have difficulty setting goals in the first place, but once goals do become set, they are difficult to change.

Prospective memory

When we have an intention to do something, for example return a library book, a goal is set to be met in the future. As we have just seen, Duncan (1986) pointed out that not only must goals be set, but they must also be maintained and then cancelled when the goal is complete. Usually we think of memory as storing what we have done or encountered in the past; this can be considered as *retrospective memory*. When we intend to do something in the future we also have a memory for what we will do, or a plan. We can think of this as *prospective memory*. Cohen (1989) identified three stages of prospective memory. First, the encoding stage, where we self-instruct ourselves to carry out an event in the future—this sets the intention. Next, the retrieval stage, when we retrieve the instruction and execute the planned act—this is the action stage. Last comes the cancellation stage, where we note the act has been performed and cancel the instruction to avoid repetition—this stage updates retrospective memory. An everyday example of failure to do this last update stage would be if you went to post a letter, but looked in your bag to discover you had posted it already. Here it is clear that retrospective and prospective memory must be interactive. The intention setting must be encoded in prospective memory, and once the intention is completed, the fact you have done it also must be entered into retrospective memory. The retrospective component of memory responsible for this sort of event is *episodic* memory, a topic covered in Chapter 11.

J. Ellis (1996) divides the phases of a prospective memory task, or the realisation of a delayed intention, into five phases (see Figure 10.3). Phase A involves the formation and encoding of intention and action: 'what' you want to do is the action, 'that' you have decided to do something is the intent, and 'when' is retrieving the intention and action to be done. J. Ellis gives the example 'I will' (that-element) 'telephone Jane' (what-element) and 'this afternoon' (when-element). Phase B is the retention interval; for example, you may set an intention to phone Jane 2 days before you plan to do it, so the retention interval would be 2 days. Phase C is the performance interval; this specifies the time window within which the intended action is to be retrieved, which might be 3 hours, between 9 am and noon. The next phase, phase D, involves the initiation of the intended action, and phase E is the evaluation of outcome stage. A record of the outcome is necessary otherwise the action might be repeated.

Having encoded the intention to do something into retrospective memory, how do we ensure we retrieve that intention at the right time? How do we remember to telephone Jane in 2 days' time, between 9 am and noon? If we fail, we demonstrate absent-mindedness, which is related to the action slips that we discussed earlier, but rather than misdirecting an action, absent-mindedness is characterised by failing to make the action at the intended time. People use a variety of

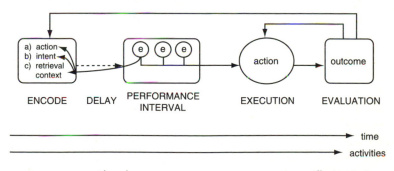

FIGURE 10.3 The phases in prospective memory. From Ellis (1996).

strategies to remember to do things. They may write a list of things to do, and check them off as they are done. In this case they set up an external memory aide. Alternatively, they may tie the intention to a routine activity, for example, 'When it is coffee break time I shall telephone Jane'. As coffee break is habitual, and bound to happen, this should trigger remembering the intention. Alternatively, they may rely on internal information to remember.

Some prospective memory is linked to habitual actions, for example cleaning your teeth before you go to bed. In this case the going to bed routine triggers the 'clean-teeth' schema. Remembering to carry out future actions that are not regularly tied to other habitual actions depends on a specific intention being retrieved at the appropriate moment in time. Meacham and Leiman (1982) tried to discover some of the ways people remember to do things using two groups of volunteers who were given cards to post back to experimenters over variable time periods. Half the volunteers were given a key-fob that was to 're-mind' them, and should have triggered the plan to send in the card. The other half were not given any formal way of remembering. The volunteers given the reminder key-fob posted their cards on time more often, and 88% of all subjects used ways of reminding themselves apart from the key-fobs. Typically these were external reminders such as marking the calendar or putting the cards in noticeable places. However, we also need to explain why we sometimes forget that we have carried out the intention.

Koriat and Ben-Zur (1988) suggested that output monitoring was necessary for knowing if an intention had been carried out. They differentiate between two kinds of process involved in output monitoring. One set of processes operate on-line and happen as the act is completed to erase or check off the act as completed. This may involve an internal erasure of the plan from an internal, mental scratch-pad, or removing the external reminder by untying the knot in your handkerchief. Alternatively, the monitoring process can be retrospective, in that when the cue for the act emerges you either search in memory for evidence that the plan still needs doing—an internal check—or note that the external reminder, the knot in your handkerchief, is still there. The problem with this view is that if plans are cancelled on-line, they cannot be reactivated, but plans can be reactivated even when they have been checked off. If a task is particularly important we are likely to check several times that we have done it. For example, when I am about to go abroad, I have the goal of finding my passport and putting it my bag. I think I remember doing this, but check to see if it really is in my bag. It is, but this does not stop me looking again several times. Despite having clear evidence that the passport is in the bag, I check again and again, as if by some magical process the passport could have got out of the bag. Some errors of prospective memory may arise because we confuse our mental rehearsal of a plan with the actual activity. In this case we may be unsure whether we imagined doing the act or really did it. In order to be sure that an action has been completed, it is necessary to uniquely specify the episode by the context of its execution. This episodic memory then provides the retrospective memorial record that the task has been done. Without this *source information* we cannot differentiate imagined from real events.

Attentional control and skill

We have seen that slips of action are most likely to occur when behaviour is controlled automatically, and earlier used the example of driving as a task that becomes more automatic with practice. Thinking back to the experiments by Shiffrin and Schneider (1977), this work showed that practice produces a learned change in the way stimuli are processed and controlled. If we have learned, then there has been a change in memory that results in a change in attentional demand. So, how can psychologists account for this change? As we saw, in the right conditions and with increasing practice, information processing begins to become automatic. A red traffic light always means 'stop', and the expert driver does this without any apparent effort. The red signal automatically triggers the sequence of activities to slow the car down and stop an appropriate distance from the car in front without stalling the engine. For the novice driver, seeing the traffic light change does not trigger a single process, but rather a set of actions to do with braking, clutch control and distance judgement, possibly accompanied by verbal self-instruction. However, skill acquisition is not a single step function change; skill increases gradually. Let's take the example of tying a particular knot, important for climbers and sailors, called a bowline. When first trying to tie the knot a novice may be given a verbal instruction, designed to be easily remembered, which involves an imaginary rabbit coming up through the hole, going round the tree and then disappearing down the hole. This is supposed to make tying the knot easier. In fact it is still quite difficult, as the 'hole' is a loop in the rope that can easily be made the wrong way round, and the 'rabbit' or free end of the rope may go the wrong way round the tree! Also, simply manipulating the rope can be difficult; the novice seems 'ham-fisted'. However, after many trials the novice begins to tie the knot more reliably and to rely less on the verbal instruction and more on what the finished knot looks like. The expert can tie the knot quickly in one fluent sequence of movements, without verbal instruction, and with their eyes closed, while talking about something else.

So, when someone learns a skill their performance changes both qualitatively and quantitatively. Newell and Rosenbloom (1981) showed that the learning curve for skill acquisition could be described by the *power law of practice* (see Figure 10.4). We never stop improving with practice, although each time we practise in the early stages has a very much greater effect on performance than later practising does. The power law shows a law of diminishing returns, with the benefits of practice getting smaller and smaller as we become more skilled. Skills can be divided into cognitive and motor skills,

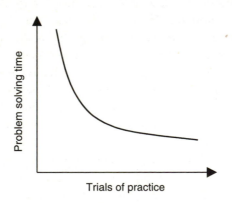

FIGURE 10.4 The power law of practice.

although most motor skills will have a cognitive component and most cognitive skills will have some sort of motor response associated with them. All skills show the same power law of practice.

One way of thinking about the way performance changes with practice was proposed by Fitts (1962) and developed by Fitts and Posner (1973). The first stage in learning a skill is the 'cognitive' phase, where the learner tries to understand the task and follows instructions such as those given for tying the knot in the example above. During this phase performance is prone to numerous errors and feedback is needed to demonstrate where the learner went wrong. As the learner begins to get better at the task, they enter the 'associative' phase. Now, the learner begins to rely more on self-monitoring for error and the activity begins to form larger chunks, and be more fluent. At this stage, the task can begin to be combined with doing something else, like talking; it has become more automatic. In the last phase in the development of skill, the 'component processes become increasingly autonomous, less directly subject to cognitive control and less subject to interference from other ongoing activities or environmental distractions' (Fitts and Posner 1973, p. 14). With most skills, frequent repetition within short periods of time leads to better results than the same amount of repetition in a large time block. Although these phases of skill learning are most usually applied to perceptuo-motor learning, they were conceived of as being applicable to all skills.

What changes with practice?

One way that this change could be brought about is if learning sets up schema in memory that become automatically activated by a particular pattern of input, or perceptual pattern. Anderson (1983) developed a computer model called ACT*, in which he distinguished between *procedural* and *declarative* knowledge (see Chapter 11). In humans, declarative knowledge can be told to someone. We can retrieve it into conscious awareness; for example, you can recite the seven times table you learnt at school—'once seven is seven, two sevens are fourteen,' etc. However, other knowledge that you have cannot be made explicit, or be told to someone else, for example, how to ride a bicycle. You have the declarative knowledge that you *can* ride a bicycle, but the skill of doing so is not available to consciousness. ACT* is a *production system* and is useful for describing how knowledge changes with practice and how skill can be acquired. Production systems can be used for computer simulations and have been used, for example, to write programs to play chess. In simple terms a production is the relation between two sets of conditions, expressed as IF . . . THEN . . . rules. These are called condition–action pairs. IF some particular condition is true, THEN a particular action is to be applied. An everyday example could be:

IF it is raining . . . THEN I take my umbrella

In ACT*, these simple condition–action pairs can become more complicated to incorporate goals, which are expressed as AND statements. For example:

IF it is raining
    AND I am going out
THEN I take my umbrella.

More complex still might be

IF it is raining
    AND I am going out
    AND I cannot find my umbrella
THEN I take the car.

Here we see that the addition of the second AND statement has modified the THEN part of the condition–action pair.

Although we have come to discuss ACT* though our discussion of automaticity and control, ACT* is also a theory of memory, and the model includes three kinds of memory; working memory, procedural memory and declarative memory (see Figure 10.5).

In ACT*, a procedure is a condition–action link between the set of conditions currently active in working memory and data or knowledge stored as schema in long-term memory. IF a condition, or set of conditions, is active in working memory, the THEN part of the rule will be applied. When a procedure runs it will result in new information entering working memory, so that another set of IF

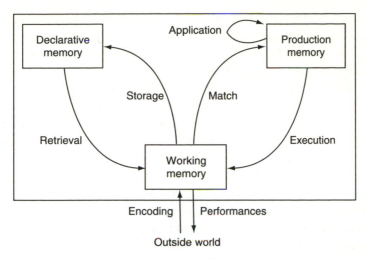

FIGURE 10.5 Anderson's (1983) ACT* model. From Anderson (1983).

conditions will be active. Working memory holds knowledge retrieved from declarative memory, the outcome of procedures and the currently active temporary information encoded from the outside world, by perception. (In the human processor, this would be equivalent to the consciously available contents of short-term working memory.) An important distinction made by memory theorists is between declarative knowledge, to which we have conscious access, and procedural knowledge, to which we have no conscious access. This distinction between procedural and declarative knowledge is fundamental to ACT*. Working memory is severely limited in the amount of information that can be concurrently represented in it. If only a small amount of task-relevant information needs to be represented in declarative form, the system could run much more efficiently. Provided the declarative system has access to the outputs from productions, there is no need for the productions themselves to be open to conscious inspection. Productions in ACT* proceed automatically as a result of pattern matching, and only the products of their execution enter working memory.

In ACT* there are three stages in learning a cognitive skill. Initially, learning involves the collection of relevant facts. So if we are learning to play chess, we must know which moves are legal and which pieces can move where. The novice then applies previous experience in problem solving to work out which is the best move. To begin with, performance is slow and error-prone because there is so much to hold in working memory while the move is worked out. If working memory becomes overloaded, relevant information may be lost and an error may result. However, with practice, the rules start to become proceduralised and, as a result, more automatic. New productions are formed from the declarative knowledge gained in the initial stages of learning. This 'proceduralisation' frees up space in working memory because the declarative knowledge has become embedded in a procedure, and no longer needs retrieving in a declarative form to be used by the system. Now, the rules governing legal moves by different chess pieces are just 'known' by the system—the player does not have to keep on retrieving that knowledge into active working memory. The player will also begin to learn that if a particular configuration of pieces is on the board, then making a particular move is likely to produce a good outcome. In the final stages of learning, new procedures are compiled from existing productions. Production rules become strengthened with use, and may become so automatic that the information within them is no longer available in declarative form. Human experts just 'know' the answer to problems and may find it extremely difficult to explain why they come to decisions. We shall look at experts and novices again when we consider implicit and explicit knowledge in Chapter 11.

A famous experiment by Chase and Simon (1973) showed that Master chess players could memorise the positions of pieces on a chess board far more quickly than novices, but only when the pieces formed part of a valid game. If the pieces were placed at random, the novices' and experts' memories appeared to be exactly the same. The experts were able to perceive the pattern of the positions of the chess pieces in much larger 'chunks' than novices. An expert can see the pieces in related groups, whereas the novice sees each piece individually. In terms of production systems like ACT*, the expert has acquired a whole set of productions in which patterns of pieces on the board specify the conditions for making particular moves. This allows information that matches previous experience to be grouped into a coherent whole. 'Random' patterns of pieces do not fit with previous experience and are no easier for the expert than for the novice.

Long-term working memory and skill

Although productions are stored in long-term memory, and as we have already explained, can be run off automatically without any demand on working memory, Ericsson and Kintsch (1995) suggested that the traditional view of memory in skilled activity needs to include a long-term working memory, LT-WM. They say that current models of memory (e.g., Anderson's, 1983, ACT*, Baddeley's working memory model, 1986) cannot account for the massively increased demand for information required by skilled task performance. They outline a theory of long-term working memory (LT-WM) that is an extension of skilled memory theory (Chase and Ericsson, 1982). They suggest that in skilled performance, say of chess players, there must be rapid access to relevant information in long-term memory. This is achieved by the use of LT-WM in addition to short-term working memory (ST-WM). The learned memory skills allow experts to use LT-WM as an extension of ST-WM in areas where they are well practised. Load on ST-WM is reduced because, rather than all the retrieval cues having to be held there, only the node allowing access to the structure in LT-WM needs to be held. So, in skilled performance, all the relevant information stored in LT-WM is rapidly accessible through the retrieval cue in ST-WM.

Ericsson and Oliver (1984) and Ericsson and Staszewski (1989) studied the ability of expert chess players to mentally represent a chess game without the presence of a chess board. Over 40 moves were presented and the chess player's representation of the resulting game position was tested in a form of cued recall task. It was found that his responses were fast and accurate, suggesting a very efficient and accurate memory representation despite the number of moves that had been made, which far exceed the capacity of ST-WM. The results suggest that the expert chess player is using this additional LT-WM to maintain and access chess positions. The ability to perform tasks automatically, therefore, depends on a variety of factors and, as we become more expert, what we have learnt modifies the way tasks are controlled.

Summary

Attention can be veiled as a resource that can be allocated according to task demands. As more resources are devoted to one task, less can be given to other concurrent tasks. Once no more resources are available a task is 'resource limited'. Data-limitations arise from insufficient data or knowledge. Some tasks can be combined if they do not compete for the same resource or stimulus-response mapping. The two process theory of attention differentiates between controlled processing, which requires attention, and automatic processing, which does not require attention. To do what we intend, automatic processing must be interrupted and controlled. Selection for action involves taking account of as much information as possible, but allowing only a part of that information to guide behaviour. Patients with frontal lobe damage have difficulty in selection for action. Norman and Shallice put forward a model for the intentional control of behaviour that involves a supervisory attentional system, SAS, that can bias schema in memory so that the intended action can be made. If attention is not maintained on the goal task, slips of action occur, when activity is captured automatically by environmental stimuli. Prospective memory is important for setting up intentions, monitoring their progress and monitoring for completion. In skilled performance, complex knowledge has become proceduralised and stored in long-term memory.

Self-assessment questions (Solutions on p. 323)

1   In terms of what you have learned in this chapter, how can you explain your performance while cooking lunch?
2   How can processing become automatic?
3   How, according to Norman and Shallice (1986), are willed actions controlled?
4   What is meant by procedural knowledge?

Further reading

Matthews, G., Davies, D. R., Westerman, S. J. and Stammers, R. B. (2000) *Human Performance: Cognition, stress and individual differences.* Hove, UK: Psychology Press. For excellent coverage and more detail on resource theory, divided attention and skill.

Styles, E. A. (1997). *The Psychology of Attention.* Hove, UK: Psychology Press. For a briefer account.

Chapter 11

Varieties of memory

The fragile present and the permanent past

IF YOU ARE REMEMBERING a telephone number and the doorbell rings, you will probably have forgotten it by the time you have dealt with the person at the door unless you write it down. When someone gives you their mobile number, you find you cannot remember it all, unless you insert pauses into the sequence of 11 digits. However, you can remember what you had for breakfast, and the school you went to, despite other things happening. What is the difference between remembering things in the short term, and for longer periods? Why is it you sometimes know a fact, but cannot remember how you found it out, or think you did something you did not do? These are some of the issues we shall address in this chapter.

In previous chapters the importance of memory in perception and the involvement of attention for learning new information has been covered. We have also seen that memory can affect how much attention is needed to carry out a task. It is evident that memory is essential for normal, effective behaviour, and unless a stimulus is a nonsense syllable, or something we have never encountered before, memory will be active in its interpretation.

Some early views of memory

Like attention, memory takes many forms. Possibly the most obvious difference was pointed out by James (1890) on the basis of his own introspection. He distinguished between *primary memory*, PM, which he described as 'the rearward portion of the present space of time', and *secondary memory*, SM, which was the 'genuine past'. James appreciated the intricate relationship between memory and attention and realised that unless the unstable memories in PM were captured by attention they would rapidly fade away. He also pointed out the difference between the small amount of fleeting information that could be consciously kept 'in mind' in PM, and the vast amount of stable knowledge that could be kept in SM. Today we refer to PM and SM as *short-term memory* (STM) and *long-term memory* (LTM).

Memory research revived

Revival of interest in human memory during the 1960s led to a better understanding of the varieties within it. Today, we know that STM and LTM can be divided even further into multiple components. STM is now referred to as 'working memory' (WM; Baddeley and Hitch, 1974). LTM is also responsible for representing a variety of information. We have already met one distinction between *procedural* and *declarative* memory in LTM, in Anderson's (1983) ACT* model.

But this is not the only difference that psychologists have proposed for distinguishing types of information represented in LTM. We shall consider these other differences in LTM representations later. First, let us look at the experimental evidence for a fundamental distinction between a short-term and a long-term memory.

Attention, short-term and long-term memory

Around the same time that Broadbent (1958) put forward his limited-capacity filter theory of information processing, another famous effect was documented. Miller (1956) presented his paper *The Magic Number Seven, Plus or Minus Two*. This magical number was the number of chunks of information that could, on average, be remembered at one time. It represents the short-term capacity for currently active information, and shows there is a limit on remembering information in the short term. Miller showed that capacity was limited not by the amount of information, but by the number of chunks, so we can remember as many words as we can letters, because although each word is made up of several letters, the letters can be grouped into one meaningful chunk. Broadbent (1958) suggested that memory for periods of more than a few seconds was handled by combination of the limited capacity system and the buffer memory store, which held information for only a very short period of time. Information fed through to the limited capacity system could be fed back into the buffer, and recycled indefinitely. Broadbent (1971, p. 325), says that: 'in introspective terms this could correspond to "saying a telephone number over to oneself" when one had heard it.' He goes on to explain that if any action is required, the recirculation, or *rehearsal*, of the items in memory must be interrupted to deal with the new signal, or if the memory is to be preserved, then the new signal must be ignored. In everyday terms, he says, if you are remembering a telephone number and someone asks you a question, you either remember the number or ignore the question. So this type of memory, held as a verbal code, is very vulnerable to interruption. For an enduring memory, a different, less vulnerable code is necessary. Broadbent (1970) suggested that 'Gradually there would be a transfer of information from this re-circulatory type of storage to a more permanent long-term store ... During the rehearsal period, the man would be unable to cope with other tasks' (p. 325). This demonstrates the close relation between attention and memory in the limited capacity system. While attention is directed to the material, and it is rehearsed, it remains in conscious awareness. However, if attention is diverted, the information is lost unless there has been sufficient rehearsal for it to have been re-coded into long-term memory. Once in long-term memory, attention is no longer required to maintain the information in conscious awareness.

A multi-store model of memory

Like Broadbent (1958), Atkinson and Shiffrin (1968) believed rehearsal was important for long-term learning. Numerous studies had shown that rehearsal seemed to transfer items from a very limited capacity system to a more durable store, and that if rehearsal is prevented, items are rapidly forgotten, e.g., Brown (1958); Waugh and Norman (1965). Atkinson and Shiffrin (1968) proposed a model of human memory and its control processes. We have already mentioned this model in connection with attentional control in Chapter 10. According to Atkinson and Shiffrin's account, memory has three permanent structural features: the sensory register, the short-term store and the long-term store (see Figure 11.1 and note the difference between store and memory).

FIGURE 11.1 A simplified version of Atkinson and Shiffrin's model of human memory (1968).

A memory store can be considered the 'receptacle' for the memory, and termed the short-term store (STS) or long-term store (LTS). On the other hand, STM or LTM refers to the type of memory task.

A stimulus first enters its appropriate sensory register: for vision this would be iconic memory; for hearing, echoic memory (see Chapters 4 and 9). The second component, the short-term store, is regarded as the subject's 'working memory'. Atkinson and Shiffrin explain that while a word may have been presented visually, it may be encoded from the visual sensory register into an auditory short-term store, but other codings are possible, such as a mental image. They used the abbreviation a-v-l to stand for the auditory-verbal linguistic store. Information in short-term store will decay, but not as quickly as that in the sensory register, because it is influenced by subject-controlled processes. The long-term memory store holds information from all the sensory modalities; it is relatively permanent, and flow of information between the components of the system is mainly under the control of the subject. Information in the sensory register is scanned, and as a result of the scan and an associated search of the long-term store, selected information enters short-term store. Here we can see the interaction between top-down and bottom-up processing and the relation between attentional control processes in the transfer of information between the memory stores. Once information is in the working memory, the most important control process, rehearsal, gets to work. Usually rehearsal involves the a-v-l component and, the more time spent on rehearsals, the more likely it is that information will become permanently stored in long-term memory. However, there are only a limited number of 'slots' for information in the rehearsal buffer, and if there are more chunks of memory than slots, items will be lost, hence explaining the limits found by Miller (1956). Atkinson and Shiffrin's model has not fared well in the light of subsequent experimental and neuropsychological evidence. It has too rigid a structure and is too serial in design. However, it does capture some of the important distinctions between remembering in the long term and remembering currently active information. It also highlighted the importance of attentional control, and provided the foundation for Baddeley and Hitch's (1974) model of working memory, which we discuss in the next chapter.

Distinctions between short-term and long-term memory:
The serial position curve

Much evidence for the short-term and long-term components of the memory system comes from studies of *free recall*. In a typical experiment, participants are presented with items one after another in a serial list. The number of items in the list is greater than could normally be recalled from STS, and the participant has to recall as many items as they can, in any order. The results are plotted onto a graph, which shows how many items were recalled and which position in the list they came from. Figure 11.2 shows a typical *serial position curve* in which items from the beginning and the end of the list are more likely to be recalled than items from the middle of the list.

Glanzer and Cunitz (1966) proposed that the items at the beginning of the list are retrieved from long-term store, and this is called the *primacy effect*. Items early in the list have had the opportunity to be rehearsed several times, and have been recoded into a more durable form that can be retrieved at recall. Items at the end of the list, which make up the *recency* portion of the curve, are simply the contents of the short-term store that were still present, and active, at the end of the serial presentation. Poor recall for words in the middle of the list suggests they have been displaced from short-term store by

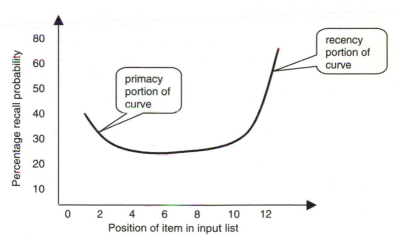

FIGURE 11.2 The serial position curve.

newly presented items, and have not yet been sufficiently rehearsed to enter long-term store. Glanzer and Cunitz tested the idea that the recency effect represented items still in STS at the end of the list by asking their participants to count backwards for 15 or 30 seconds before recall. The logic was that counting backwards would displace the items currently in STS, leaving only those items already in LTS available for later recall. The results showed that backward counting destroyed the recency effect, supporting the view that recency reflected the output from a fragile STS.

Rundus (1971) manipulated the number of times an item was rehearsed in a serial position experiment. He found that increasing rehearsal improved the primacy effect but not the recency effect, suggesting that the primacy reflected retrieval from LTS. Craik (1970) engaged his participants in a session of free recall trials for lists of words, all of which showed the normal primacy and recency effects. However, when given a surprise test recall for all of the lists again at the end of the session, Craik found that all recency effects had completely disappeared. This effect was termed *negative recency*. Craik interpreted the results as showing that the most recent parts of the list had not been rehearsed, and were therefore recalled worst of all.

Evidence such as this seemed to support a distinction between a transient STS and a more permanent LTS. However, doubts about whether the recency effect really reflects the capacity of STS have weakened this evidence. A number of experiments have demonstrated recency effects in LTS. For example, Baddeley (1986) found that rugby players showed recency effects in remembering aspects of the current season's games. This suggests that recency reflects a retrieval strategy. Other experiments have shown recency effects in lists where a distraction task is given in between each item (e.g., Baddeley, 1986). Glenberg *et al.* (1980) suggested that the recall probability of any information is governed by a constant ratio rule. Basically the probability of an item being recalled is a function of the time interval between the presentation of each item and the time that has elapsed between initial presentation and subsequent recall. Crowder (1976) gives the following analogy, which can account for the way in which recent items are more distinct than more distant ones and so show recency. 'Items in a memory list presented at a constant rate pass by with the same regularity as do telegraph poles when one is on a moving train. Just as each telegraph pole in the distance becomes less distinctive from its neighbours, like-wise each item in memory becomes less distinctive as the presentation episode recedes to the past' (p. 462). Baddeley (1986) suggests that recency is an important property of memory with ecological significance. It allows us to know where we have just been, or what we have just been doing, and enables us to orient ourselves in time and space.

Coding differences in memory

As well as serial position effects, a number of experiments tested for coding differences between STS and LTS. Conrad (1964) showed that confusable consonants such as S and F, or P and V, were likely to be misreported as each other. It appeared that the acoustic features of the sound of the letter, or its 'phoneme', were more important for encoding a letter than its visual features (see speech perception in Chapter 7). Further evidence for the importance of phonemic encoding in STS was provided in a study reported by Conrad and Hull (1964). Participants were more accurate at recalling sequences of letters that were phonemically dissimilar—such as R,H,Z,F,K—than phonemically similar letters such as B,P,V,T,C. This evidence was taken to show that STS uses a phonemic or speech-based code. Hence the importance of the a-v-l for rehearsal in Atkinson and Shiffrin's (1968) model. LTS was assumed to rely on semantic coding, or meaning. Baddeley (1986) contrasted short-term and long-term learning using words that were either acoustically or phonemically similar. Results were consistent with acoustic coding in STM and semantic coding in LTM. Other experiments have shown that acoustic confusability affects the recency portion of the serial position curve, while semantic confusability affects the primacy portion. Taken together, it appeared at that time as if short-term storage was in an acoustic code, while long-term storage was semantic.

Selective memory loss in amnesia

Imagine what it would be like to have no memory beyond the present contents of conscious awareness. This is what it would be like if

249

you had lost the ability to transfer current information into a more permanent record. You would be introduced to someone and talk with them, but if the conversation went on too long, you might lose track of what it was about. If the person left the room and returned, you would have no knowledge of meeting them before or who they are. This is rather what it must be like to suffer from *amnesia*. Scoville and Milner (1957) reported the case study of an amnesic patient HM, who had been operated on in an attempt to relieve his intractable epilepsy. The operation had involved removal of parts of the cortex and the hippocampus and amygdala, subcortical structures now known to be important in memory consolidation. The operation was a success, but HM was left with profound amnesia. He could retain very little about what had happened to him since his operation, and Scoville and Milner report that HM would do the same jigsaw puzzles day after day or read the same magazines over and over again. He would have his dinner, but moments later not be able to remember what he had eaten. In a follow-up study, Milner, Corkin and Teuber (1968, p. 217) describe how HM appeared to them and to himself. 'His experience seems to be that of a person who is just becoming aware of his surroundings, without fully comprehending the situation, because he does not remember what went before.' In describing himself, HM said his situation was 'like waking from a dream'. However, although HM was unable to learn new information, he could recall events from his early life; he could also remember old skills such as mowing the lawn, and other abilities such as language were also preserved.

Despite HM's inability to learn new information, his STS, or primary memory, appears to be normal. This has been demonstrated with other amnesic patients by Baddeley and Warrington (1970). So, HM and other amnesic patients can have a normal digit span and show normal recency effects, but not be able to learn, or retain information about new events. It appears that STS is intact but LTS is damaged. There is a 'dissociation' between the types of memory. In neuro-psychology a dissociation is interesting, but more important is the discovery of a *double dissociation*. When Shallice and Warrington (1970) reported their patient KF, such a dissociation was found. KF had a severely impaired STS for immediate verbal memory, but normal LTS. Taken together, these patients and others like them provide very convincing evidence that there is a real distinction between a STS and a LTS, but at the same time they provide evidence against the multi-store model of Atkinson and Shiffrin (1968). If KF had a severe impairment of auditory verbal memory, then how could it be that he was able to demonstrate normal long-term learning? According to Atkinson and Shiffrin, the a-v-l was essential for the rehearsal process that resulted in learning. Other evidence concerning the role of rehearsal in learning was also beginning to threaten the model.

Memory as processing rather than structure

The *levels of processing approach* to memory arose out of a number of demonstrations that the length of time rehearsing items in psychological tests, or the frequency of dealing with everyday items, did not necessarily result in any learning. If you stop reading for a moment and, from memory, draw both sides of a 2-pence piece, you can test your own memory for a familiar object. Once you have made your attempt it will be apparent to you that, despite handling 2-pence pieces frequently, you know very little about what they look like. Morton (1967) asked his participants to do a similar task, in which they were to reproduce the letters and digits that were in the finger holes on the dial of the kind of telephone used at that time. His results again showed very poor memory for frequently encountered information. In a laboratory study, Tulving (1966) demonstrated that simply exposing a stimulus many times did not result in learning, although the information must have been in STS many times.

On the other hand, other evidence showed that even without the intention to learn, people did sometimes do so. Hyde and Jenkins (1973) involved their participants in an incidental learning task where, unknown to the participants, they would be tested for their memory of the material they were working on at the end of the experiment. Different groups of participants were given different orienting tasks, that is, tasks that directed them to process different aspects of the stimuli. Performance on each condition was compared with that of participants who had been told to learn the words for subsequent recall. The orienting tasks included looking for a particular letter in a word, judging the part of speech, and rating for pleasantness. Results showed that participants who had intended to learn did so, and the amount they learnt depended on the processing activity required by the orienting task, with checking for letters being worse than judging for part of speech, and rating for pleasantness being best of all. What was astonishing was that the participants who had not been told to learn the words recalled them just as well as those who had been intending to learn, in all conditions. This evidence demonstrates that the kind of processing we undertake during task performance determines how well we recall the information we have processed.

Levels of processing

Craik and Lockhart (1972) proposed a levels of processing approach to memory that was different from the structural theories of memory that had come before. They reviewed the case for the multi-store models, as is summarised in Figure 11.3, and then discussed the flaws and inconsistencies in dividing memory into stores along the lines discussed in the previous section. Craik and Lockhart propose that 'retention is a function of depth and various factors such as the amount of attention devoted to the stimulus, its compatibility with the analyzing structures and the processing time available will determine the depth to which it is processed' (p. 676). Processing level was seen as a continuum from the fleeting products of sensory analysis to the highly durable products of semantic association. In addition, stimuli could be retained by recirculating information at one level of processing, and this was equivalent to keeping an item in consciousness, holding the items in a rehearsal buffer or retaining items in what they, like James (1890), termed primary memory, PM. The recirculation of information was controlled by a limited-capacity, attentional, central processor. Depending on the level at which the processor was operating, more or fewer items could be retained. So, at higher levels, where past knowledge or learned rules could be used, material could be more efficiently handled, and more could be retained. Repetition at the same level of analysis simply prolongs, or maintains, processing in PM for as long as the material is being processed and attended to, but as soon as attention is diverted, information is lost at a rate appropriate to its level of processing, and the deeper the level the slower the

Commonly accepted differences between the three stages of verbal memory

Feature	Sensory register	Short-term store	Long-term store
Entry of information	Preattentive	Requires attention	Rehearsal
Maintenance of information	Not possible	Continued attention	Repetition
Format of information	Literal copy of input	Phonemic Probably visual Possibly semantic	Organisation Largely semantic Some auditory and visual
Capacity	Large	Small	No known limit
Information loss	Decay	Displacement Possibly decay	Possibly no loss Loss of accessibility or discriminability by interference
Trace duration	0.25 – 2 seconds	Up to 30 seconds	Minutes to years
Retrieval	Readout	Probably automatic Items in consciousness Temporal/phonemic cues	Retrieval cues Possibly search processes

FIGURE 11.3 Craik and Lockhart's analysis of the differences between STM and LTM. From Craik and Lockhart (1973).

decay. Craik and Lockhart (1972) call this *Type I processing*. In contrast, *Type II processing* involves additional, deeper analysis of the stimulus and leads to a more durable trace. This view that memory duration is dependent upon the type of processing carried out on the stimulus could more easily explain incidental learning and the finding that simple repetition does not lead to learning.

The levels of processing approach soon ran into trouble, as it proved very difficult to establish depth of processing in any other way than by measuring memory. Johnston and Heinz (1979) claimed to have an independent measure, which they called 'expended processing capacity'. In their experiment, participants were engaged in a dichotic listening task and shadowed a message on the basis of either voice, a relatively easy task assumed to demand fewer attentional resources than the other task, which required shadowing on the basis of the semantic content of the message. At the same time as shadowing, participants were asked to detect the onset of a light, and their reaction time was measured. The rationale was that reaction time to the light would indicate the amount of processing dedicated to the shadowing task. Johnson and Heinz discovered that reaction times to the light were faster when shadowing was by voice, but on an unexpected recall task of information in the shadowed message, recall was better for the semantic condition. Whilst this measurement of processing dedicated to each task goes some way to solving the problem of measuring depth, other evidence undermined the levels of processing approach. It was found that people showed evidence of durable memory for material processed to only shallow, perceptual levels, and that factors such as elaboration and distinctiveness of the stimulus were also shown to be important.

Transfer appropriate processing

In addition to the problems just described, interactions were found between the conditions at learning and the conditions at retrieval. Morris, Bransford and Franks (1977) found, for example, that if an incidental learning task oriented the participant to process a word for rhyme, later recognition was better when tested on a rhyme task than on a semantic task. On the other hand, if the orienting task involved making a semantic judgement on whether a sentence was true or not (a *sentence verification task*), incidental learning of semantics but not of rhyme was found (see Figure 11.4).

Morris *et al.* suggested that participants engage in *transfer appropriate processing*, that is, they process information according to the task demands. This discovery is rather difficult to reconcile with the levels of processing approach, which assumed that semantic processing was always superior to non-semantic processing. The finding of a relationship between the processing used during learning and the processing used at recall fits well with Tulving's (1972) 'encoding specificity principle', ESP, which we shall discuss in Chapter 12.

The contribution of Craik and Lockhart (1972)

Despite all its problems, the levels of processing approach, which placed an emphasis on the nature of memory processes rather than on the structure of memory, was an important shift in the way psychologists thought of memory, and provided an impetus for new directions in memory research. For a critical review of levels of processing, see Baddeley (1997).

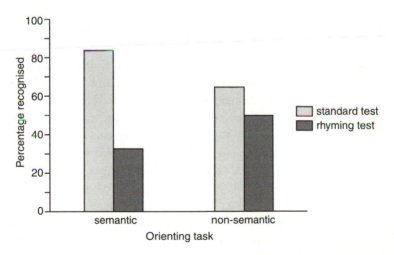

FIGURE 11.4 An illustration of transfer appropriate processing. From Parkin (2000).

Preserved learning in amnesia: Dividing the long-term store

Whether a structural or a process view of memory is the correct interpretation, there are further issues that need accounting for. Remember
HM, the amnesic patient described earlier, whose STS seemed intact
yet who had severe difficulty in learning new facts or new people, and
repeatedly did the same jigsaw puzzle with no apparent memory of
having done it before? Well, like other patients with the amnesic syndrome, HM does actually still have some preserved learning abilities.
An early report of learning in an amnesic patient is given by Claparede
(1911/1951) in Schacter (1987). One morning he hid a pin in his hand
when he shook hands with one of his patients. The lady, who suffered
from Korsakoff's amnesia induced by alcohol abuse, refused to shake
hands with him the following morning. When asked why she would
not shake hands, she had no idea why she did not want to, but had
clearly learned not to shake hand with the doctor. Prince (1914)
reviewed a variety of evidence from hypnosis, dreams and hysterical
patients that, he argued, demonstrated that memories can reveal themselves without any conscious recollection. With the fall from fashion
of unconscious processing this line of enquiry was not pursued, and
experimental psychologists largely ignored what Schacter calls *implicit
memory*. With the development of cognitive psychology, evidence
of dissociations between memory and awareness began to be seen as
important sources of evidence for understanding normal memory. For
example, Talland (1965) demonstrated preserved learning in Korsakoff
amnesics who were introduced to novel tools, and Corkin (1968)
showed that amnesics benefit from practice on perceptuo-motor
tasks such as pursuit motor tasks, and on mirror drawing, despite
having no recollection of doing the task many times. Many other
studies have shown similar effects. Studies have also found improve-
ments in amnesics' ability in solving puzzles (Brooks and Baddeley,
1976), and they show priming effects (Jacoby and Witherspoon, 1982;
Warrington and Weiskrantz, 1968, 1978) amongst many others.
Schacter, Harbuck and McLachlan (1984) demonstrated that amnesics
can learn fictitious information about people, such as 'Bob Hope's
father was a fireman', but could not explicitly remember that they had
just been told this information. There is a wealth of evidence for a

dissociation between memory and awareness in amnesia. Amnesic patients demonstrate normal learning on a variety of tasks at the same time as denying any conscious memory for having practised the task (see Parkin, 1997, and Schacter, 1987, for reviews). The dissociation of learning from subjective awareness in some memory tasks is important evidence for specifying the memory system that is spared in amnesia, and in helping psychologists understand the nature and composition of long-term memory. Clearly there are some forms of memory that do not require conscious recollection of the learning experience for performance of the task. The type of learning that appears to be preserved in amnesia is revealed in tasks that do not require conscious recollection for performance and in which learning can be demonstrated by doing the task. Any theory of memory must be able to account for both normal memory and the breakdown of memory in amnesia.

Episodic and semantic memory

Tulving (1972) proposed a distinction between *semantic* and *episodic* memory. Semantic memory stores all our knowledge about the world, including the meaning of words, what they refer to, facts and their associations, and the rules and formulae that allow us to manipulate symbols. Semantic knowledge is not tied to any particular personal experience, although all the knowledge we have must have been acquired by some now-forgotten experience. For example, you know Paris is in France, and it is the capital city, but you probably do not know when you first learned this. Episodic memory, on the other, has personal connotations. Your memory of being in Paris, going up the Eiffel tower or trying to speak French there is episodic; an episode in your own personal experience. Initially, Tulving used this semantic / episodic distinction to differentiate between the memory tested by asking a participant to retrieve the answers to general knowledge questions and the memory tested by asking people to recall lists of words learnt in an experiment. The experiment was, in his view, a specific episode, tagged to being in particular place, the lab, at a particular time—i.e., it has a particular spatio-temporal context. So, semantic memory has no personally associated context, whereas episodic memory does. Patients with amnesia appear to have defective episodic memory; their general knowledge remains, but they have great difficulty in remembering any new episodes. However, if new semantic memories rely on the encoding of new episodes, they should also have difficulty in acquiring new semantic knowledge. This does seem to be the case. Generally, amnesics are unable to learn who people are, or who the current prime minister is, so while performing quite well on identifying famous people from before the onset of their amnesia, they are very poor at learning new famous people (Baddeley, 1997). So, it appears that selective loss of episodic memory is not the reason for amnesia.

Tulving equated episodic memory with autobiographical memory, but today autobiographical memory is viewed as a particular kind of episodic memory since not all episodes become part of autobiographical memory. In practice, there cannot be a complete distinction between semantic and episodic memory, because when you learn a fact, such as 'a glurk is a small furry animal that lives in South America', the episode, reading this book, is the source of the fact. As you learn more about glurks in other episodes, such as watching a television programme, or going to the zoo, you may learn their feeding habits, range of coat colour and so on. Over repeated episodes, this information must gradually become compiled into your general knowledge about glurks, and the specifics of each episode will be lost. So, while semantic memory and episodic memory may become differentiated, they must interact to allow the acquisition of new semantic knowledge. Another way of thinking about the difference between semantic and episodic knowledge is to consider episodic memories as specific, 'my dog barked at the postman this morning', and semantic knowledge as general, 'all dogs bark'.

Source amnesia

When we lose the source or episode that led us to know a fact, we have lost the associated sensory and spatio-temporal information of the episode, and demonstrate source amnesia. We know we know something, but we do not know how we came to know it. Janowsky, Shimamura and Squire (1989) demonstrated that patients with frontal lobe damage were particulary likely to suffer from source amnesia, and suggest that the frontal lobes are involved in episodic memory and the retrieval of *source information*. Johnson (1988) suggests that memories for events we actually perceive, rather than events we imagine, are much richer in sensory and contextual information, and it is these sensory properties that allow us to distinguish real and imaginary events. This ability is called *reality monitoring*, and is also important for differentiating between intending to do something and knowing that we actually did it. For example, you may find yourself wondering if you locked the door as you left home, or whether you only thought you did it. Sometimes you can retrieve some episodic information that lets you know you did lock the door; you may remember hearing the mechanism click. This recent perceptual information allows you to differentiate the intention from the performed action.

False memories

Johnson *et al.* (1979) showed that thinking about or imagining words increased the likelihood that people thought they had actually seen those words. Goff and Roediger (1998) performed an experiment in which participants sometimes listened to simple action statements, such as 'flip a coin', and sometimes also performed the actions, or imagined performing the actions. Later participants were asked to recognise whether an action had been presented at all and whether they had imagined performing it, actually performed it or had simply heard it. The results clearly showed that the more times a participant had imagined an action the more likely they were to falsely remember carrying it out. Falsely remembering flipping a coin is of little consequence, but for other memories it may be of much more importance. It could be that imagination can lead to false childhood memories, or that imagination actually triggers recall of a real event. Some researchers have proposed that events will only be implanted in memory if they are plausible. Pedzek, Finger and Hodge (1997) suggested that script-relevant information is necessary to generate a false memory. A script is stored knowledge about a body of knowledge, similar to a schema (see Chapter 12). In their study, Pedzek *et al.* found that the more unusual information is, the less likely it is to be falsely remembered as having actually happened. Thomas and Loftus (2002) suggest that with numerous TV programmes, books and films regarding childhood abuse, this script-relevant knowledge is now widely available, making such events less unusual and hence more plausible. It is well documented that unusual or bizarre information is actually remembered better than common information. Schacter, Israel and Racine (1997) suggest that distinctiveness is important in allowing participants to decide if an event has really happened or has only been imagined. Thomas and Loftus tested the idea that bizarre actions will elicit fewer false memories than common actions, and that the more times an action is imagined, the more likely it is to be falsely remembered. In session 1, participants heard a mixture of common action statements such as 'pick up the dice', and bizarre action statements such as 'kiss the magnifying glass'. All items on which actions could be made were on a table in front of them. Some actions were to be made and some were only to be imagined. In the second session, participants only ever imagined making actions, but same actions were imagined only once, with others imagined five times. Some objects on the table were not imagined at all. Two weeks later the participants were given a recognition test, which asked them to recall if the action was presented in session 1; if they replied 'yes', a source monitoring test asked if the action was performed or imagined, and a 'remember/know' test asked how vivid the memory was. 'Remember' was for memories for which participants had explicit recollection of the event, and 'know' judgements were for when there was only a feeling of knowing about the event. The proportion of 'did' responses for novel actions that were never even presented was 4%, indicating a false memory for these actions. For familiar actions imagined five times, false reports rose to 24%, and for bizarre actions, to 14%. So, although bizarre and never performed, imagining an event can produce a false memory. These results show that repeated imaginings can lead people to believe they have performed both common and bizarre actions. Thomas and Loftus suggest that repeated imagination can lead to participants to develop 'false contextual cues to support their false memories or performance' (p. 429), and that repeated imagination of an event decreases recognition accuracy. They suggest that contextual and episodic memory information is created in association with the false memory and that imagination provides visual and other sensory detail for the event, even if it is bizarre.

Attention and episodic memory

Allport (1977), Coltheart (1980) and Styles and Allport (1986) proposed that perceptual integration could be necessary for the production of episodic memories. If episodic, physical and semantic properties are not integrated there can be no confident report of the event, although activation of semantic memory structures could give rise to priming at a level below conscious awareness (e.g., Marcel, 1983). When a brief visual display is followed by a pattern mask, this interferes with the physical information that is needed for perceptual integration (see feature integration theory, Chapter 5), leaving semantic activation in an unreportable form. This activation may modify memory and be inaccessible by voluntary recall, but recognition time to a semantically related stimulus may show a priming effect due to the residual semantic activation. Patients with amnesia show better recognition than recall and may exhibit a *feeling of knowing* (Huppert and Piercy, 1976; Schacter and Tulving, 1982). Stern (1981) suggests this effect arises from a failure to integrate contextual or physical information with an object or event. Unless there is integration of the physical, sensory properties of the learning episode there will be no episodic trace to allow subsequent recall. Baddeley (2000) added a new component, which he called the 'episodic buffer', to his model of working memory. It is proposed that this buffer allows for perceptual integration between information in different codes. Whilst it has some properties in common with Tulving's conception of episodic memory, the episodic buffer has limited capacity and acts as a temporary store at the interface of other memory systems. The episodic buffer is explained in more detail in the following chapter. *Change blindness* is the phenomenon in which people fail to notice episodic changes in the environment, and was used as an example of the importance of attention for memory in Chapter 5.

Wheeler, Stuss and Tulving (1997) suggest that the major distinction between semantic and episodic memory is the subjective experience that accompanies the encoding and retrieval of the two kinds of memory. Taking evidence of source amnesia into account, together with evidence from PET studies on normal participants, they proposed that as additional brain areas, in particular the left pre-frontal cortex, are involved in episodic memory tasks, the underlying processes involved in semantic and episodic memory are different. In particular, episodic memory is associated with a subjective self-awareness of a personal event, whereas semantic memory lacks these properties. Despite their differences, both semantic and episodic memory share the property that they can be made explicit. We can tell someone what we know about dogs, or that my dog is called Fido. There is, however, an important distinction that we have already made between knowledge that requires conscious recollection to be demonstrated and knowledge that can only be accessed indirectly, out-side conscious awareness. It is this type of knowledge that is evidently preserved in amnesia, and that underlies unconscious priming and skill learning in the normal case.

Memory without awareness

A number of frameworks and definitions have been proposed to account for memory that does or does not need conscious recollection to be demonstrated. Graf and Schacter (1985) and Schacter (1987) draw a related distinction between explicit and implicit memory. In essence, procedural memory, as in ACT* (see Chapter 10) is usually limited to motor and mental skills, which run off automatically with-out the need for attention or conscious awareness of the knowledge being used, whereas implicit memory is similar but incorporates priming and rule learning as well. If implicit learning relies on dif-ferent memory processes or structures to explicit memory, then we might expect to find dissociations between their effects, not only in patients with amnesia, but also in other people in experimental tasks. Tulving, Schacter and Stark (1982) involved their participants in a *fragment completion task*. In such an experiment, participants first study a list of words, such as VENDETTA, or TOBOGGAN. Some time later (from minutes to hours, or even weeks), the participants are called back and asked to do another test, which is presented to them as a 'word puzzle'. They are given incomplete fragments of words, for example _ EN _ _ T _ _, or _ _ B_GG _ _, and asked to complete them to make a word. Half the fragments would make words from the previously studied list, and half were new words. It would be expected that participants would show a 'repetition priming' effect, and would complete more words from the list they had studied than new words. The participants were also given a test of explicit recognition to evaluate how many words from the list they could recognise. So, this experiment provides two ways of assessing memory for the studied words. One, the fragment completion, is an implicit test; the other, the recognition task, is an explicit test. Tulving *et al.* discovered that the probability of a participant successfully completing a word fragment did not predict success at recognising the word that corresponded with that fragment, and vice versa. Further tests showed that the rate of forgetting for the recognition test was faster than that for the fragment completion. It would appear that the two tests access different, independent memories. There has been some debate over the reliability of this data (Hintzman, 1991), but given the dissociation in memory from patients with amnesia, it appears that the difference is real.

Attention and implicit memory

Jacoby, Ste-Marie and Toth (1993) used the process-dissociation procedure to examine the effect of attention on implicit and explicit memory. Process dissociation is based on the principle that attention to an event is required for later, intentional use of memory (explicit memory) but not for automatic or unconscious influences of memory (implicit memory). A test situation is devised that sets the automatic and intentional use of memory in opposition to each other, allowing the processes to be dissociated. Jacoby *et al.* combined list learning with an attention-demanding listening task. They reasoned that if attention were necessary for explicit memory but not implicit memory, then dividing attention would selectively damage performance on an explicit memory test.

Participants were asked to study a list of names, which they were told belonged to people who were not famous, in either full attention or divided attention conditions. When attention was divided, subjects were to concurrently monitor a list of digits for a run of three odd numbers. Next, the participants were given another list in which some of the names from the first list were mixed with other non-famous names and some famous names. As participants had been told that no name in the first list was famous, they should know that, if they consciously recalled one of those names, it belonged to a non-famous person. If they recalled a name and said it was famous (when consciously they should have known it was not), then the mistake must be due to unconscious processing. So, non-famous names from the first list would be mistakenly recalled as famous only if the name was familiar, an outcome of automatic implicit memory, and not consciously or explicitly remembered as being from the first list. Dividing attention was expected to reduce the probability of conscious explicit memory and therefore increase the chance of a name being judged only on implicit familiarity. In the divided attention condition the old non-famous names were more likely to be mistaken as famous, showing that when attention was divided subjects were less able to use conscious recollection to oppose the familiarity produced by reading the names earlier. This 'false fame' effect is also shown by the elderly, and amnesic patients. These results support the suggestion that explicit, conscious, intentional memory is affected by attentional processing, but feelings of familiarity are served by implicit, automatic, unconscious processing.

Tulving and Schacter (1990) distinguished between perceptual and conceptual implicit tests of memory. In typical perceptual tests the participant is presented some study material and then tested with a fragment of the stimulus, or some kind of degraded representation that shares perceptual features with the initial stimulus. In contrast, a conceptual implicit test shares only conceptual features with the material studied. Gabrielli (1998) has found a double dissociation between these forms of tests in neuropsychological patients. This provides evidence that different brain areas underlie implicit perceptual and implicit conceptual memory tasks.

Learning without awareness

For implicit memory to arise, there must be learning processes associated with it, of which the learner is unaware. We have discussed already how rehearsal or type and level of processing can lead to long-term learning, but these are conscious and effortful processes that we intentionally engage in when we want to learn. There is also evidence that we learn quite complex information quite unintentionally. The two main areas of complex, non-conscious learning are artificial grammar learning (e.g., Berry and Deines, 1993; Reber, 1967) and the control of complex systems (e.g., Berry and Broadbent, 1984). Both these types of study reveal a dissociation between measured performance and explicit verbal knowledge of the rules on which performance was based.

In these implicit learning tasks participants have to try to solve a complex problem, and after repeated efforts and with feedback on their success, they eventually are able to do it, even though they are unable to explain what they have learned in terms of the rules they are evidently applying. Berry and Broadbent (1984) asked their participants to maintain control over sugar production in a computer simulation of a sugar factory by manipulating the size of the workforce. Unbeknown to the participant, there were hidden rules governing sugar output that related to levels set on previous trials. Eventually the participants learned to control the factory, but their verbal reports showed that the more they thought they knew about what they were doing, the less well they actually did the task. So, there is a dissociation between performance and verbal knowledge that suggests the task is performed on the basis on implicit knowledge. In learning artificial grammars, similar results are found (Reber, 1967). In the first part of the experiment, participants were given strings of letters to learn, which were generated according to rules that specify which letters can follow others in a sequence. The participants were not told of the rules' existence. Next, they were told about the existence of the grammar, and asked to classify a new list of letter strings as being grammatical or not. In comparison to the control group, the experimental participants were able to classify the strings as grammatical or not, even though they were unable to explain how they made their decisions or what the rules of the grammar were.

Retrieval from memory

If information is stored in memory, it can only be of use if it can be accessed when needed. The question of how memory search and retrieval are achieved has produced a number of theoretical explanations. These explanations must not only be able to account for successful retrieval, but also for memory failures. We are all familiar with being unable to remember something that we know we know. This knowing what we know is called 'metamemory'—for example, knowing a person's name, or the word for a particular article. Sometimes the memory is temporarily inaccessible; sometimes it may appear lost for ever until something triggers it, or provides a cue that accesses the memory, and we can recall it. Evidently we are usually able to recall information and recognise things as familiar, but sometimes we fail. Psychologists must be able to account for both successful and unsuccessful memory retrieval. We shall turn to some of these explanations next.

If you remember, the evidence from incidental learning experiments discussed in the preceding sections suggests that when the conditions at encoding match the conditions at retrieval, memory is more likely to be successful than if there is a mismatch. Before we discuss any theory, we must distinguish different ways of retrieving stored information. Experiments can involve recognition or recall; remembering refers to any form of retrieval. Recognition means to 'know again', and refers to testing memory by presenting a stimulus that has been seen before, and asking the participant if they recognise it as having been presented previously in the test. Of course, if the stimuli were a list of words, the words would already be familiar, and would be recognised as being known already. However, in experimental recognition tests, the participant must be able to tell if the word was seen before in the 'context' of the experiment. So, there must be a mechanism that allows us to distinguish one encounter with a word from another encounter. This is similar to the difference we discussed between semantic and episodic memory earlier in the chapter. The words are represented in semantic memory, but each encounter with the word will have an associated episode.

Recall can also take a variety of forms. In *free recall* a participant is simply asked to recall what they can remember—for example, a list of previously studied words. *Cued recall*, as its name suggests, provides a *cue* to recall, for example, recall all the words beginning with a particular letter, or all the animal words from a list. This verbal cue was not presented at the time of learning, but can act as a prompt for retrieval. Another type of cued recall task might involve a participant learning pairs of words, such as cat–table, hat–car. At recall, one of each pair is presented again and the participant has to recall the other word of the pair. Typically, cued recall gives better memory performance than free recall. Tulving and Osler (1968) found that given one half of a pair of previously learned words, for example cat as a cue to table, recall levels were higher than in free recall. However, it is usually the case that recognition is better than all types of recall.

Generate-recognise theory

Anderson and Bower (1972) and Kintsch (1970) proposed that retrieval is a reconstructive process, in which the processing system 'generates' possible candidates for the memory being searched for. As the candidate memories become available they are examined to discover if they are recognised. If they are not recognised they are rejected, but if they are recognised they are accepted. Hence the name for this class of theory is *generate-recognise theory* (GR). Imagine that a participant has been trying to memorise a list of words, and then is asked to recall them. In essence, GR models assume that words are represented by 'nodes' in semantic memory. When the words are studied some additional information, or episodic 'tag', is associated with each word in the list to mark it as a member of the memorised list. If the test of memory is free recall, candidate words are generated in the retrieval phase of the experiment, and are examined for evidence of the 'tag' that allows them to be recognised as a member of the list, or not, as the case may be. If the test of memory is recognition, a list of candidate words is presented, so no candidates need generating, and nodes are activated automatically. All that needs to be done in this case is to ascertain if the tag is present. The GR account of retrieval can account for the superiority of recognition over cued recall, and of cued recall over free recall, quite well. Recognition does not require the generation of any candidates, and so cuts out one stage of the retrieval process altogether; cued recall is better than free recall because it helps to guide generation. In free recall there is no additional information to guide the search for candidates at all.

The GR account can also explain why, in free recall, participants remember high-frequency words better than low-frequency words. This is because high-frequency words are more likely to be generated as possible candidates for the recognition stage. The effect of word frequency on recognition tests of memory can also be explained. In recognition, rather than recall, high-frequency words are often harder to recognise as having been in the study list, and this is because they will have a number of tags associated with them by being used frequently, and so the decision about where they were last encountered is more difficult.

Encoding specificity and synergistic ecphory

According to GR theory, it should not be possible to recall words that cannot be recognised. However, a number of experiments have shown that this can happen (e.g., Tulving and Thomson, 1973). To account for recognition failure of recallable words, Tulving and Thomson proposed the *encoding specificity principle* (ESP). According to this view, recognition and recall are both part of the same retrieval process, and successful retrieval depends on the effectiveness of the retrieval cue in accessing a memory. Tulving and Thomson summarise ESP as follows: 'Specific encoding operations performed on what is perceived determine what is stored, and what is stored determines what retrieval cues are effective in providing access to what is stored' (p. 369). Later, Tulving (1983) used the term *synergistic ecphory* to describe the way in which information in the retrieval cue combines with the memory trace to produce 'a conscious memory of certain aspects of the original event'. The normal superiority of recognition over recall arises because in a recognition test the complete item is presented again. It is a copy cue and a correct recognition simply requires a familiarity judgement. Successful recall requires greater overlap of information because the original event must be named. Tulving assumes that when a memory trace is created the learning does not simply attach a tag to the trace, but contextual, episodic information present at the time of learning is also encoded. This context can include not only environmental information, but also emotional states. At the time of retrieval the combination of information in the cue with the memory trace, or *engram*, work together to produce ecphoric information that can either give rise to a positive identification of the event, or to a further state of *recollective experience*, which is a conscious awareness of having experienced the event.

According to ESP, a cue will only be effective if it was specifically encoded with the target event, and this is why free recall, cued recall and recognition differ in effectiveness. The basic assumptions of encoding specificity are useful in understanding some of the powerful effects of context on memory. One problem for ESP is that it involves a circular argument, as there is no way of independently finding out whether or not a cue was encoded with the trace. If a cue is effective then it was encoded, but if it is not effective, then it must be assumed it was not encoded. Despite this problem there is a great deal of data consistent with ESP.

Divided attention during the retrieval of words

Fernandes and Moscovitch (2002) examined the effect of divided attention on the encoding and retrieval of lists of words in tests of episodic memory. They found large effects of divided attention on recall when the distracting task involved words or word-like material. In contrast, experiments that combined list retrieval with a non-verbal task, such as card sorting (Baddeley, *et al.*, 1984a), digit monitoring (Fernandes and Moscovitch, 2002) or visuo-spatial tasks (Craik, 2001) show much smaller interference effects. However, all tasks that involve dividing attention have some detrimental effect on retrieval. These results suggest that retrieval is not an automatic process; otherwise, drawing attentional resources from the retrieval task should have no effect (see dual tasks and attentional resource theory in Chapter 10). Fernandes and Moscovitch suggest that retrieval requires setting up and maintaining a retrieval mode, which involves reactivating the memory trace by its interaction with memory cues. This process involves ecphory and activation from pre-frontal cortex, which we have seen is important in intentional behaviour. They go on to suggest that ecphory is interfered with when a concurrent task involves word-like material because the information in the memory trace is also representing word-based material. It would seem, therefore, that retrieval from episodic memory requires attention.

Context effects on memory

Context can take at least two forms: *intrinsic context* and *extrinsic context* (Hewitt, 1973). Intrinsic context refers to features that are integral with the stimulus at the time it is encoded, for example, when *cold* is associated with *ground* at presentation. Extrinsic context refers to features of the environment at the time the stimulus was presented, but which are not a part of the stimulus itself, for example the room in which the experiment was done. To take a more personal example, imagine returning to your old school for a reunion. As you enter a particular classroom, a flood of memories to do with that year-group may come to mind. Here, the context of the classroom was extrinsic to the events at the time of encoding, but is still capable of accessing memory. Similarly, the smell from a restaurant may evoke the memory of a foreign holiday.

Smith, Glenberg and Bjork (1978) conducted an experiment in which people were asked to learn lists of words and then were tested either in the same or a different room. They found that when rooms were changed between learning and recall, performance was worse than when learning and recall were in the same room. Another example of the effect of extrinsic factors on learning and memory comes from studies on deep-sea divers (Godden and Baddeley, 1975, 1980). The participants were deep-sea divers who learned lists of words either on shore or underwater, and then were asked to recall the words either in the same or the opposite environment. Results showed that when the environment was the same at both encoding and retrieval, recall was better than when the environment was different. However, this context-dependency effect is not found for recognition.

State dependency

Not only can the external environment affect memory, but so, too, can a person's internal environment, such as their psychoactive state or mood. A number of studies have shown that when the psychoactive state is the same at both learning and retrieval, memory is enhanced. This is known as *state dependency*. For example, Goodwin (1974) tested recall and recognition in participants who had either consumed a soft drink, or several shots of good vodka. The following day the participants returned to perform the same tests again, and were allotted to either the same or opposite group as the day before. When the state changed between learning and test, recall was significantly reduced in both groups, i.e., learn sober, test intoxicated or learn intoxicated, recall sober. However, recognition was unaffected.

Similar effects are found for mood, and are called *mood-congruency* effects. It is possible to induce people into different mood states, such as 'happy' or 'sad', by playing different types of music or asking them to think happy or sad thoughts. Bower, Gilligan and Monteiro (1981) induced their participants into either happy or sad mood. Next, all participants were told a story about the life of a fictitious person. The story included an equal proportion of positive and negative events. When asked to recall events from the life of the person in the story, 'happy' participants recalled positive events and 'sad' participants recalled negative events. Like environmental context and state-dependent effects, the mood-congruency effect was only found for recall, not for recognition.

Of course, some people are in depressed mood due to illness, so no mood induction is necessary. Clark and Teasdale (1981) tested patients who exhibited natural mood changes during their depressive illness. They found that when patients were relatively happy they recalled more positive and pleasant memories than when in more depressed mood. During the more depressed period, more negative and unpleasant memories were recalled. The mood congruency effect may help to explain why, as people become depressed, they find it more and more difficult to retrieve positive memories, and hence can become more depressed. Williams and Broadbent (1986) demonstrated that suicidally depressed patients found it more difficult to retrieve memories when cued with positive words than with negative words. Similarly, in depressed patients, Lloyd and Lishman (1975) found that the time to retrieve negative experiences became faster as depression deepened. It is clear from these studies that mood can also have strong effects on memory.

Summary

Atkinson and Shiffrin's multistore model of memory proposed a series of memory stores through which information was transferred and transformed by rehearsal and attentional control processes. This model could not account for learning without rehearsal, or the fact that rehearsed material may not be learned. The serial position curve has been taken to represent the activity of two separate memory stores; the primacy portion reflects LTM and recency is the output from STM. Evidence from patients with amnesia and coding differences also suggests the existence of two distinct memory stores. According to the levels of processing approach, learning is a result of the type of processing done on material and memory varies in durability according the depth to which it has been processed. Tulving distinguished between semantic and episodic memory; semantic memory is knowledge for facts but episodic memory has personal associations. Episodic memory additionally appears to involve the pre-frontal cortex. Memory without awareness and implicit memory are preserved in amnesia and do not require conscious recollection to be utilised. Imagined events can sometimes become confused with real events, producing a false memory. Retrieval from memory has been suggested to be a generate-recognise process, but this cannot account for the recognition failure of recallable words. The encoding specificity principle can account for recognition failure effects and proposes that recognition and recall rely on the same process of synergistic ecphory between cues at retrieval and the memory trace. Retrieval from episodic memory appears to require attention. Context effects on memory can be interpreted in terms of the match between conditions at encoding and retrieval.

Self-assessment questions (Solution on p. 324)

1 How would Atkinson and Shiffrin's (1968) model explain the serial position curve?
2 What is meant by Type I and Type II processing?
3 What kinds of knowledge can be represented implicitly?
4 Why is recognition failure of recallable words a problem for generate-recognise theory?

Further reading

Baddeley, A. D. (1997) *Human Memory: Theory and practice.* Hove, UK: Psychology Press.

Parkin, A. J. (1997) *Memory and Amnesia: An introduction* (2nd ed.). Oxford: Blackwell. For full, clear overviews of all types of memory.

Chapter 12

Representing and manipulating information

Thinking about your holiday

C LOSE YOUR EYES and go back to a time when you sat by the sea on a distant beach. Now think of what topics you learned for your last exam. I guess your memories of the beach were associated with an image; you could recreate what it was like to be there again. Possibly there were also images associated with your last exam—the episodic information about the room, who else was there, and what you did afterwards. However, unlike the holiday memory, the actual topics you learned for your exam are probably not easily pictured. You might remember one topic, and then be able to remember the theories or experiments you learned in association with it. If you remember another topic, you can probably remember other theories and experiments that go together. Next, I could ask you what happens when you go to a restaurant. Although you will be able to recall memories about a restaurant that you are familiar with, you will also know what to expect if you go to a new one that is recommended to you. The questions we shall look at in this chapter are concerned with the way in which different types of knowledge are represented. Are the representations in memory that allow you to picture your holiday, remember knowledge in an organised way or know what happens in restaurants all the same or are they different? We shall also look at storage of temporary information. Think again of sitting on the beach, and now imagine turning to look behind you; can you see the town, or the hotel or the hills? An important issue for psychologists is to explain how, once retrieved, information from long-term memory can be manipulated in short-term working memory. In this example the information is visual, but another example could involve verbal information. Let's say I ask you to recite your five times table. To be able to do this you must retrieve the knowledge from long-term memory and convert it into speech. However, it is probably the case that you can recite your tables at the same time as imagining the scene on the beach, so in this case, different memory codes must be active at once. If you were asked to imagine the beach at the same time as telling me what your bedroom looks like, this would prove difficult. Try it!

In the previous chapter we distinguished between short-term memory and varieties of long-term memory. In the following sections we shall discover that the short-term store needs further differentiation to account for its flexibility in representing information in the short term. Later we shall turn to how knowledge is represented and organised in long-term memory.

Working memory: Representing information for use in the short term

First, let us remind ourselves where we have met the conception of working memory already. The term *working memory* was used by

Atkinson and Shiffrin (1968) to imply that STS was not only responsible for storage, but also for manipulating and controlling information. It was considered the work space where currently active information was held for further processing. However, according to this model there was a strict limit on the number of chunks of information that could be maintained before the short-term capacity was exceeded and information would be displaced. Anderson's (1983) ACT* model also incorporated a working memory (WM). According to this model, WM is the interface between incoming perceptual information and other information stored in the *procedural* and *declarative* memory. However, neither of these accounts of WM goes into detail about the WM component in terms of different types of information or processing that can go on within it, or exactly how it is controlled. Although all these models appreciate the important role that WM plays in cognition, they do not account in any detail for the complex role WM plays in the human information-processing system.

Testing the conception of working memory

Baddeley and Hitch (1974) realised that existing approaches to understanding WM were inadequate and asked the basic, but profound question: 'What is working memory for?'. They realised that evidence from dual-task experiments demonstrated that if WM was solely an auditory verbal system, as proposed by Atkinson and Shiffrin (1968), then people should be unable to combine tasks that demanded a capacity greater than the number of items that could be held in the span of the auditory-verbal loop (a-v-l.). We have already seen that some tasks can be combined quite easily, provided the input–output relationships between the tasks are not competing for the same modality-specific subsystem.

In a series of experiments, Baddeley and Hitch (1974) combined standard memory span tasks with a variety of other tasks. They reasoned that if WM was equivalent to the span held in an a-v-l then once the loop was completely filled by the rehearsal of a list of items, there should be no further capacity available to do any other task at the same time. In one experiment, participants were given span-length memory loads to repeat aloud at the same time as being required to do a verbal reasoning task, judging if the letters shown in a visual display were consistent with a verbal statement. For example, the visually displayed letters might be A followed by B; the task was to decide if the statement 'A follows B' was true or false. In this case the statement is true, and the participant should answer 'yes'. Alternatively the statement could be more complicated, and so make greater demands on WM, for example 'A is not preceded by B'. This statement is also true, but requires the manipulation of the statement. An example of a false statement might be 'B is not preceded by A'. The results from this experiment showed that reasoning time increased with the complexity of the reasoning task, as was expected. However, and most importantly, the participants were able to maintain the series of digits at the same time. Although they became slower on the reasoning task, their errors on the digit task remained constant. Evidently, these concurrent verbal tasks could be combined, although they should have far outstripped the capacity of the STS (see Figure 12.1).

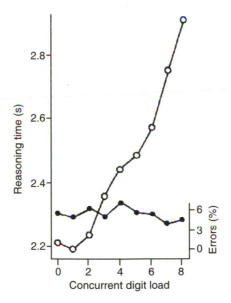

FIGURE 12.1 The relationship between concurrent digit load and reasoning time. From Baddeley (1997).

Other experiments revealed that the *recency* portion of the *serial position curve* survived for a list of unrelated words, even when accompanied by a digit load of three or six items. A three-digit load had no effect on performance at all, and a six-digit load impaired *primacy*, but had no effect on recency. (The serial position curve is covered in Chapter 11.) This evidence suggests that the recency portion of the serial position curve and span are supported by different memory components. In addition a digit span load had little effect on comprehension or learning and, together with many other experiments, the inadequacies of previous explanations of WM were revealed. See Baddeley (1986) for a full review and Baddeley (2000) for a summary and update.

Baddeley and Hitch's model of working memory

It was clear that a new conception of short-term storage was required. The evidence for a multicomponent system seemed irrefutable, and Baddeley and Hitch (1974) put forward their new conception of working memory (see Figure 12.2).

Rather than a single system, Baddeley and Hitch proposed that WM comprises an attentional controller, or *central executive*, that supervises and coordinates a number of subsystems. Two of the subsidiary 'slave' systems have been studied in most detail: these are

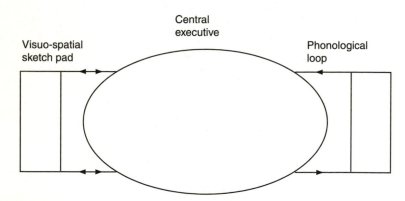

FIGURE 12.2 The working memory model proposed by Baddeley and Hitch (1974). From Baddeley (1997).

the *phonological loop*, which deals with speech-based information, and the *visuo-spatial sketch pad*, which deals with visually based information. We have discussed each of these components in respect to their role in maintaining auditory-verbal and visual information in Chapter 7 on hearing, and Chapter 4 on vision. If words are presented visually, they can only enter the phonological loop indirectly via a process of *subvocal articulation*. At the time the model was initially proposed, rather little was known about executive control processes, but developments in attention research have since led to a number of accounts of supervisory control. We also discussed this aspect of WM when we considered Norman and Shallice's (1986) model of the control of willed and automatic behaviour in Chapter 10. Baddeley (1986) proposed that the SAS component of Norman and Shallice's model could be analogous to the central executive of working memory.

The central executive of working memory

At its inception, and for a number of years, the central executive (CE) was not well explained and was considered an area of residual ignorance. It was in danger of becoming a depository for all WM functions not accounted for by the phonological loop or the visuo-spatial sketch pad. The CE was assumed to be the part of WM that could undertake verbal reasoning when the phonological loop was occupied (Hitch and Baddeley, 1976), and was also responsible for 'controlling' recoding from one component of WM to the next. Baddeley (1986) points out that before 1986 there was little in the attention literature that could contribute to an understanding of executive control. However, a publication by Norman and Shallice (1986) changed this state of affairs. Baddeley proposed that the central executive component of the working memory system is comparable to the supervisory attentional system (SAS) in Norman and Shallice's model. Baddeley (1986, 1997) went on to interpret a number of experimental findings that were said to involve CE terms of this model, including deficits in patients with frontal lobe damage, slips of action and the effects of automaticity. We have reviewed this evidence already in Chapter 10, where the development of Norman and Shallice's model is explained. Another set of data that Baddeley (1993) considered is that concerning random generation, in which participants are asked to produce a random sequence of letters from the alphabet. They are asked to imagine drawing letters from a hat, wherein each letter is written on a slip of paper. There is only one instance of each letter in the hat, and letters are replaced after being taken out and 'read'. When asked to imagine doing this task at a slow rate subjects are able to produce more or less random sequences; however, if asked to do the task quickly randomness is reduced and repeated or familiar sequences tend to occur. Baddeley explains this, in terms of the Norman and Shallice model, by assuming that the production of letter names is dominated by powerful schema that, for example, represent the normal sequence of the alphabet, or acronyms such as BBC, USA. In order to generate truly random sequences, these well-learned schema must be over-ridden by attentional biasing from the SAS, and this takes time. When fast generation is required the SAS is unable to inhibit well-learned sequences and non-random generation results.

Although Baddeley (1986) claims that the SAS from Norman and Shallice's model of willed and automatic behaviour is an appropriate central executive, it is not entirely clear how to combine these two approaches. If you refer back to the original WM model you will notice that there is no contact with any other aspects of the human information processing system. On the other hand, Norman and Shallice's model incorporates perceptual processes and schema in long-term memory, but no component called working memory. We need to ask ourselves 'where are the phonological loop and visuo-spatial sketch pad?' in terms of the Norman and Shallice model, and 'where are perception and long-term memory in the WM model?' If we consider WM to be the currently active part of LTS, as Atkinson and Shiffrin (1968) suggested, then WM emerges when schema in LTS are activated above a threshold level. The schema activated could depend on the modality of input, for example speech sounds could activate different schema to those representing knowledge about visual proper-ties. In terms of what is known about the modularity of cognitive processing, this would make sense. Different modules represent and process different types of information. The selective loss of cognitive abilities in neuropsychological patients supports this view. For example, patient PV, reported by Vallar and Baddeley (1984), appeared to have a specific deficit of the phonological storage component of the phonological loop. Other patients show a deficit in drawing or describing objects from memory, a visual task, but can still perform spatial tasks such as pointing to the location of cities on a map (Levine, Warach and Farah, 1985).

Clearly, cognitive abilities can break down along the lines of the WM model, but at present only some components are identified. Presumably there are also other components of temporary storage that represent other modalities and varieties of processing. For example, Reisberg, Rappaport and O'Shaughnessy's (1984) experiment showed that people could remember numbers encoded by positions on their fingers. Does this show that there is a WM component for tactile stimuli? If so, how many other WM components might there be? Monsell (1984) sees WM as an 'umbrella term' for temporary storage 'distributed over diverse cognitive subsystems' (p. 328).

Working memory and the control of attention

Baddeley (1993) speculated that the CE may not actually store any information, and that not all working memory tasks necessarily involve memory. Rather, he suspected, all working memory tasks draw, at least partially, on the attentional resource of CE and that perhaps the working memory system could be considered 'working attention'. He discounted this suggestion for a number of reasons, not least because temporary storage is the basis of the WM system, although the CE component itself 'is concerned with attention and co-ordination rather than storage' (p. 168). However, recent work has implicated working memory in the control of attention in tasks where a target must be selected from distractors, that is, when attention has to be focused on relevant material amongst other, irrelevant material. De Fockert et al. (2001) combined two unrelated tasks, one requiring selective visual attention and the other a working memory task. The selective visual attention task required the participants to classify written names as pop stars or politicians while ignoring the face over which the word was written. Half the faces and names were congruent, for example the name of pop star written over the face of a pop star; the other half were incongruent, for example the name of a pop star written over the face of a politician. Participants were to ignore the faces and respond to the names. Reaction time (RT) to congruent stimuli is normally faster than to incongruent stimuli, and the slowing of RT to incongruent stimuli is taken as an indication of the degree of processing devoted to the irrelevant aspect—in this case, the face. This selective attention task was embedded in a working memory task that asked the participant to remember five digits while they did the attention task and then decide if a single digit presented had been in the memory list. The difficulty of the working memory task was manipulated either by using the same list of digits on every trial (easy), or by changing the list of digits on every trial (difficult). The results were that when name classification was combined with the difficult working memory task, the RT to the name was slower in the incongruent condition, indicating that when working memory was having to work harder, selective visual attention was less effective. The authors then repeated the experiment using fMRI to measure activity in face processing areas of the brain, and found that activity was greater in the high than the low memory load condition. Related findings by Conway *et al.* (2001) suggest that people with low memory span (a measure of working memory) are more likely to hear intrusions from the unattended channel in a dichotic listening experiment. This pattern of results is explained by Lavie *et al.* (2004) in their load theory and shows that ability to ignore distractors is determined by the available capacity of working memory.

The episodic buffer: A new component of working memory

Baddeley (2000) introduced the possibility of a new, fourth, component of working memory called the episodic buffer. After reviewing the effectiveness of the original model of working memory to account for the accumulated data, Baddeley concludes that although the phonological loop and visuo-spatial sketch pad can account for a wide range of data, there is a need for some other system that can provide an additional kind of storage. This is necessary to account, for example, for the effects of visual similarity on verbal recall, and the effect of meaning, which is stored in long-term memory on immediate recall from short-term memory. These effects suggest that more information is available at one time than is contained in a single system alone. The episodic buffer allows information represented in different codes to be temporarily bound together. Baddeley suggests that the episodic buffer is a limited capacity store that acts as an interface between systems which have different codes by using a common multidimensional code. The episodic buffer has the effect of integrating, or binding together, information from a variety of sources. It is controlled by the central executive, which can retrieve information from the episodic buffer into conscious awareness. The central executive can also '. . . influence the contents of the episodic buffer by attending to a given source of information, whether perceptual, from other components of working memory, or from LTM' (Baddeley, 2000, p. 421). Figure 12.3 shows this new conception of working memory including the episodic buffer.

The episodic buffer is similar to Tulving's concept of episodic memory, which we discussed in the last chapter, in the sense that it holds episodes of integrated information over space and time. However, unlike long-term episodic memory, the episodic buffer is only temporary and is limited in capacity and separate from LTM,

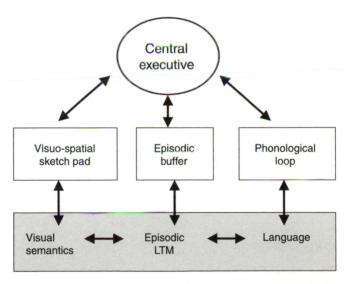

FIGURE 12.3 The new revision of working memory including the episodic buffer. From Baddeley (2000).

although Baddeley suggests it is an important stage in long-term epi-sodic learning. The episodic buffer would also appear to be rather like the temporary object file proposed in Treisman's feature integration theory of attention, in which attention binds together the separable visual attributes of objects, but with the capability of binding across more and different codes.

However many components of WM representing different types information there might be, the problem of how they are all controlled remains. Although Baddeley (1986) adopted the SAS as an appropriate control system, there are questions concerning how the SAS is itself controlled (see Chapter 10) and how the SAS version of the central executive can achieve recoding from one modality to another. These difficulties are not unique to the working memory model of Baddeley and Hitch (1974) or Baddeley (2000). Other models of WM such as Broadbent's (1984) Maltese Cross model and Anderson's (1983) ACT* account for the mechanism of control by using a production system architecture, in which patterns in WM specify actions or processes to be carried out. However, there is still the problem of how the intended process can gain control of the system in the face of competition.

Representation of knowledge in long-term memory

In the previous chapter we considered evidence for different kinds of long-term storage, and made some distinctions between semantic/episodic memory, procedural/declarative memory and implicit/explicit knowledge. Although we mentioned some aspects of the way this knowledge was coded, we must now tackle the problem in more detail. Some questions that need answering are 'What is a representation?'; 'Are there different kinds of representation?' and 'How is knowledge organised?'. We shall take these in turn.

What is a representation?

Basically, a *representation* is something that stands for something else. The represent*ation* is responsible for represent*ing* in the brain the object or situation in the world that is represent*ed*. The represent*ation* can be considered as a mapping between what is doing the represent*ing* and what is represent*ed*. For example, the word 'cup' is a representa-*tion* that maps between the object that is represent*ed* and the cognitive system that is represent*ing* it. The word *cup* is a 'symbol' for the object, it bears no relationship to the visual properties of a cup, but is used to represent it. On the other hand, a picture of a cup is analogous to the real object.

Are there different kinds of representation?

There are obviously a number of different ways for representing the same information in the external world. For example, imagine the pattern spots on a dice that has fallen to show 'three'. The word *three* represents the number of spots, but the pattern of dots could be repre-sented as the numerical symbol 3, or as a spatial image, or as a verbal description such as 'the black spots form a diagonal line from the top left to the bottom right'. However, the fact that we can describe the information on a dice in different ways does not tell how the cognitive system represents that information. It is possible that the information is represented in one form only, but the cognitive system is able to interpret it in different ways.

If we consider semantic knowledge, for example 'some animals are birds', 'birds can fly', 'canaries sing', it is difficult to think of many different ways of representing this knowledge. Although we know what birds look like and may be able to generate an image of a bird, or a singing bird, this type of knowledge seems best represented by truth statements, or propositions, and is referred to as propositional knowledge. From these propositions it would be possible to generate images that appear to be analogues of the real objects, provided they had associated visual properties. However, concepts such as 'peace' or 'willpower' are difficult to associate with any particular image. You might be able to think of associations such as a peace-rally, or trying to give up chocolate, but these are not images of the concept itself. There has been considerable debate in cognitive psychology about the nature of representation, particularly whether there really are analogue representations.

Analogue representations: Mental rotation and the mind's eye

We discussed Shephard and Metzler's (1971) experiments on mental rotation in connection with the use of the *visuo-spatial sketch pad* of working memory. The evidence suggested that people can represent a visual image in a form that is analogous to the object in the real world and can manipulate it in the same way as a real object. This is therefore an analogue representation. It is assumed that the internal representation passes through all the stages of transformation, in a one-to-one correspondence to what would happen to the external object. Other experiments have provided support for the existence of analogue representations. Kosslyn (1980) involved his participants in image scanning experiments. The task was to memorise a map with landmarks on it, such as a house, trees and mountains. Then the participants were asked to imagine scanning the map to move from one object to the next and tell the experimenter when they got there. Kosslyn found that the time to 'move' the scan was proportional to the distance between objects, and so in accordance with an analogue representation of the map. Kosslyn suggested that there were many similarities between perception and scanning mental images. In one study his participants were asked to imagine a rabbit beside an elephant, or beside a mouse, and then asked to answer questions about details of the rabbit, such as its eye. When the rabbit was imagined beside the mouse, responses were faster than when the rabbit was imagined beside the elephant. This was assumed to arise because when the elephant was fitted into the imagined scene, the scale meant that the rabbit was very small, and so details were more difficult to 'see' in the 'mind's eye'. In contrast, when the rabbit and mouse were together, the rabbit was much larger and its details easier to 'see'. Another example, which you can do for yourself, is to imagine a friend in the distance, walking toward you. Kosslyn found that people reported the image of the person expanding as it came closer, analogous to the way in which real objects expand on the retina in the real world. Kosslyn developed a computational model of imagery that incorporated image files and propositional files that both store information about objects from which images can be generated. The images are represented in a *spatial medium* that can be scanned and manipulated. The spatial medium has a central area of high resolution rather like the retina on the physical eye.

Propositional representations

Pylyshyn (1981) argued that mental images are not analogue representations, and are not like perception at all. He proposed that all representations are propositional, and that when people engage in mental imagery, they simply behave in the way they know they do when dealing with real images. So, according to Pylyshyn, images are nor 're-perceptions' and there are no 'pictures in the head'. The biggest problem Pylyshyn draws attention to is the question of the 'mind's eye', that is, if there really are images stored as analogues of the perceptual world, what mechanism could look at them? Further, he suggested, even if it were possible to store images, they would be difficult to search for, and people do not seem to have to search for images at all, rather they appear to generate them directly and quickly. This is done from propositional knowledge. The power of *propositional representations* is that they can represent relations between objects, such as 'John hit James with the cricket bat' and include our understanding of agents and objects, so that, given three objects and the verb 'hit', 'the cricket bat hit John with James' cannot be true. See Eysenck and Keane (2000) for a thorough discussion of propositional knowledge.

Dual coding hypothesis

Pavio (1986) proposed that mental representation could be coded both visually and verbally. He reports an experiment in which his participants were given lists of pictures or lists of words to remember. It was assumed that when the participants named the pictures in the list this would activate both the word and picture representations. However, participants who were only given the words would only have the word code in memory. Pavio found that participants who had been given the pictures to name recalled the words better than participants who had only seen the words. Therefore, the dual code improved memory. In other experiments he showed that the more concrete and imageable a word is, the better it is remembered. Figure 12.4 shows the two coding systems: logogens are activated by verbal information, and imagens are activated by non-verbal information. The probability that an imagen or logogen will be activated is a result of all the stimulus attributes and contextual information, and one or both systems may be activated at the same time.

The logogen and imagen systems can refer to each other via connections to enable a word to create an image or an image to give rise to a word. This association between images and words is used in a number of mnemonic techniques to improve memory. See Richardson (1999) for a full review of imagery and competing theories.

The organisation of knowledge

Knowledge is stored in semantic memory, and there is good evidence that it is stored in an organised way. For example, when people are

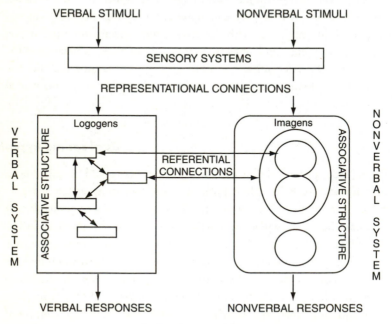

FIGURE 12.4 Paivio's dual coding model. From Paivio (1986).

asked to recall a list of words that comprise different categories, say vegetables, animals and furniture, even if the categories were mixed up in the list, they tend to be clustered together at recall (Mandler, 1967). Likewise, if asked to generate words, people tend to cluster them by category or by association (Deese, 1959). So, how might knowledge be represented to give rise to this organisation?

A model for semantic memory: Collins and Quillian (1969)

An early attempt to model semantic memory in a propositional system was proposed by Collins and Quillian (1969); this was also an early attempt at artificial intelligence. To discover some of the properties of search for conceptual information in semantic memory, participants were given *sentence verification* tasks. In sentence verification, a statement is presented and the participant has to judge as quickly as possible whether the statement is true or false. Examples of some sentences and their response times are: 'A canary is yellow'; this generates a fast response. 'A canary can fly'; this generates a medium response. 'A canary eats food'; this generates a slow response.

It was assumed that the time to judge the sentence as true or false measured the time to retrieve that knowledge from memory. The graded response times were taken to suggest a hierarchy of information storage, where the specific properties are stored with the 'canary' concept, specific properties of birds with the 'bird' concept, and properties of animals with the 'animal' concept. Figure 12.5 shows a version of such a memory hierarchy.

This semantic network represents knowledge about concepts in such a way that the characteristics of concepts at a higher level are 'inherited' by concepts at a lower level. Each concept is represented at a 'node' in memory. This is an economical way of representing knowledge as it removes the necessity to store all information about the properties of animals, for example, with every fish or bird. Exceptions to the general characteristics are stored with the concept, for example, the fact that ostriches cannot fly is coded with ostrich.

Semantic networks are highly interconnected and activation spreads from node to node, so that when 'canary' and 'wings' are

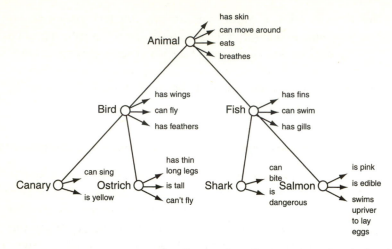

FIGURE 12.5 A version of Collins and Quillian's (1969) hierarchical model of semantic memory. From Parkin (2000).

activated, excitation spreads to other connected nodes. When the two sources of activation meet, this allows a 'yes' response. This concept of *spreading activation* is important in accounting for priming by association. Meyer and Schvanaveldt (1971) demonstrated that if people have just responded to 'nurse', they are faster to respond to 'doctor' on a following trial. This effect can be accounted for by the activation spreading to doctor from nurse and raising activity in the 'doctor' node. If doctor is presented before this activation has decayed, response is speeded, or primed. There are, of course, some problems for this model. In particular, some false sentences are rejected quickly, such as 'a canary can swim'. This result is not predicted by the model, as it should take a long time, or be impossible for activation from 'canary' to reach 'can swim'. Other problems include the finding that not all members of a category are responded to with the same speed, so the time to decide that 'a robin is a bird' is far quicker than that to decide 'a chicken is a bird' (Rosch, 1973). This *typicality effect* is not accounted for by Collins and Quillian (1969).

Accounting for typicality effects

A number of theories have proposed that category membership is not stored at nodes of semantic memory, but is computed by comparison of features. Smith, Shoben and Rips (1974) suggested a *feature comparison model*, in which the meaning of a concept is represented as a bundle of features. One set of features is that of the *defining features*, which are necessary for category membership, the other is that of *characteristic features*, which will apply to most members, but not all, and which are not essential for category membership. Given a sentence such as 'a canary is a bird', a two-stage comparison process begins. The first stage is a quick comparison of all features listed with the instance, and if this is successful, a response is made. However, if this search is not conclusive, a slower search of all the defining features must be carried out. This model can account for typicality effects, as the more typical instance is likely to share more features with the category than an atypical instance. However, as this model is not propositional, it has difficulty in accounting for our ability to know that 'a canary is a bird' is true, but 'a bird is a canary' is false.

Rosch (1973) and Rosch and Mervis (1975) explored the representation of the *prototype*. A prototype is no particular instance or example, but a more general kind of 'family resemblance', an idea put forward by Wittgenstein. No two members of the family may be exactly the same, but a typical family member will share more features with the rest of the family than a less typical family member. Rosch and Mervis asked people to rate instances as good or bad members of a category, and also asked another group to list as many attributes as they could for each category. Results showed that participants generated rather few attributes for each category, but nevertheless, typical instances of categories such as fruit, furniture and clothing tended to share more features with other members of the category. These feature comparison approaches are more in accordance with the data but are less powerful in accounting for spreading activation, or priming between related concepts.

The problem with features and attributes

Any model that proposes that knowledge about objects or concepts is stored in terms of attributes has difficulty in determining which features are necessary and sufficient for category membership. This is a philosophical problem, but an important constraint on theory. Other problems arise from the effects of context on category judgements. For example, Barsalou (1983) asked people to generate items from arbitrary artificial categories like 'things you can fit into a matchbox', or 'things to take on holiday'. This proved quite easy to do, yet it is unlikely that we have pre-stored features for these types of categories. Our knowledge base must be far more flexible and interconnected to allow us access to information according to novel categories.

Bartlett's schema theory

Knowledge is more sophisticated, flexible and interdependent than is captured in the models we have considered so far. Bartlett (1932) in his book *Remembering* proposed that knowledge is held in structures called *schema*, and that we remember and interpret new information in terms of these pre-existing structures. If you consider for a moment the kinds of semantic memory tasks described in the previous section, you can appreciate the narrowness of their scope. How often does someone ask you 'Does a canary have legs?'. If they did you might assume it was because they had some purpose in knowing. Claxton (1980) points out 'If someone asks me "Can canaries fly?" in the pub I will suspect either that he is an idiot or that he is about to tell me a joke. How I react will be a function of the entire circumstances, as I perceive them.' This emphasises the point that cognitive processes do not operate in isolation: they work to interpret the environment, and as Bartlett suggested, learning and remembering are active processes, with people showing 'effort after meaning'. People apply the knowledge in schema to help them understand ongoing situations and disambiguate the ambiguous. In his classic study of remembering, Bartlett asked his participants to classify ambiguous pictures, for example one shape was somewhat like an anchor, or somewhat like an umbrella. Later he asked them to draw the pictures again and found that, depending on how the picture had been classified, the drawing was changed to be more like an anchor or more like an umbrella. People had remembered their interpretation of the picture, rather than the picture itself.

In another study Bartlett gave people a North American folk tale to read, called *The war of the ghosts*. The content of the story was strangely structured; it was not always clear what exactly was going on, and the content was unfamiliar. When asked to recall the story, Bartlett found that people did a number of things. First, the story was very much shorter, second, it had been reconstructed rather than remembered verbatim, and most importantly, participants omitted or added information to make sense of the story in terms with which they were familiar.

Schema scripts and frames

Following Bartlett's work, little interest was shown in schema theory until the 1970s, when a number of related works proposed the importance of knowledge structures that were broader in scope than those that concentrated at the level of concepts. Schanck (1975) revived Bartlett's ideas in schema in the structure of episodes in memory. Minsky (1975) introduced the notion of framework for representing knowledge in *frames*. Schanck introduced the idea of *scripts* and Abelson (1975) suggested that *plans* provide a framework of knowledge for interpreting social situations. Rumelhart (1975) suggested that schema were used in understanding stories.

Whilst these different authors have slightly different interpretations of schema, their proposals have a number of common features, which are well summarised by Rumelhart and Norman (1985). All these interpretations of schema-like knowledge propose that a schema represents 'generalised concepts underlying objects, situations and events, sequences of events, actions and sequences of actions' (p. 36). We met schema for action sequences in our discussion of action slips in Chapter 10. The example given was of a hierarchical system of parent and child schema representing how to make a cup of tea. Slips of action were accounted for in Norman and Shallice's (1986) model for willed and automatic behaviour by the correct or incorrect activation of schema in long-term memory. Rumelhart and Norman go on to explain that schema are 'like models of the outside world. To process information is to determine which model best fits the incoming information' (p. 36). This explanation of the use of schema in making sense of the world is similar to the hypothesis testing view of perception proposed by Neisser (1967) and Gregory (1980). We interpret the world in terms of what we know and what we expect. Here again the influence of memory on perception is evident.

Schema have variables, and can be embedded in each other. So, for example, the schema for going to eat in a restaurant will have a core of relatively fixed features, such as sitting at a table and eating food. Variable features might include whether it is self-service, or if there will be waiters serving you. Another variable may be what you will eat, but again this may be contained by another schema, as schema can embed one within another. For example, depending on whether it is a Chinese or an Italian restaurant, another set of core and variable features will apply within the superordinate schema for eating in a restaurant. Figure 12.6 shows a theoretical restaurant script.

Schema can represent knowledge at all levels of abstraction. They do not only apply to concrete examples like those just given; we also have schema for abstract constructions like 'democracy' or 'justice' that represent knowledge rather than concepts, so rather than a definition for a democracy, the schema for it will incorporate what you know about democratic societies and how you expect their governments to be structured. Lastly, schema are active in recognition, working top-down to interpret and make sense of scenes, situations, stories or social situations. Schema theory is usually criticised for being too vague to generate testable predictions: How can we specify what knowledge is in a schema? How can schema act top-down to interpret situations? With advances in computational modelling, some answers are beginning to emerge from connectionist or parallel distributed models of memory,

Connectionist representations

More recently, a new approach to the representation of knowledge has been provided by connectionist or parallel distributed processing

Name: Restaurant
Props: Tables
    Menu
    Food
    Bill
    . Money
    Tip
Entry Conditions: Customer hungry
                      Customer has money

Roles: Customer
    Waiter
    Cook
    Cashier
    Owner

Results: Customer has less money
       Owner has more money
       Customer is not hungry

Scene 1: Entering
    Customer enters restaurant
    Customer looks for table
    Customer decides where to sit
    Customer goes to table
    Customer sits down

Scene 2: Ordering
    Customer picks up menu
    Customer looks at menu
    Customer decides on food
    Customer signals waitress
    Waitress comes to table
    Customer orders food
    Waitress goes to cook
    Waitress gives food order to cook
    Cook prepares food

Scene 3: Eating
    Cook gives food to waitress
    Waitress brings food to customer
    Customer eats food

Scene 4: Exiting
    Waitress writes bill
    Waitress goes over to customer
    Waitress gives bill to customer
    Customer gives tip to waitress
    Customer goes to cashier
    Customer gives money to cashier
    Customer leaves restaurant

FIGURE 12.6 The Restaurant Script, adapted by Rumelhart and Norman (1985) from Schank and Abelson (1977).

(PDP) models. One of their advantages is that the information represented in them is *content addressable* in that it can be accessed by only a partial description of an item or object. Like the human cognitive system, they can use stored knowledge to form a hypothesis about what is represented and come to a decision on the basis of the best evidence available. The pandemonium model (Selfridge, 1959), which we used to try and understand pattern recognition, was to some extent an early ancestor of PDP models. So, too, were semantic network models such as that of Collins and Quillian (1969), which proposed a network of knowledge within which activation could spread. However, the problem for these earlier accounts was that they did not offer the flexibility of processing that humans possess; nor did they allow content addressability. If I ask you 'Who was the King of England who had six wives?', you know the answer is Henry VIII. This is not all you know about him; he was also the father of Queen Elizabeth I, reigned in the middle of the 16th century, was a member of the royal family and so on. Any of these questions may allow you access to your knowledge of 'Henry VIII', and once one part is accessed it can allow access to other knowledge you have, such as what he looked like. We have already considered the interactive activation model (IAM) of word recognition (McClelland and Rumelhart, 1981) and the interactive competition (IAC) model of person recognition (Burton and Bruce, 1993) in Chapter 6. These models allow access to stored representations on the basis of partial knowledge because the representation is distributed over many units.

Which gang does he belong to? The Jets and the Sharks

McClelland (1981) devised another influential model that is able to capture conceptual knowledge in a PDP architecture. In the musical *West Side Story* there were two gangs, the Jets and the Sharks. McClelland used these gangs to illustrate how knowledge about individuals in each gang could give rise to a concept of what a Jet or Shark was typically like. He gave each member of the fictitious gang personal attributes, such as where they went to college, whether they were married, their occupation and their name. Each attribute is represented in an attribute map, and is connected to an instance node that allows communication between attribute maps. Activation of any attribute activates all other sources of information about that person, but within each attribute map there is mutual inhibition. So, if you are given the name 'Lance' you will know he is in his 20s, went to junior high school, is a Jet, is single and is a burglar. This model also shows how if you are asked 'What are Jets like?' this would send activation to the properties associated with Jets in general, allowing you to know what a prototype Jet is. This process is called *spontaneous generalisation*. So, if you are introduced to Bill and told he is a member of the Jets, you would immediately have a stereotype to judge him by. This model also has the property of *graceful degradation*, in that some information can be lost or damaged, but the system will still work. This model explains how particular instances, or episodes— say, meeting members of the gang at parties—can give rise to general semantic knowledge and can explain how conceptual categories can be represented without having to define features that are necessary for category (gang) membership.

Representing schema in a parallel distributed model

Rumelhart *et al.* (1986) produced a PDP model for representing schematic knowledge. In their view schema are not 'things', and there is no specific representation that is a schema. Rather, schema emerge as they are needed from simpler elements in memory working together, and are created by the environment they are trying to interpret. When information begins to enter the perceptual system, units are activated that feed onto memory units. The perceptual input and the knowledge stored in the connections between units in the system provide constraints on interpretation until a stable state is formed. At this point the best interpretation of the data is settled at, and in this way it appears that schema exist, although in fact all that has happened is that appropriate knowledge has been activated during processing. Given a different input, a different set of relevant knowledge will be active. In this way schema are flexible.

The model is designed to capture knowledge about rooms. We all know what a typical kitchen, bathroom or living room is like and the items we expect to find, or not find, in them. For example, a kitchen has an oven and a sink, but not a bath. A bathroom does have a bath, but probably not a coffee table. Rumelhart *et al.* (1986) asked subjects to generate lists of items they expected to find in different types of room, and putting them all together chose 40 items to put into the PDP network. All the room items were connected together in the network, and then the network was 'presented' with 80 descriptions of rooms. So a sink, cooker and coffee pot would be presented as 'kitchen'; a sofa, lamp and coffee table would be a 'living room'; a computer, a desk and a lamp would be 'office', and so on. Items that were presented together were 'learned' by the program in terms of strengthening the connections between them; connections to non-presented items were inhibitory. Once the learning was complete the system was presented with a combination of items it had never seen before, and left to settle to an 'answer'. It was shown that it would settle to the best answer possible on the available information, so if presented with an oven, a sink and a coffee pot, it would produce a 'kitchen' schema, and fill in the other items associated with the schema it had learned, such as toaster and refrigerator. If items that did not fit the schema were presented, such as a bed, together with kitchen items, the bed would gradually be inhibited. In this simple model we can see how repeated experiences of rooms or other events can produce knowledge structures in memory that act like schema in the interpretation of the perceptual input. What we expect is constructed on the basis of knowledge; this is like the constructivist view of perception discussed in Chapter 4.

Over the last 20 years PDP and connectionist modelling has become the most widely used and powerful computer metaphor for cognitive processing.

Summary

Information must be represented both temporarily while it is worked on and in the long-term, for it to be accessed as required. The working memory model allows for information to be held in modality-specific stores that are controlled by a supervisory, executive attentional system. This system is responsible for controlling coding between subsystems and for planning and coordination of actions. Breakdown of executive control and random sequence generation support the view of an executive component involved in working memory. Knowledge in long-term memory may be represented as images or propositions. An image is an analogue representation that mirrors the real world. Propositions are verbal statements that represent truth values. Pavio suggests that both forms of representation are used in his dual coding hypothesis. Semantic memory can be probed with sentence verification tasks and Collins and Quillian proposed a hierarchical network representing features of concepts. This model has difficulty in accounting for typicality effects. Feature comparison models have difficulty in explaining which features are necessary and sufficient to define concepts. Schema represent knowledge in larger units than concepts and have been suggested to be involved in interpreting stories, plans and social situations. Schema can represent knowledge at all levels of abstraction, but it is difficult to specify what knowledge is contained in a schema. Connectionist representations of knowledge can represent information in a content-addressable form and allow for general, prototypical knowledge to emerge from individual instances.

Self-assessment questions (Solutions on p. 324)

1 Explain the function of each of the components of Baddeley's model of working memory.
2 What is the difference between analogue and propositional representations?
3 How do you know how to behave in a restaurant?
4 What is meant by a 'distributed representation'?

Further reading

Baddeley, A. D. (1997) *Human Memory: Theory and practice*. Hove, UK: Psychology Press. For a good account of different types of memory representation and connectionist modelling.

Ellis, R. and Humphreys, G. (1999) *Connectionist Psychology: A text with readings*. Hove, UK: Psychology Press. For more detail on PDP and connectionism, see Chapter 1.

Eysenck, M. W. and Keane, M. T. (2000) *Cognitive Psychology: A student's handbook* (4th ed.). Hove, UK: Psychology Press. For a shorter review.

Glossary

Absolute threshold. The point at which a stimulus can be detected 50% of the time. It is the lower limit of sensation.

Accommodation. The thickening or thinning of the lens in the eye, controlled by muscles that provide feedback to the brain about the degree of change in the lens. A cue for distance.

Acoustic signal. A sound pattern of frequency and amplitude detected by the auditory system.

Action schema. A schema organised in a hierarchical way, with parent and child schemas that are recruited as necessary to complete an action sequence.

Adequate stimulus. The stimulus that is normally encoded by a sensory receptor; in vision, for example, it is light.

Afferent. A neural signal from the sense organs going to the brain.

Amnesia. A neuropsychological disorder in which new information cannot be encoded into long-term storage such that it can be made consciously available in the future. Implicit learning, which can be demonstrated without conscious recollection, is preserved.

Amplitude. The peak-to-peak measurement of a sound wave, measured as sound pressure level in decibels. The psychological correlate is loudness.

Analysis by synthesis. A term coined by Neisser (1967) to refer to the interpretation of a stimulus in terms of the way it is expected to be on the basis of existing knowledge.

Anterior attentional orienting system. An attentional system within the frontal lobes involved in selecting and enhancing attention processing to a visual location.

Articulatory suppression. A procedure to occupy the articulatory apparatus with irrelevant articulation, such as repeating 'the', 'the', 'the', to prevent articulation of other verbal experimental stimuli.

Attention for action. The type of attention necessary for planning controlling and executing responses, or actions.

Attention for perception. The type of attention necessary for encoding and interpreting sensory data.

Auditory input lexicon. A store of word representations within which word detectors collect evidence for their occurrence. If there is sufficient evidence for a word it will output its associated information to the rest of the processing system.

Automatic processing. Processing that does not demand attention. It runs off outside intentional control and is not capacity limited or resource limited, or interfered with by another task. Automatic processes are not available for conscious inspection.

Basilar membrane. The membrane within the cochlea covered with hair cells that is responsible for transducing the physical properties of sound into a neural code.

Basket cells. Receptors wrapped around the base of the hair shaft in the skin sensitive to movement of the hair.

Behavioural rigidity. The inability to change from one mental task to another. A symptom of frontal lobe damage.

Binding problem. As the brain codes many perceptual properties of objects in separate specialised cells and pathways, the problem is how all the different properties are correctly put together, or bound, into the correct combination.

Blind spot. The place where the optic nerve leaves the back of the eye. At this point the retina effectively has a 'hole' in it, and so no visual information is coded over this area.

Bottom-up. A term that refers to processing driven by the information in the stimulus, proceeding upward from low levels of analysis toward the higher levels.

Break through. The ability of some information to capture conscious awareness despite being unattended, usually used with respect to the unattended channel in dichotic listening experiments.

Canonical view. The typical view of an object that reveals the principal axes.

Capture. The ability of one source of information to take over from another. For example, if visual and tactile information are in conflict, vision may capture touch so that an object is recognised by the way it looks rather than the way it feels. A different example would be the sudden onset of novel information within a modality, for example an apple falling may interrupt ongoing attentional processing.

Categorical perception. The phenomenon whereby a stimulus that gradually changes is only heard as one thing or another, with no perception of the graded change. Usually applied to auditory stimuli such as phonemes, which are never heard as ambiguous, but always categorised.

Central cue. A symbol, such as an arrow, presented to indicate which side of visual space a target will arrive.

Central executive. A hypothetical attentional system whose purpose is to direct controlled processing. Part of Baddeley and Hitch's (1974) model of working memory and equated with the supervisory attentional system in Norman and Shallice's (1986) model of willed behaviour.

Change blindness. The phenomenon of the inability of participants to notice gross changes in the environment that occur while attention is diverted.

Characteristic features. The features that an object usually has, none of which are necessary and sufficient to define it as a category member, but which are shared by most members.

Closed loop. Performance controlled this way demands attention and ongoing activity is monitored for errors and for moving towards the intended goal.

Cochlea. The spiral-shaped structure of the inner ear, which is divided along its length by the basilar membrane.

Cocktail party effect. The ability to selectively listen to one of a number of concurrent conversations.

Cognitive neuropsychology. A branch of cognitive psychology concerned with the analysis of functional loss in patients who have suffered brain damage. One of its assumptions is that the brain is modular and that functions can be selectively lost. Evidence can be used to support or refute theories or models of normal function.

Cognitive neuroscience. The combined approach of cognitive psychology, cognitive neuropsychology, neuropsychology and neurophysiology to understanding the brain at both the biological and cognitive levels. Modern imaging techniques such as PET and fMRI are used to observe the intact brain in action, together with other physiological methods.

Conjunction. A term from the feature integration theory of attention that describes a target defined by at least two separable features, such as a red O amongst green Os and red Ts.

Connectionist. Applied to parallel distributed processing models that comprise a large number of units that are highly interconnected by inhibitory and excitatory links. In such models knowledge is held as a pattern of activity distributed across the units in a network.

Consistent mapping. A task in which distractors are never targets and targets are never distractors; there is a consistent relationship between the stimuli and the responses to be made to them.

Content addressable memory. A memory system that can be accessed on the basis of any of the information held within it.

Contention scheduler. A component of Norman and Shallice's (1986) model that is responsible for the semi-automatic control of schema activation to ensure that schema run off in an orderly way.

Controlled processing. Processing that is under conscious, intentional control. It requires attentional resources, or capacity, and is subject to interference.

Conscious processing. See **controlled processing**.

Constructivist approach. The view that perception involves hypothesis testing, and that interpretation of stimuli is guided by what the observer knows and expects. It acknowledges top-down influences on bottom-up processing. Similar to analysis-by-synthesis.

Convergence. The movement of the eyes as they turn in towards each other when an object moves closer to them. A cue to depth perception at close distances.

Copy cue. The presentation of a stimulus that has been seen before in a test of recognition memory.

Cortical space. The area of cortex that corresponds to the site of activity associated with the presentation of a visual stimulus.

Covert attentional orienting. Orienting attention without making any movement of the eyes.

Cue. Any signal that indicates what is to be done in a psychological task.

Cued recall. Recall in response to the presentation of a word that was presented at the same time as the stimulus word. For example, if the word pair was *cold–ground*, and *cold* has been responded to in the first test, *ground* would be presented as the cue to recall *COLD*.

d prime. The distance between the means of two distributions, used in signal detection theory to measure the overlap between signal and noise.

Data-limited. A task that cannot be performed any better no matter how much attentional resource is allocated to it, because there is insufficient perceptual data or knowledge.

Declarative knowledge. Knowledge that can be retrieved from memory into conscious awareness, and told to someone.

Decouple. A term that describes the necessity for preventing all stimuli from concurrently activating their associated responses in order that the selected action can be made.

Defining features. The features of an object that are necessary and sufficient to define it as a member of a category. All category members will have the defining features of their category.

Dichotic listening. A task in which two messages are delivered concurrently, one to each ear, and the participant has to selectively listen to one designated message and ignore the other.

Difference threshold. The smallest change in the physical properties of a stimulus that give rise to a noticeable psychological change. The same as a just-noticeable difference.

Direct perception. The view of J. J. Gibson (1950), that perception could proceed directly from the perceptual input without need for interpretation from memory or top-down processes.

Doppler shift. The compression of a sound wave to the front of a moving object produces a rise in pitch, while the sound wave behind the moving object is expanded, producing a drop in pitch. This has the effect of producing pitch changes as the object moves past. An auditory cue to movement.

Dorsal stream. A pathway for visual information that encodes what an object is.

Double dissociation. Refers to the case where one neuropsychological patient can do task A but not task B, and another patient can do task B but not task A. Taken as evidence for the tasks being processed by independent modules in the brain.

Early selection. Selective attention that operates on the physical information available from early perceptual analysis.

Ecological approach. An approach to perception taken by J. J. Gibson (1950), that emphasises the importance of perception and action in processing environmental information.

Efference copy. A copy of the signal for a muscle movement that informs the rest of the brain that it should expect a change related to that movement. Used to differentiate between whether we are touching ourself or are being touched, and to distinguish between movement across the retina produced by an eye movement, and that of an object crossing visual space.

Efferent. A neural signal that leaves the brain to go to (for example) the muscles.

Encapsulated end organs. The primary receptors for touch in the hairless regions of the body.

Encoding specificity principle. Proposed by Tulving (1972), the principle states that only a cue that is encoded with a memory trace can act as a cue for retrieval of that memory at a later time.

Endogenous attention. Attention that is controlled by the intention of a participant.

Endorphin. A neurotransmitter substance that is the body's natural pain killer. It is related to opiate drugs such as morphine, which have the same effect.

Engram. Tulving's (1972) term for a memory trace in long-term memory.

Episodic memory. Long-term memory that has contextual information associated with it. The memory for having experienced an event that can be remembered as such.

Exogenous attention. Attention that is drawn automatically to a stimulus without the intention of the participant. Processing by exogenous attention cannot be ignored. It is attracted, for example by a peripheral cue, in visual orienting experiments.

Extinction. A phenomenon sometimes exhibited by patients with unilateral visual neglect, in which the introduction of a second stimulus toward the good side of visual space 'extinguishes', or makes invisible, the previously seen stimulus.

Extrinsic context. Context surrounding an event that is not integral to the stimulus being processed; for example, the room you are reading this book in is extrinsic context.

Feature comparison model. A model from Rips, Shoben and Smith (1974) of how object category decisions are made, which involves the comparison of the object's features to those that are, first, characteristic of the category, and then, if a match is not made, to the defining features of the object category.

Feature integration theory. Treisman and Gelade (1980) proposed that when a conjunction of features is necessary to identify an object in visual search, serial search of object locations with focal attention is required, and attention is the 'glue' that binds features together. Search for individual features is parallel and does not require attention. Without focal attention, illusory conjunctions may be formed where features in the display are incorrectly combined.

Feature map. A component of feature integration theory. The feature map represents the location of individual features on the map for that feature. There are separate maps for colour and orientation, for example.

Feeling of knowing. A term introduced by Huppert and Piercy (1976) for the effect observed in patients with amnesia who did not recognise a stimulus as having been seen before, but had a less definite feeling that they knew it in some way.

Filtering. The selective process whereby a class of stimuli meeting some criterion, such as 'in the left ear', or 'red Os' are allowed access to further processing, while stimuli not meeting that criterion are blocked from further processing. A central aspect of Broadbent's (1958) model of information processing.

Fixation. The time the fovea of the eye dwells on a location in visual space, during which time information is collected.

Fourier analysis. Used to analyse the component sine waves from the wave form of a complex sound.

Fovea. The area of the retina with highest resolution and the highest concentration of cones for detecting colour.

Fragment completion task. A task introduced by Warrington and Weiskrantz (1976) in which a fragmentary outline of a picture is presented and the participant is asked to name the object represented. Previous presentation of the complete picture primes recognition of the fragment in patients with amnesia, despite their inability to remember the learning trial.

Frames. A type of schema introduced by Minsky (1975) for representing an organised system of knowledge about particular areas of understanding.

Free nerve endings. The most common skin receptor found all over the body.

Free recall. A memory test in which after the learning episode a participant is simply asked to recall as much as they can without any additional cues being given.

Frequency. In acoustics, the period of the sine wave that gives rise to the psychological property of pitch. In language, the number of times a word appears in regular usage of the language. The word frequency effect is the finding that frequent words are recognised more quickly than less frequent words.

Frontal lobe syndrome. The pattern of deficits exhibited by patients with damage to the frontal lobes. These patients are distractable, show behavioural rigidity, are poor at planning and may exhibit utilisation behaviour.

Galvanic skin response. A measurable change in the electrical conductivity of the skin when emotionally significant stimuli are presented. Often used to detect the unconscious processing of stimuli.

Generate-recognise theory. A theory of retrieval from long-term memory that suggests candidate words are first generated, and then examined to see if they can be recognised. Does not account for recognition failure of recallable words.

Gestalt principles. Principles of perceptual grouping proposed by the Gestalt school of psychology. Predominantly German, the Gestalt movement is most famous for the saying 'the whole is more than the sum of its parts'. The principles emphasise the organisation of perceptual patterns that emerge from the overall information in the display. Examples are: proximity—things that are close to each other tend to be grouped together; continuity—things that follow one from another are grouped together; and similarity—things that are similar tend to be grouped together.

Global processing. Processing of the overall shape of an object rather than its local elements. For example, processing a 'tree' rather than its leaves.

Graceful degradation. A property of connectionist and parallel processing models in which some units can be destroyed without the system failing.

Hypothetical stage. A stage of information processing that can be hypothesised to exist in order for a particular operation to be achieved or be possible. For example, a buffer memory for sensory information is a hypothetical stage, during which sensory information is held in memory while selective processes act to transform the information to a different, more durable code.

Iconic memory. A high capacity, fast decay memory for visual information, from which only a subset can be reported before the memory is lost.

Ideomotor compatibility. The compatibility between the stimulus and its required response in terms of, usually, spatial relations. For example, if the task is to indicate if a stimulus was to the left or to the right, response times are faster if the responses for left and right involve pressing a button on the left and right. If the responses are crossed, reaction time is slowed.

Implicit memory. Memory that cannot be explicitly reported, but can be demonstrated to exist by the performance of a task. Memory that a person does not have conscious access to.

Intensity difference. If a sound source is placed closer to one ear than the other the intensity of sound is greater at the closer ear. A binaural cue for location, most useful for high frequencies.

Interaural time difference. The difference between the time of arrival of a sound signal at each ear. A binaural cue to location.

Intrinsic context. Properties of a stimulus that are an integral part of it for example, a word may be in italics or in upper case.

Introspection. A method used by early psychologists to examine the contents of the mind. A participant who introspects reports the contents of their experience to the experimenter. The data produced is subjective and not open to objective verification. If I tell you the sky looks red to me, you have no way of proving otherwise.

Just-noticeable-difference. The minimum difference in the physical properties of two stimuli that can be subjectively reported. The same as a difference threshold.

Levels of processing. An approach to memory proposed by Craik and Lockhart (1972), that suggested the durability of memory is related to the depth of processing carried out on the stimulus.

Linear perspective. A pictorial cue to depth based on the convergence of parallel lines as they recede into the distance.

Local processing. Processing of the local elements of a larger shape, for example, attending to the shape of the leaves on a tree rather than the global shape of the tree.

Long-term memory. Memory for information that has left short-term memory and is unconscious until retrieved. Varieties of long-term memory include semantic, episodic, procedural, declarative, implicit, explicit, prospective, autobiographical and meta memory.

Master map of locations. A component of feature integration theory. In order to combine features represented on individual feature maps, the master map is referred to, which represents all features present at a particular location on all maps.

Mental rotation. The ability to mentally manipulate an image to determine if it matches another shape. Mental rotation appears to be an analogue process.

Modality effect. The finding that visually presented word lists are better recalled than auditorily presented lists.

Monocular cues. Cues to the visual perception of depth that only require the use of one eye.

Mood congruency. The finding that items learned in a particular mood state are best recalled if the same mood state is reinstated at the time of memory retrieval.

Negative recency. If a number of lists have been recalled in a serial position experiment, and then at the end all lists are asked for again in a final recall test, items that previously showed recency are now recalled worst of all.

Neurotransmitter substance. A range of chemicals that are released into the synapse between neurons that allow neural transmission to cross the synaptic gap.

Nociceptor. A receptor in the skin that detects damage and signals pain.

Object-centred. A representation of an object that is centred on its major axis and allows an object to be recognised irrespective of viewpoint.

Object file. A temporary representation of the results of feature integration that allows an object to be recognised.

Olivocochlear bundle. The final stage of auditory processing in the auditory system that sends information from the brain to the hair cells of the basilar membrane. Thought to be involved in setting selective attention.

Open-loop control. An action system controlled in such a way that the action sequence is triggered automatically and output is not constantly monitored or modified by feedback from the environment.

Optic array. The structured pattern of light falling on the retina.

Pacinian corpuscle. The major receptor in hairless areas of skin.

Parallel distributed processing. A computational model in which processing is distributed over many interconnected units working in parallel.

Partial report. Selective report of a subset of information on the basis of a cue.

Perceptual constancy. The phenomenon where, despite changes in the size or shape in the retinal image, an object is perceived as a constant shape or size; e.g., a person running toward you expands on the retina but is not perceived as growing.

Performance operating characteristic. A graph plotting the performance of one task against the performance of another concurrent task. If attentional resources are equally shared the graph will be a straight line, but if one task begins to demand more resources and the other task suffers, the line will reflect the way resources are allocated between tasks.

Perseveration. The persistent repetition of a previous action or mental process despite the intention to change it. A symptom of frontal lobe damage.

Phoneme. The smallest unit of the speech signal that can carry meaning.

Phonemic confusability. The confusion in memory of phonemes that share articulatory features.

Phonological loop. A component of Baddeley and Hitch's (1974) model of working memory, comprising a phonological store and articulatory loop. Responsible for maintaining short-term verbal information.

Pictorial cues. Monocular cues to depth in a two-dimensional representation, such as occlusion and linear perspective.

Pigeon-holing. A concept introduced by Broadbent (1970) to account for conceptual effects in selective attention.

Plans. A version of schema for representing generalised knowledge about everyday life.

Point localisation. The ability to point accurately to the place on the skin surface that is touched. This ability varies over the skin surface depending on the distribution of receptors.

Pop-out. An object will pop out from a display if it is detected in parallel and is different from all other items in the display.

Posterior attentional orienting system. A system believed to control low-level aspects of attention such as disengagement.

Power law of practice. The relationship between the amount of practice and improvement in performance. A law of diminishing returns: early in practice, improvement is much greater than later in practice.

Primacy effect. The recall advantage for the first few items in a list. Part of the serial position curve.

Primal sketch. The first level of processing in object description in Marr and Nishihara's (1978) model. It derives a representation of intensity changes, edges and contours.

Primary memory. An alternative term for short-term memory.

Primary motor cortex. The area of cortex responsible for sending signals to the muscle for making movements. Closely associated with the somatosensory cortex and arranged somatotopically.

Procedural knowledge. Knowledge for skills that cannot be made explicit and can only be demonstrated by performance.

Production system. A computational model based on IF–THEN condition action pairs. IF the rule is represented in working memory THEN the production stored in long-term memory is applied; e.g., Anderson's (1983) ACT* model.

Proprioception. Information from sensors in the joints and muscles tell the brain the positions of body parts.

Propositional representations. Language-like memory representations stored as truth statements.

Prospective memory. Long-term memory for actions and plans to be carried out in the future.

Prototype. A representation of the characteristic attributes, or best example of a concept.

Psychological refractory period. The time delay between the response to two overlapping signals that reflects the time required for the first response to be organised before the response to the second signal can be organised.

Random dot stereogram. A pair of dot patterns, one of which is displaced in relation to the other, such that when viewed binocularly a three-dimensional shape appears as a result of retinal disparity.

Reality monitoring. A term used to describe the differentiation of real from imagined events on the basis of episodic and source information.

Recency effect. The report advantage of the most recently presented items in a supraspan list.

Receptive field. The receptive field of a cell; for example, in vision, it is the area of retina that, when stimulated, will affect the firing of that cell.

Recollective experience. The experience in memory retrieval of the event of the memory itself.

Redundancy. This refers to the fact that more information than necessary for identification is present in the incoming data and so decisions can be made on the basis of only partial information, the remainder being redundant.

Rehearsal. The vocal or subvocal repetition of verbal information used to retain it in short-term memory.

Representation. Any symbol or set of symbols that stands for or represents something, usually in the absence of what is being represented.

Resource-limited. A task is resource limited when there are no more attentional resources available to improve or support performance.

Retinotopic. A representation of a pattern of stimulation in the brain that is distributed in space in the same way as it is distributed on the retina.

Retrospective memory. Memory for past events.

Saccade. The movement of the eyes during which information uptake is suppressed. Between saccades the eyes make fixations during which there is information uptake at the fixated area.

Schema. Organised packets of knowledge stored in long-term memory involved in the encoding and interpretation of the environment, events and people.

Scripts. A version of schema, particularly concerned with how to act in social situations.

Secondary memory. Another term for long-term memory, used by William James (1890), Waugh and Norman (1965) and Craik and Lockhart (1972).

Semantic memory. Long-term memory for facts, general knowledge, language. The store for what we know.

Sensory homunculus. A distorted shape of a person that represents body parts in proportion to the area of sensory cortex dedicated to processing information from the different areas of the body.

Sentence verification task. A task in which a participant is asked to decide as quickly as possible whether the given sentence is true or false. For example, 'Can canaries fly?' Used to probe the structure of semantic memory.

Serial position curve. When a list of words that must be remembered is longer than that which can be held in short-term memory, the first and last items in the list are more accurately recalled than items from the middle of the list.

Shadowing. Used in a dichotic listening task. Participants repeat aloud, or shadow, the attended message.

Short-term memory. A memory system that holds information in conscious awareness. Usually applied to verbal material, but can also hold visual images. See also **working memory**, the **phonological loop** and the **visuo-spatial sketch pad**.

Simultanagnosia. The phenomenon in which a patient is unable to 'see' two stimuli at once. Usually a result of parietal damage and associated with visual neglect.

Size constancy. A pictorial cue to depth based on the known size of objects.

Slips of action. Errors in carrying out sequences of actions, e.g., where a step in the sequence is omitted, or an appropriate action is made but to the wrong object.

Somatosensory cortex. The strip of cortex running over the top of the head, roughly from ear to ear, that is responsible for processing information received from the receptors in the skin.

Somatotopic map. The orderly pattern of representation of body parts and the skin surface that is laid out in the cortex in the same spatial relationship as the body parts.

Source information. Information encoded with a memory that specifies the time and place that the information was encoded.

Spatial medium. A hypothetical component of Kosslyn's computational theory of imagery, which preserves the spatial relations between parts of an image and has properties similar to the retina.

Spinal gate control theory. A theory of pain perception that allows for the influence of cognitive factors in opening or closing the 'gate' for pain perception.

Split span technique. Used in dichotic listening experiments. A sequence of words is presented alternately to the ears, but the participants asked to report the messages from each ear in turn.

Spontaneous generalisation. A property of connectionist and parallel distributed models that allows the properties or features of known examples to be applied to new examples.

Spreading activation. The concept that activity spreads among related concepts in semantic memory, which is used to account for priming effects between related stimuli.

State dependency. When material is learned in a particular mood or physiological state, memory performance is best when the participant is in the same state at recall.

Stereopsis. A cue to depth perception based on the retinal disparity.

Stimulus–response compatibility. This refers to how direct the mapping between a stimulus and its response is. A stimulus of a spoken word is more compatible with repeating the word than, for example, with pointing to a written word on a page.

Stroop effect. The effect of a well-learned response to a stimulus slowing the ability to make the less well-learned response. For example, naming the ink colour of a colour word.

Subvocal articulation. Making movements of the vocal apparatus used to pronounce words without producing the words aloud.

Suffix effect. The effect of an irrelevant item presented at the end of a list for serial recall, such as 'recall', on reducing the probability for recall of the last item of a list.

Supervisory attentional system. A component of Norman and Shallice's model of intentional control. It is the system that uses attentional biasing to allow the intended schema to take control of action.

Supplementary motor area. A part of the cortex adjoining the rest of the motor cortex that is involved in making voluntary movements.

Synergistic ecphory. The combined activity of a cue and a memory trace, or engram, that work together to retrieve a memory.

Template theory. An early theory of pattern recognition that proposed that recognition involves matching perceptual input to templates stored in memory. Not successful, as there are too many variations in the perceptual features of patterns.

Texture density gradient. The change in visible texture of a surface as it recedes into the distance.

Timbre. A complex sound form that is characteristic of a musical instrument. In addition to the frequency of the musical tone produced, resonances in the instrument add harmonics that change the sound property of the tone.

Top-down processing. Processing in which knowledge and expectations in memory act back on the stimulus to interpret it.

Transfer appropriate processing. Processing in which the most appropriate level is selected for the ongoing task. A flexible approach allowing for a fit between task and memory demands.

Type I processing. One of the types of rehearsal in the levels of processing approach, in which information is recirculated at the same level with no additional processing for depth.

Type II processing. According the levels of processing approach, this type involves recoding of information to another level of depth and leads to a more durable memory trace.

Typicality effect. The finding that more typical members of a category are recognised or categorised more quickly than less typical members.

Unilateral visual neglect. The inability of patients with brain damage (usually right parietal) to orient visual attention to the left side of space or an object, so that they effectively ignore it.

Utilisation behaviour. The inability to inhibit the action most frequently made to an object whenever an object is presented, for example, if a glass and water are in view a patient with this problem will fill the glass and drink, even if they have no conscious intention to do so.

Varied mapping. The condition in which a stimulus and its response are changed from trial to trial.

Ventral stream. A pathway in the brain that deals with the visual information for what objects are.

Viewer-centred. An object representation that is dependent on the viewpoint of the observer, which means as the observer or object moves, the representation will change.

Visual capture. In a situation where there is information from a number of sensory modalities but the information from vision dominates.

Visuo-spatial sketch pad. A component of Baddeley and Hitch's (1974) working memory model that holds visuo-spatial information necessary for manipulating images and predominantly spatial information.

Willed behaviour. The term used by James (1890) and Norman and Shallice (1986) for intentional, consciously controlled behaviour.

Word-length effect. The finding that the number of words that can be held in short-term memory depends on how long the words take to be articulated.

Working memory. A term used to encompass all components of short-term memory and the attentional control required to hold, rehearse and manipulate the information while it is worked on by other processes. Sometimes considered the active part of long-term memory and conscious awareness.

Solutions

Chapter 2, p. 25

1 Introspection is not objectively verifiable because no one can check if what the person introspecting is saying is true or not. Therefore it is not scientific. Introspection cannot be used for unconscious processes.

2 Hypothetical processing stages can be proposed and tested by measuring speed and accuracy of responses, which are objective measures. Both conscious and unconscious processes can be experimented on. Cognitive models can be tested using computer simulation and the performance of brain-damaged patients.

3 Top-down processes involve interpretation of incoming information in terms of existing knowledge. Bottom-up processing is dependent only on the information in the stimulus.

4 (a) Attention can be selective, divided, executive. Attention may be for perception or for action. It is sometimes considered a limited resource of processing capacity. In other models it is necessary for binding the properties of objects together.

(b) Perception involves the encoding of the physical world into sensory properties that the brain can represent. Perception produces interpretations of the state of the world and is involved in the identification of objects where they are and how we can act on them. The final output is a perceptual experience.

(c) Memory stores information, with different memories for different purposes. Memory may be for very brief storage of sensory data, short-term or long-term. Some memory is declarative, but procedural memories can only be demonstrated by doing a task. There is semantic memory for facts and general knowledge and episodic memory for personal experiences. Memory may also be implicit.

Chapter 3, p. 45

1 The absolute threshold is the physical magnitude at which a stimulus can be detected as being present. A just-noticeable difference is the difference in physical magnitude at which two stimuli can be judged as different.

2 People vary in confidence, they may get tired, bored or fail to maintain attention. There may be variability in the stimulus itself. Depending on instructions, observers may adopt different criteria.

3 It not only looks at correct detection, but also uses correct rejections, false alarms and misses to calculate the criterion being used, and the overlap between signals and noise in the system.

4 You were not sure if you heard your friend because the noise was a weak signal arriving in a noisy environment. Finding the stars in the sky is a similar problem. You friend could see the moving star, but you may not have been able to look in exactly the right place, or have had a different absolute threshold for detecting light or difference threshold for movement. The reason why stars to the edge of vision seem bright until you look at them will be explained if you read the next chapter.

Chapter 4, p. 72

1 All the binocular and monocular cues to depth and motion are in the scene in the park. You know the jogger is running toward you as his shape expands on the retina, and the children are in the distance because they are very small, and you know the size of children. The bird shows up when it moves because its shape moves as a whole against the background. You will find out why you were misled by the milk carton in the next chapter.

2 This is the problem of explaining how all the different features and properties of objects are correctly combined when we perceive an object.

3 This approach believes the percept is guided by stored knowledge. What we know helps us to construct an interpretation of the world in terms of what we know and expect.

4 No, because context can affect perception, and context is due to knowledge, which acts top-down.

5 Because the visual world is distributed in space, even simple features such as colour cannot be seen without also having a location.

Chapter 5, p. 99

1 Endogenous orienting is internally controlled by intention. Exogenous orienting is automatic and driven by external stimuli.

2 Unilateral neglect can be of visual space, reaching space, oro-facial space, representational space or object space.

3 Feature search is parallel and automatic and so not dependent on display size. Conjunction search is serial, necessary for forming a conjunction of features, and search time depends on display size.

4 It shows that more information is available in the visual display than can be reported before the initial representation is lost.

Chapter 6, p. 127

1 The patterns of visual information from the environment have been grouped into objects. Perceptual processes and feature integration (see previous chapters) have produced an organised set of shapes to be recognised. Object recognition processes allow the identification of the shapes of objects we know, even as we and they move. The dogs and people can be distinguished on the basis of the hierarchical arrangement of their axes, which also allow us to see them as invariant shapes despite their movement. We can read all different kinds of writing, even if it is obscured, using top-down knowledge of language.

2 There are too many variations in features for there to be memory representations for all possibilities.

3 Without a viewer-centred representation, objects would appear to change shape as we, or they, moved. It is important, therefore, for producing an invariant representation of an object.

4 As different modules are responsible for encoding different aspects of person knowledge, partial information can arise from the most activated modules leaving other information unavailable. Patients with prosopagnosia may have damage that prevents a module from working at all.

Chapter 7, p. 156

1 The sounds can be localised using the binaural cues of interaural intensity and time of arrival differences. Sounds that are similar will be grouped and localised together. We identify the sounds of objects because their auditory properties are stored in long-term memory. The conversation is easy to follow when there is redundancy in the language, but when you are unfamiliar with the topics, redundancy is reduced and in the noisy environment analysis can be aided by top-down knowledge. The siren is an illustration of the Doppler shift.

2 The visual environment is distributed in space, and persists in time, so if we need to we can look again. The auditory environment is composed of sounds that are distributed in time; it is not possible to listen to them again. We can move our eyes to search the environment, and close them if we wish. We cannot move or close our ears; searching the auditory environment must be based on internal mechanisms of selection.

3 Because phonemes change depending upon which other phonemes they are combined with, there is variation in the auditory signal. The problem then is how we perceive sounds as the same when in fact they are different.

4 As phonemes that are confusable are those that are similar in the way they are articulated, and the phonological loop uses articulation to maintain information, any errors are likely to be between phonemically similar words or letters.

Chapter 8, p. 181

1 This is the minimum distance on the skin at which the difference between being touched by two points and one is apparent. You can measure it using a psychophysical method (see Chapter 3) with two cocktail sticks.

2 When we touch our own skin, an efference copy of the motor command tells the brain to expect a sensory event at the place the action was directed to. The skin is always sensitive to touch, but the unpredictability of the sensation due to the absence of an efference copy when someone else touches us increases ticklishness.

3 Cognitive and emotional factors that might be intense during competition can close the gate that allows pain to be sensed. Once these have passed the gate will open and pain will be felt.

4 The somatosensory cortex once allocated to the amputated limb can be

invaded by neuronal input from the immediately adjacent cortical areas, so the sensation of a phantom limb will appear in the part of the body served by neighbouring regions of somatosensory cortex.

Chapter 9, p. 209

1 The faces on screen have moving lips to which we attribute the sounds of their voices. The theme music is not attributed to anything on the screen and is heard as background. Selective auditory attention can be directed to the people behind, but as the conversation is selected the auditory information from the film cannot be processed at the same time.

2 Broadbent (1958) proposed that only information with the physical properties used for selective passage through the filter would be available for report. However, it was shown that semantic information without the to-be-selected physical properties could sometimes break through the filter, which should not be possible.

3 A ventriloquist exploits visual dominance. By speaking without moving his mouth, but moving the dummy mouth in synchrony with the speech we can hear, the ventriloquist is able to produce the illusion that the dummy is speaking. We hear the sound as originating from where we see it.

4 Whichever sense data provides the best information about the judgement a task requires will dominate.

Chapter 10, p. 238

1 You are not practised at cooking dinner and so many aspects require attentional resources because they are not automatic. Holding a conversation demands attention, which if withdrawn from cooking leads to errors. You mother is more practised and so needs to use less attentional processing. When you drive home, this is a skill you are practised at, and so you have attentional resources available for talking at the same time.

2 By practice. The more we practise, the more automatic a task becomes provided the relationship between stimuli and the responses they require remains the same.

3 By the attentional biasing of schema in memory so that the intended schema is the most active.

4 This is knowledge for how to do something, usually applied to skills, and not explicitly available. It can only be demonstrated by doing the task.

Chapter 11, p. 273

1 The primacy portion of the serial position curve reflects the output of information that has been sufficiently rehearsed to enter long-term memory. The recency portion is the current contents of short-term memory. The list items in between these portions have not entered long-term memory because they have not been rehearsed enough, and have been displaced from short-term memory.

2 Type I processing recirculates information at the same level without engaging in any deeper processing. Type II processing involves deeper processing and leads to a more durable trace.

3 The rules for solving complex problems involving control, rules of grammar and primed semantic knowledge.

4 As recognition is dependent on a previous recall stage, recall should not be possible for any item not recognised.

Chapter 12, p. 301

1 The phonological loop holds and manipulates verbal information, and is automatically accessed by speech. The visuo-spatial sketch pad holds and manipulates visual information and images; it is predominantly spatial. The central executive is the control system that is involved in problem solving and planning and controlling the other systems.

2 Analogue representations have a one-to-one relationship with the real-world information they represent, and are usually applied to mental imagery. Propositions are language-like statements of truth and can represent knowledge that is abstract, and in principle all other types of knowledge.

3 We have schematic knowledge, sometimes referred to as scripts, that enables us to use past experiences to interpret and act in social situations.

4 A representation in which knowledge is distributed across many small interconnected units that work in parallel to come to a best-guess solution to any information by the interaction between top-down and bottom-up processes.

References

Abelson, R. (1975) Concepts for representing mundane reality in plans. In: D. G. Bobrow and A. M. Collins (eds) *Representation and Understanding: Studies in Cognitive Science.* New York: Academic Press.

Aitkenhead, A. M. and Slack, J. M. (1985) *Issues in Cognitive Modelling.* Hove, UK: Lawrence Erlbaum Associates Ltd.

Allport, A. (1987) Selection for action: Some behavioural and neurophysiological considerations of attention and action. In: H. Heuer and A. F. Sanders (eds) *Perspectives on Perception and Action.* Hillsdale, NJ: Lawrence Erlbaum Associates Inc.

Allport, A. (1988) What concept of consciousness? In: A. J. Marcel and E. Bisiach (eds) *Consciousness in Contemporary Science.* Oxford, Oxford University Press.

Allport, A. (1989) Visual attention. In: M. I. Posner (ed) *Foundations of Cognitive Science.* A Bradford book. Cambridge MA. MIT Press.

Allport, A. (1993) Attention and control: Have we been asking the wrong questions? A critical review of twenty-five years. In: D. E. Meyer and S. M. Kornblum (eds) *Attention and Performance, XIV:*

Synergies in Experimental Psychology, Artificial Intelligence and Cognitive Neuroscience. A Bradford book. Cambridge, MA: MIT Press.

Allport, A. Styles, E. A. and Hseih, S. (1994) Shifting intentional set: Exploring the dynamic control of tasks. In: C. Umilta and M. Moscovitch (eds) *Attention and Performance XV, Conscious and Nonconscious Information Processing.* Cambridge, MA: MIT Press.

Allport, D. A. (1977) On knowing the meaning of words we are unable to report: The effects of visual masking. In: S. Dornic (ed) *Attention and Performance VI.* Hillsdale, NJ: Lawrence Erlbaum Associates Inc.

Allport, D. A. (1980) Attention and performance. In: G. Claxton (ed) *Cognitive Psychology: New Directions.* London: Routledge and Kegan Paul.

Anderson, J. R. (1983) *The architecture of cognition.* Cambridge, MA: Harvard University Press.

Anderson, J. R. and Bower, G. H. (1972) Configural properties in sentence memory. *Journal of Verbal Learning and Verbal Behavior,* 11, 594–605.

Atkinson, R. C. and Shiffrin, R. M. (1968) Human memory: A proposed system and control processes. In: K. W. Spence and J. D. Spence (eds) *The Psychology of Learning and Motivation, Vol. 2.* New York: Academic Press.

Baddeley, A. D. (1986) *Working Memory.* Oxford: Oxford University Press.

Baddeley, A. D. (1993) Working memory or working attention? In: A. Baddeley and L. Weiskrantz (eds) *Attention: Selection, Awareness and Control: A Tribute to Donald Broadbent.* Oxford: Oxford University Press.

Baddeley, A. D. (1997) *Human Memory: Theory and Practice* (rev ed) Hove, UK: Psychology Press.

Baddeley, A. D. (2000) The episodic buffer: A new component of working memory? *Trends in Cognitive Sciences,* 4(11), 417–423.

Baddeley, A. D. and Hitch, G. J. (1974) Working memory. In: G. H. Bower (ed) *The Psychology of Learning and Motivation, Vol. 8.* London: Academic Press.

Baddeley, A. D., Lewis, V., Eldridge, M. and Thomson, N. (1984) Attention and retrieval from long-term memory. *Journal of Experimental Psychology: General,* 113, 518–540.

Baddeley, A. D., Lewis, V. J. and Vallar, G. (1984) Exploring the articulatory loop. *Quarterly Journal of Experimental Psychology,* 36, 233–252.

Baddeley, A. D. and Lieberman, K. (1980) Spatial working memory. In: R. Nickerson (ed) *Attention and Performance VIII.* Hillsdale, NJ: Lawrence Erlbaum Associates Inc.

Baddeley, A. D., Thomson, N. and Buchanan, M. (1975) Word length and the structure of short-term memory. *Journal of Verbal Learning and Verbal Behavior*, 14, 575–589.

Baddeley, A. D. and Warrington, E. K. (1970) Amnesia and the distinction between long- and short-term memory. *Journal of Verbal Learning and Verbal Behavior*, 9, 176–189.

Barsalou, L. W. (1983) Ad hoc categories. *Memory and Cognition*, 11, 211–217.

Bartlett, F. C. (1932) *Remembering: A Study in Experimental and Social Psychology*. Cambridge: Cambridge University Press.

Beck, J. (1966) Effect of orientation and shape similarity on perceptual grouping. *Perception and Psychophysics*, 1, 300–302.

Beecher, H. K. (1956) Relationship of significance of wound to pain experienced. *Journal of the American Medical Association*, 161, 1609–1613.

Berry, D. C. and Broadbent, D. E. (1984) On the relationship between task performance and associated verbalisable knowledge. *Quarterly Journal of Experimental Psychology*, 36A, 209–231.

Berry, D. C. and Deines, Z. (1993) *Implicit Learning: Theoretical and Empirical Issues*. Hove, UK: Lawrence Erlbaum Associates Ltd.

Berti, A., Allport, A., Driver, J., Deines, Z., Oxbury, J. and Oxbury, S. (1992) Levels of processing for visual stimuli in an 'extinguished' field. *Neuropsychologia*, 30, 403–415.

Bianchi, L. (1985) The functions of the frontal lobes. *Brain*, 18, 497–530.

Biederman, I. (1987) Recognition by components: A theory of human image understanding. *Psychological Review*, 94, 115–147.

Biederman, I. and Cooper, E. E. (1991) Priming contour deleted images: Evidence for intermediate representations in visual object recognition. *Cognitive Psychology*, 23, 393–419.

Biederman, I. and Gerhardstein, P. C. (1993) Recognising depth rotated objects: Evidence for 3-D viewpoint invariance. *Journal of Experimental Psychology: Human Perception and Performance*, 19, 1162–1182.

Bisiach, E. (1988) Language without thought. In: L. Weiskrantz (ed) *Thought without Language*. Oxford: Oxford University Press.

Bisiach, E. and Luzatti, C. (1978) Unilateral neglect of representational space. *Cortex*, 14, 128–133.

Bisiach, E. and Vallar, G. (2000) Unilateral neglect in humans. In: F. Boller, F. Graffman and G. Rizolatti (eds) *Handbook of Neuropsychology, Vol. 1* (2nd ed). Amsterdam: Elsevier Science.

Blakemore, S.-J., Frith, C. D. and Wolpert, D. M. (1999) Spatio-temporal prediction modulates the perception of self-produced stimuli. *Journal of Cognitive Neuroscience*, 11, 551–559.

Blakemore, S. J., Wolpert, D. M. and Frith, C. D. (1998) Central cancellation of self-produced tickle sensation. *Nature Neuroscience*, 1, 635–640.

Blakemore, S.-J., Wolpert, D. M. and Frith, C. D. (2000) Why can't we tickle ourselves? *NeuroReport*, 11, R11–16.

Blanz, V., Tarr, M. J. and Bulthoff, H. H. (1999) What object attributes determine canonical views? *Perception*, 28, 575–600.

Bliss, J. C., Crane, H. D., Mansfield, P. K. and Townsend, J. T. (1966) Information available in brief tactile presentations. *Perception and Psychophysics*, 8, 273–283.

Bodamer, J. (1947) Die Prosop-Agnosie. *Archiv für Psychiatrie und Nervenkrankheiten*, 179, 6–53.

Bower, G. H., Gilligan, S. G. and Monteiro, K. P. (1981) Selective learning caused by affective states. *Journal of Experimental Psychology: General*, 110, 451–473.

Brandimonte, M. A., Einstein, G. O. and McDaniel, M. A. (eds) (1996) *Prospective Memory: Theory and Applications*. Mahwah, NJ: Lawrence Erlbaum Associates Inc.

Bregman, A. S. (1990) *Auditory Scene Analysis*. Cambridge, MA: MIT Press.

Broadbent, D. E. (1954) The role of auditory localisation in attention and memory span. *Journal of Experimental Psychology*, 47, 191–196.

Broadbent, D. E. (1958) *Perception and Communication*. London: Pergamon Press.

Broadbent, D. E. (1971) *Decision and Stress*. London: Academic Press.

Broadbent, D. E. (1982) Task combination and selective intake of information. *Acta Psychologia*, 50, 253–290.

Broadbent, D. E. (1984) The Maltese Cross: A new simplistic model for memory. *Behavioural and Brain Sciences*, 7, 55–68.

Brooks, L. (1968) Spatial and verbal components in the act of recall. *Canadian Journal of Psychology*, 22, 349–368.

Brooks, L. and Baddeley, A. D. (1976) What can amnesic patients learn? *Neuropsychologia*, 14, 111–122.

Brown, J. (1958) Some tests of the decay theory of immediate memory. *Quarterly Journal of Experimental Psychology*, 10, 12–21.

Bruce, V. (1996) Introduction: Soluble and insoluble mysteries of the mind. In: V. Bruce (ed) *Unsolved Mysteries of the Mind*. Hove, UK: Erlbaum (UK) Taylor and Francis.

Bruce, V., Green, P. R. and Georgeson, M. A. (1996) *Visual Perception:*

Physiology, Psychology and Ecology (3rd ed). Hove, UK: Psychology Press.

Bruce, V. and Young, A. W. (1986) Understanding face recognition. *British Journal of Psychology*, 77, 305–327.

Bruce, V. and Young, A. (1998) *In the Eye of the Beholder: The Science of Face Perception*. New York: Oxford University Press.

Bruner, J. S. and Goodman, C. D. (1947) Value and need as organising factors in perception. *Journal of Abnormal and Social Psychology*, 42, 33–44.

Bunderson, C. (1990) A theory of visual attention. *Psychological Review*, 97, 523–547.

Burton, A. M. and Bruce, V. (1993) Naming faces and naming names: Exploring an interactive activation model of person recognition. *Memory*, 1, 457–480.

Campbell, R. and Dodd, B. (1980) Hearing by eye. *Quarterly Journal of Experimental Psychology*, 32, 85–99.

Carlson, N. R. (1999) *Physiology of Behaviour* (6th ed). Needham Heights, MA: Allyn and Bacon.

Carlyon, R. P., Cusack, R., Foxton, J. M. and Robertson, I. H. (2001) Effects of attention and unilateral neglect on auditory stream segregation. *Journal of Experimental Psychology: Human Perception and Performance*, 27, 115–127.

Chase, W. G. and Ericsson, K. A. (1982) Skill and working memory. In: G. H. Bower (ed) *The Psychology of Learning and Motivation, Vol. 16* (pp. 1–58). New York: Academic Press.

Chase, W. G. and Simon, H. A. (1973) Perception in chess. *Cognitive Psychology*, 4, 55–81.

Cherry, E. C. (1953) Some experiments on the recognition of speech with one and two ears. *Journal of the Acoustical Society of America*, 25, 975–979.

Cinel, C., Humphreys, G. W. and Poli, R. (2002) Cross-modal illusory conjunctions between vision and touch. *Journal of Experimental Psychology: Human Perception and Performance*, 28, 1243–1266.

Clark, D. M. and Teasdale, J. D. (1982) Diurnal variation in clinical depression and accessibility of positive and negative experiences. *Journal of Abnormal Psychology*, 91, 87–95.

Claxton, G. (1980) Cognitive psychology: A suitable case for what sort of treatment? In: G. Claxton (ed) *Cognitive Psychology: New Directions*. London: Routledge and Kegan Paul.

Cohen, G. (1989) *Memory in the Real World*. Hove, UK: Lawrence Erlbaum Associates Ltd.

Cohen, G. (1996) *Memory in the Real World* (2nd ed). Hove, UK: Psychology Press.

Cohen, G., Eysenck, M. W. and Le Voi, M. E. (1986) *Memory: A Cognitive Approach*. Milton Keynes, UK: Open University Press.

Colle, H. A. and Welsh, A. (1976) Acoustic masking in primary memory. *Journal of Verbal Learning and Verbal Behavior*, 15, 17–32.

Collins, A. M. and Quillian, M. R. (1969) Retrieval time from semantic memory. *Journal of Verbal Learning and Verbal Behavior*, 8, 240–247.

Coltheart, M. (1980) Iconic memory and visible persistence. *Perception and Psychophysics*, 27, 183–228.

Conrad, R. (1964) Acoustic confusions in immediate memory. *British Journal of Psychology*, 55, 75–84.

Conrad, R. and Hull, A. J. (1964) Information, acoustic confusion and memory span. *British Journal of Psychology*, 55, 429–432.

Conway, R. A., Cowan, N. and Bunting, M. F. (2001) The cocktail party revisited: The importance of working memory capacity. *Psychonomic Bulletin and Review*, 8, 331–335.

Corkin, S. (1968) Acquisition of motor skill after bi-lateral medial temporal-lobe excision. *Neuropsychologia*, 6, 255–265.

Corteen, R. S. and Dunn, D. (1973) Shock associated words in a non-attended message: A test for momentary awareness. *Journal of Experimental Psychology*, 94, 308–313.

Corteen, R. S. and Wood, B. (1972) Autonomous responses to shock associated words in an unattended channel. *Journal of Experimental Psychology*, 94, 308–313.

Craik, F. I. M. (1970) The fate of primary memory items in free recall. *Journal of Verbal Learning and Verbal Behavior*, 9, 143–148.

Craik, F. I. M. (2001) Effects of dividing attention on encoding and retrieval processes. In: H. L. Roediger III, J. S. Nairne, I. Neath and A. M. Suprenant (eds) *The Nature of Remembering: Essays in Honour of Robert G. Crowder*, Washington, DC: American Psychological Association.

Craik, F. I. M. and Lockhart, R. S. (1972) Levels of processing: A framework for memory research. *Journal of Verbal Learning and Verbal Behavior*, 11, 671–684.

Crowder, R. G. (1976) *Principles of Learning and Memory*. Hillsdale, NJ: Lawrence Erlbaum Associates Inc.

Crowder, R. G. and Morton, J. (1969) Pre-categorical acoustic storage. *Perception and Psychophysics*, 5, 365–373.

Cutting, J. E. and Rosner, B. S. (1974) Categories and boundaries in speech and music. *Perception and Psychophysics*, 16, 564–570.

Darwin, C., Turvey, M. and Crowder, R. (1972) An auditory analogue of the Sperling partial report procedure: Evidence for brief auditory storage. *Cognitive Psychology*, 3, 255–267.

Deese, J. (1959) Influence on inter-item associative strength on immediate free recall. *Psychological Reports*, 5, 305–312.

de Fockert, J. W., Rees, G., Frith, C. D. and Lavie, N. (2001) The role of working memory in visual selective attention. *Science*, 291 (5509), 1803–1806.

Deutsch, D. (ed) (1982) *The Psychology of Music*. New York: Academic Press.

Deutsch, J. A. and Deutsch, D. (1963) Attention, some theoretical considerations. *Psychological Review*, 70, 80–90.

Dick, A. O. (1969) Relations between the sensory register and short-term storage in tachistoscopic recognition. *Journal of Experimental Psychology*, 82, 279–284.

Driver, J. (1996) Enhancement of selective listening by illusory mislocation of speech sounds due to lip-reading. *Nature*, 381, 66–68.

Driver, J. and Halligan, P. W. (1991) Can visual neglect operate in object centred co-ordinates? An affirmative case study. *Cognitive Neuropsychology*, 8, 475–496.

Driver, J. and Spence, C. J. (1994) Spatial synergies between auditory and visual attention. In: C. Umilta and M. Moscovitch (eds) *Attention and Performance XV: Conscious and Nonconscious Information Processing*. Cambridge MA: MIT Press.

Driver, J. and Spence, C. J. (1999) Cross-modal links in spatial attention. In: G. W. Humphreys, J. Duncan and A. Treisman (eds) *Attention, Space and Action*. Oxford: Oxford University Press.

Duncan, J. (1986) Disorganisation of behaviour after frontal lobe damage. *Cognitive Neuropsychology*, 3, 271–290.

Duncan, J. (1999) Converging levels of analysis in the cognitive neurosciences. In: G. W. Humphreys, J. Duncan and A. Treisman (eds) *Attention, Space and Action*. Oxford: Oxford University Press.

Duncan, J. and Humphreys, G. W. (1989) Visual search and visual similarity. *Psychological Review*, 96, 433–458.

Duncan, J. and Humphreys, G. W. (1992) Beyond the search surface: Visual search and attentional engagement. *Journal of Experimental Psychology: Human Perception and Performance*, 18, 578–588.

Eccleston, C. (1994) Chronic pain and attention: A cognitive approach. *British Journal of Clinical Psychology*, 33, 535–547.

Eccleston, C. (1995) Chronic pain and attention: An experimental investigation into the role of sustained and shifting attention in the processing of chronic pain. *Behavioural Research Therapy*, 33, 391–404.

Eccleston, C. and Crombez, G. (1999) Pain demands attention: A cognitive-affective model of the interruptive function of pain. *Psychological Bulletin*, 125, 356–366.

Eimas, P. D. and Corbit, J. D. (1973) Selective adaptation of linguistic feature detectors. *Cognitive Psychology*, 4, 99–109.

Eimas, P. D., Miller, J. L. and Jusczyk, P. W. (1971) Speech perception in infants. *Science*, 171, 303–306.

Ekman, P. (1982) *Emotion and the Human Face*. Cambridge: Cambridge University Press.

Ekman, P. (1992) Facial expressions of emotion: An old controversy and new findings. *Philosophical Transactions of the Royal Society of London, B*, 335, 63–69.

Ellis, A. W. and Young, A. W. (1988) *Human Cognitive Neuropsychology*. Hove, UK: Lawrence Erlbaum Associates Ltd.

Ellis, A. W. and Young, A. W. (1996) *Human Cognitive Neuropsychology* (2nd ed). Hove, UK: Psychology Press.

Ellis, J. (1996) Prospective memory for the realisation of delayed intentions: A conceptual framework. In: M. Brandimonte, G. O. Einstein, and M. A. McDaniel (eds) *Prospective Memory: Theory and Applications*. Hillsdale, NJ: Lawrence Erlbaum Associates Inc.

Ericsson, K. A. and Kintsch, W. (1995) Long-term working memory. *Psychological Review*, 102, 211–245.

Ericsson, K. A. and Oliver, W. (1984, November) *Skilled Memory in Blindfold Chess*. Paper presented at the annual meeting of the Psychonomic Society, San Antonio, TX.

Ericsson, K. A. and Staszewski, J. (1989) Skilled memory and expertise: Mechanisms of exceptional performance. In: D. Klahr and K. Kotovsky (eds) *Complex Information Processing: The Impact of Herbert A. Simon* (pp 235–267) Hillsdale, NJ: Lawrence Erlbaum Associates Inc.

Eriksen, C. W. and Murphy, T. D. (1987) Movement of attentional focus across the visual field: A critical look at the evidence. *Perception and Psychophysics*, 42, 299–305.

Eriksen, C. W. and St. James, J. D. (1986) Visual attention within and around the field of focal attention: A zoom lens model. *Perception and Psychophysics*, 40, 225–240.

Eslinger, P. J. and Damasio, A. R. (1985) Severe disturbance of higher cognition after bi-lateral frontal ablation: Patient E.V.R. *Neurology*, 35, 1731–1741.

Eysenck, M. (1982) *Attention and Arousal: Cognition and Performance*. New York: Springer.

Eysenck, M. W. and Keane, M. T. (2000) *Cognitive Psychology: A Student's Handbook* (4th ed). Hove, UK: Psychology Press.

Farah, M. J. and Aguirre, G. K. (1999) Imaging visual recognition: PET and fMRI studies of the functional anatomy of human visual recognition. *Trends in Cognitive Sciences*, 3, 179–186.

Farah, M. J., Wilson, K. D., Drain, M. and Tanaka, J. N. (1998) What is special about face perception? *Psychological Review*, 105, 482–498.

Fechner, G. (1860) *Elements of psychophysics*. (English edition: Vol. 1, edited by H. E. Adler, D. H. Howes, and E. G. Boring, 1966.) New York: Holt Rinehart and Winston.

Fernandes, M. A. and Moscovitch, M. (2002) Factors modulating the effect of divided attention during retrieval of words. *Memory and Cognition*, 30, 731–744.

Fernandez, E. and Turk, D. C. (1989) The utility of cognitive coping strategies for altering pain perception: A meta-analysis. *Pain*, 38, 123–135.

Fitts, P. M. (1962) Factors in complex skill training. In: R. Glaser (ed) *Training Research and Education*. Pittsburgh PA: University of Pittsburgh Press. [Reprinted 1990. In: M. Venturino (ed) *Selected readings in human factors* (pp. 275–296) Santa Monica, CA: Human Factors Society.]

Fitts, P. M. and Posner, M. I. (1973) *Human Performance*. Basic Concepts in Psychology series. London: Prentice Hall.

Flanagan, J. R., Wing, A. M., Allison, S. and Spenceley, A. (1995) Effects of surface texture on weight perception when lifting objects with a precision grip. *Perception and Psychophysics*, 57, 282–290.

Fodor, J. A. (1983) *Modularity of Mind*. Cambridge MA: MIT Press.

Foley, J. M. (1980) Binocular distance perception. *Psychological Review*, 47, 411–435.

Frith, C. D. (1992) *The Cognitive Psychology of Schizophrenia*. Hove, UK: Lawrence Erlbaum Associates Ltd.

Gabrielli, J. D. E. (1998) Cognitive neuroscience of human memory. *Annual Review of Psychology*, 49, 87–115.

Gabrielli, J. D. E., Carillo, M. C., Cermak, L. S., McGlinchey Berroth, R., Gluck. M. A. and Disterhoft, J. F. (1995) Intact delay-eye blink classical conditioning in amnesia. *Behavioural Neuroscience*, 109, 819–827.

Gardiner, J. Gathercole, S. E. and Gregg, V. H. (1983) Further evidence of interference between lip-reading and auditory recency. *Journal of Experimental Psychology: Learning Memory and Cognition*, 9, 328–333.

Gathercole, S. E., Gregg, V. H. and Gardiner, J. M. (1983) Influences of delayed distraction on the modality effect in free recall, *British Journal of Psychology*, 74, 223–232.

Gautier, I., Behrmann, M. and Tarr, M. J. (1999) Can face recognition really be dissociated from object recognition? *Journal of Cognitive Neuroscience*, 11 (4), 349–370.

Gautier, I., Skudlarski, P., Gore, J. C. and Anderson, A. W. (2000) Expertise for cars and birds recruits brain areas involved in face recognition. *Nature Neuroscience*, 2 (6), 191–197.

Gentilucci, M. and Rizzolatti, G. (1990) Cortical motor control of arm and hand movements. In: M. A. Goodale (ed) *Vision and Action: The Control of Grasping*. Norwood, NJ: Ablex.

Gibson, J. J. (1950) *The Perception of the Visual World*. Boston: Houghton Mifflin.

Gibson, J. J. (1966) *The Senses Considered and Perceptual Systems*. Boston: Houghton Mifflin.

Gibson, J. J. (1979) *The ecological approach to vision*. Boston: Houghton Mifflin.

Gillie, T. and Broadbent, D. E. (1989) What makes interruptions disruptive? A study of length, similarity and complexity. *Psychological Research*, 50, 243–250.

Glanzer, M. and Cunitz, A. R. (1966) Two storage mechanisms in free recall. *Journal of Verbal Learning and Verbal Behavior*, 5, 351–360.

Glenberg, A. M., Bradley, M. M., Stevenson, J. A., Kraus, T. A., Tkachuk, M. J., Gretz, A. L., Fish, J. H. and Turpin, B. A. M. (1980) A two process account of long-term serial position effects. *Journal of Experimental Psychology: Human Learning and Memory*, 8, 355–369.

Glucksberg, S. and Cowan, G. N. (1970) Memory for non-attended auditory material. *Cognitive Psychology*, 1, 149–156.

Godden, D. and Baddeley, A. D. (1975) Context-dependent memory in two natural environments: On land and under water. *British Journal of Psychology*, 66, 325–331.

Godden, D. and Baddeley, A. D. (1980) When does context influence recognition memory? *British Journal of Psychology*, 71, 712–724.

Goff, L. M. and Roediger, H. L., III (1998) Imagination inflation for action events: Repeated imaginings lead to illusory recollections. *Memory and Cognition*, 26, 20–33.

Goodale, M. A. and Milner, A. D. (1992) Separate visual pathways for perception and action. *Trends in Neuroscience*, 15, 20–25.

Goodwin, D. W. (1974) Alcoholic blackout and state dependent learning. *Federation Proceedings*, 33, 1833–1835.

Graf, P. and Schacter, D. L. (1985) Implicit and explicit memory for new associations in normal and amnesic subjects. *Journal of Experimental Psychology: Learning Memory and Cognition*, 11, 501–518.

Green, D. M. and Swets, J. A. (1966) *Signal detection theory and psychophysics*. New York: John Wiley.

Greenberg, G. and Larkin, W. (1968) Frequency-response characteristic of auditory observers detecting signals of a single frequency in noise: The probe-signal method. *Journal of the Acoustical Society of America*, 44, 1513–1523.

Greenwald, A. G. and Shulman, H. G. (1973) On doing two things at once: II. Elimination of the psychological refractory period. *Journal of Experimental Psychology*, 101, 70–76.

Gregory, R. L. (1967) *Eye and Brain: The Psychology of Seeing*. Oxford: Oxford University Press.

Gregory, R. L. (1970) *The Intelligent Eye*. London: Weidenfeld and Nicholson.

Gregory, R. L. (1980) Perception as hypotheses. *Philosophical Transactions of the Royal Society of London, B*, 290, 181–197.

Gregory, R. L. (1998) *Eye and Brain* (5th ed). Oxford: Oxford University Press.

Gray, J. A. and Wedderburn, A. A. (1960) Grouping strategies with simultaneous stimuli. *Quarterly Journal of Experimental Psychology*, 12, 180–184.

Gross, R. and McIlveen, R. (1999) *Perspectives in Psychology*. London: Hodder and Stoughton.

Guttman, N. and Julesz, B. (1963) Lower limits of auditory periodicity analysis. *Journal of the Acoustical Society of America*, 35, 610.

Handel, S. (1989) *Listening*. Cambridge MA: MIT Press.

Hasselmo, M. E., Rolls, E. T. and Baylis, G. C. (1989) The role of expression and identity in the selective responses of neurons in the temporal visual cortex of the monkey. *Behavioural Brain Research*, 32, 203–218.

Hay, J. C., Pick, H. L. and Ikeda, K. (1965) Visual capture produced by prism spectacles. *Psychonomic Science*, 2, 215–216.

Hernandez-Peon, R., Scherrer, H. and Jouvet, M. (1956) Modulation of selective activity in cochlear nucleus during 'attention' in unanesthetized cats. *Science*, 123, 331–332.

Hewitt, K. (1973) *Context Effects in Memory: A Review*. Cambridge: Cambridge University Psychological Laboratory.

REFERENCES

Hitch, G. J. and Baddeley, A. D. (1976) Verbal reasoning and working memory. *Quarterly Journal of Experimental Psychology*, 28, 603–631.

Hollingworth, A. and Henderson, J. M. (2002) Accurate visual memory for previously attended objects in natural scenes. *Journal of Experimental Psychology: Human Perception and Performance*, 28, 113–136.

Hubel, D. H. and Wiesel, T. N. (1959) Receptive fields, binocular interaction and functional architecture in the cat's visual cortex. *Journal of Physiology*, 160, 106–154.

Hubel, D. H. and Wiesel, T. N. (1970) Stereopsis vision in the macaque monkey. *Nature*, 225, 41–42.

Humphreys, G. W. and Bruce, V. (1989) *Visual Cognition: Computational, Experimental and Neuropsychological Perspectives*. Hove, UK: Lawrence Erlbaum Associates Ltd.

Humphreys, G. W. and Riddoch, M. J. (1993) Interactions between object and space systems revealed through neuropsychology. In: D. E. Meyer and S. M. Kornblum (eds) *Attention and Performance, Vol. XVI*. London: MIT Press.

Huppert, F. A. and Piercy, M. (1976) Recognition memory in amnesic patients: Effect of temporal context and familiarity of material. *Cortex*, 12, 3–20.

Hyde, T. S. and Jenkins, J. J. (1973) Recall of words as a function of semantic, graphic and syntactic orienting tasks. *Journal of Verbal Learning and Verbal Behavior*, 12, 471–480.

Igarashi, M., Alford, D. R., Gordon, W. P. and Nakai, V. (1974) Behavioural auditory function after transection of crossed olivo-cochlear bundle in the cat: Conditioned visual performance with intense white noise. *Acta Otolarangol* (Stockholm), 77, 311–317.

Jacoby, L. L., Ste-Marie, D. and Toth, J. P. (1993) Redefining automaticity: Unconscious influences, awareness and control. In: A. Baddeley and L. Weiskrantz (eds) *Attention Awareness, and Control: A Tribute to Donald Broadbent*. Oxford: Oxford University Press.

Jacoby, L. L. and Witherspoon, D. (1982) Remembering without awareness. *Canadian Journal of Psychology*, 36, 300–324.

James, W. (1890) *The Principles of Psychology*. New York: Holt.

Janowsky, J. S., Shimamura, A. P. and Squire, L. R. (1989) Source memory impairment in patients with frontal lobe lesions. *Neuropsychologia*, 27, 1043–1056.

Jarvis, M. (2000) *Theoretical Approaches to Psychology*. London: Routledge.

Johnson, M. K. (1988) Reality monitoring: An experimental phenomenological approach. *Journal of Experimental Psychology: General*, 117, 390–394.

Johnson, M. K., Raye, C. L., Wang, A. and Taylor, T. (1979) Facts and fantasy: The role of accuracy and variability in confusing imaginations with perceptual experiences. *Journal of Experimental Psychology: Human Learning and Memory*, 5, 229–246.

Johnston, W. A. and Heinz, S. P. (1979) Depth of non-target processing in an attention task. *Journal of Experimental Psychology*, 5, 168–175.

Jones, D. M. (1999) The cognitive psychology of auditory distraction: The 1997 BPS Broadbent lecture. *British Journal of Psychology*, 90, 167–187.

Jonides, J. (1981) Voluntary versus automatic control over the mind's eye. In: J. Long and A. D. Baddeley (eds) *Attention and Performance XI*. Hillsdale, NJ: Lawrence Erlbaum Associates Inc.

Julesz, B. (1971) *Foundations of Cyclopean Perception*. Chicago: Chicago University Press.

Kahneman, D. (1973) *Attention and Effort*. Englewood Cliffs, NJ: Prentice Hall.

Kahneman, D. and Treisman, A. M. (1984) Changing views of attention and automaticity. In: R. Parsuraman and D. R. Davies (eds) *Varieties of Attention*. Orlando, FL: Academic Press.

Kanwisher, N. (2000) Domain specificity in face perception. *Nature Neuroscience*, 3(8), 759–763.

Kanwisher, N., McDermott, J. and Chun, M. (1997) The fusiform face area: A module in human extrastriate cortex specialised for face perception. *The Journal of Neuroscience*, 17, 4302–4311.

Kennedy, J. M. (1984) The tangible world of the blind. *Encyclopedia Britannica Medical Health Annual*. Chicago, IL: Encyclopedia Britannica.

Kintsch, W. (1970) *Learning memory and conceptual processes*. New York: Wiley.

Kofka, K. (1935) *Principles of Gestalt Psychology*. New York: Harcourt Brace.

Koriat, A. and Ben-Zur, H. (1988) Remembering that I did it: Processes and deficits in output monitoring. In: M. M. Gruneberg, P. E. Morris and R. N. Sykes (eds) *Practical Aspects of Memory: Current Research and Issues, Vol. 1* (pp. 203–208). Chichester, UK: Wiley.

Kosslyn, S. M. (1980) *Image and Mind*. Cambridge, MA: Harvard University Press.

Kuhl, P. K. and Meltzoff, A. N. (1982) Bimodal perception of speech in infancy. *Science*, 218, 1138–1141.

Kuhl, P. K. and Miller, J. D. (1978) Speech perception by the chinchilla: Identification function for synthetic VOT stimuli. *Journal of the Acoustical Society of America*, 63, 905–917.

Kunnapas, T. M. (1968) Distance perception as a function of available visual cues. *Journal of Experimental Psychology*, 77, 523–529.

Laberge, D. (1983) Spatial extent of attention to letters and words. *Journal of Experimental Psychology: Human Perception and Performance*, 9, 371–379.

Laberge, D. (2000) Networks of attention. In: M. S. Gazzaniga (ed) *The new cognitive neurosciences* (pp. 711–724). Cambridge, MA: MIT Press.

Lackner, J. R. and Garrett, M. F. (1972) Resolving ambiguity: Effect of biasing context in the unattended ear. *Cognition*, 1, 359–372.

Laming, D. (1994) Psychophysics. In: R. L. Gregory and A. M. Colman (eds) *Sensation and Perception*. Harlow, UK: Longman.

Lavie, N. (1995) Perceptual load as a necessary condition for selective attention. *Journal of Experimental Psychology; Human Perception and Performance*, 21, 451–468.

Lavie, N., Hirst, A., deFockert, J. W. and Viding, E. (2004). Load theory of selective attention and cognitive control. *Journal of Experimental Psychology General*, 135(3), 339–354.

Leder, H. and Bruce, V. (2000) When inverted faces are recognised. *The Quarterly Journal of Experimental Psychology*, 53(a), 523–536.

Lederman, S. J., Thorne, G. and Jones, B. (1986) Perception of texture by vision and touch: Multidimensionality and intersensory integration. *Journal of Experimental Psychology: Human Perception and Performance*, 12, 169–180.

Levine, M. W. and Shefner, J. M. (2000). *Fundamentals of Sensation and Perception*. Oxford: Oxford University Press.

Levine, D. N., Warach, J. and Farah, M. J. (1985) Two visual systems in mental imagery: Dissociation of 'what' and 'where' in imagery disorders due to bilateral posterior cerebral lesions. *Neurology*, 35, 1010–1018.

Lhermitte, F. (1983) Utilisation behaviour and its relation to lesions in the frontal lobes. *Brain*, 106, 237–255.

Liberman, A. M., Cooper, F. S., Shankweiler, D. P. and Studdert-Kennedy, M. (1967) Perception of the speech code. *Psychological Review*, 74, 431–461.

Lien, M.-C., Procter, R. W. and Allen, P. A. (2002) Ideomotor compatibility in the psychological refractory period effect: 29 years of oversimplification. *Journal of Experimental Psychology: Human Perception and Performance*, 28, 396–409.

Lindsay, P. H. and Norman, D. A. (1972) *Human Information Processing*. New York: Academic Press.

Livingstone, F. and Hubel, D. H. (1987) Psychophysical evidence for separate channels for the perception of form, colour, movement and depth. *Journal of Neuroscience*, 7, 3416–3468.

Lloyd, G. G. and Lishman, W. A. (1975) Effect of depression on the speed of recall of pleasant and unpleasant experiences. *Psychological Medicine*, 5, 173–180.

Locke, J. (1929) *An Essay Concerning Human Understanding*. London: Oxford University Press. [First published 1690.]

Logan, G. D. (1996) The CODE theory of visual attention: An integration of space-based and object-based attention. *Psychological Review*, 103, 603–649.

Logie, R. H. (1986) Visuo-spatial processing in working memory. *Quarterly Journal of Experimental Psychology*, 38A, 229–247.

Lovinenko, A. D. and Belpolskii, V. I. (1994) Convergence as a cue for distance. *Perception*, 23, 207–217.

Luria, A. R. (1966) *Higher cortical functions in man*. London: Tavistock.

MacKay, D. G. (1973) Aspects of the theory of comprehension, memory and attention. *Quarterly Journal of Experimental Psychology*, 25, 22–40.

Macken, J. M., Tremblay, S., Houghton, R. J., Nicholls, A. P. and Jones, A. M. (2003) Does auditory streaming require attention? Evidence from attentional selectivity in short term memory. *Journal of Experimental Psychology: Human Perception and Performance*, 29, 43–51.

MacPhail, E. M. (1998) *The Evolution of Consciousness*. New York: Oxford University Press.

Mandler, G. (1967) Organisation and memory. In: K. W. Spence and J. T. Spence (eds) *The Psychology of Learning and Motivation. Vol. 1*. New York: Academic Press.

Mann, V. A. and Repp, B. H. (1980) Influence of vocalic context on perception of the [f]-[s] distinction. *Perception and Psychophysics*, 28, 213–228.

Marcel, A. J. (1980) Conscious and preconscious recognition of polysemous words: Locating the selective effects of prior verbal context. In: R. S. Nickerson (ed) *Attention and Performance, VII*, Hillsdale, NJ: Lawrence Erlbaum Associates Inc.

Marcel, A. J. (1983) Conscious and unconscious perception: An approach to the relations between phenomenal experience and perceptual processes. *Cognitive Psychology*, 15, 238–300.

Marcel, A. J. (1988) Phenomenal experience and functionalism. In: A. J.

Marcel and E. Bisiach (eds) *Consciousness and Contemporary Science.* Oxford: Oxford University Press.

Marr, D. (1976) Early processing of visual information. *Philosophical Transactions of the Royal Society of London, B207*, 187–217.

Marr, D. (1982) *Vision.* San Francisco. Freeman.

Marr, D. and Nishihara, H. K. (1978) Representation and recognition of the spatial organisation of three-dimensional shapes. *Proceedings of the Royal Society of London, Series B*, 200, 269–294.

Marshall, J. and Halligan, P. (1988) Blindsight and insight into visuo-spatial neglect. *Nature*, 336, 766–767.

Massaro, D. W. (1970) Pre-perceptual auditory images. *Journal of Experimental Psychology*, 85, 411–417.

Massaro, D. W. and Cohen, M. M. (1983) Evaluation and integration of visual and auditory information in speech perception. *Journal of Experimental Psychology: Human Perception and Performance*, 9, 753–771.

Matthews, G., Davies, R. D., Westerman, S. J. and Stammers, R. B. (2000) *Human Performance: Cognition, Stress and Individual Differences.* Hove, UK: Psychology Press.

Mattingley, J. B., Driver, J., Beschin, N. and Robertson, I. J. (1997) Attentional competition between modalities: Extinction between touch and vision after right hemisphere damage. *Neuropsychologia*, 35, 867–880.

McClelland, J. L. (1981) Retrieving general and specific knowledge from stored knowledge of specifics. *Proceedings of the Third Annual Conference of the Cognitive Science Society*, 170–172.

McClelland, J. L. and Rumelhart, D. E. (1981) An interactive activation model of context effects in letter perception: Part 1. An account of basic findings. *Psychological Review*, 85, 375–407.

McGurk, H. and MacDonald, J. (1976) Hearing lips and seeing voices. *Nature*, 264, 746–748.

McLeod, P. D. (1978) Does probe RT measure central processing demand? *Quarterly Journal of Experimental Psychology*, 30, 83–89.

Meacham, J. A. and Leiman, B. (1982) Remembering to perform future action. In: U. Neisser (ed) *Memory Observed: Remembering in Natural Contexts.* San Francisco: Freeman.

Melzak, R. and Dennis, S. G. (1978) Neurophysiological foundations of pain. In: R. A. Strenbach (ed) *The Psychology of Pain.* New York: Raven.

Melzak, R. and Wall, P. D. (1965) Pain mechanisms: A new theory. *Science*, 150, 971–979.

Melzak, R. and Wall, P. D. (1982) *The Challenge of Pain.* New York: Basic Books.

Merikle, P. M. (1980) Selection from visual persistence by perceptual groups and category membership. *Journal of Experimental Psychology: General*, 109, 279–295.

Mewhort, D. J. K. (1967) Familiarity of letter sequences, response uncertainty and the tachistoscopic recognition experiment. *Canadian Journal of Psychology*, 21, 309–321.

Meyer, D. E. and Schvanaveldt, R. W. (1971) Facilitation in recognising pairs of words: Evidence of a dependence between retrieval operations. *Journal of Experimental Psychology*, 90, 227–234.

Miller, G. A. (1956) The magical number seven, plus or minus two: Some limits on our capacity for processing information. *Psychological Review*, 63, 81–97.

Miller, G. A. (1962) *Psychology: The Science of Mental Life*. USA: Penguin Books.

Miller, G. A., Heise, G. A. and Lichten, W. (1951) The intelligibility of speech as a function of the context of test materials. *Journal of Experimental Psychology*, 41, 329–335.

Miller, G. A. and Isard, S. (1963) Some perceptual consequences of linguistic rules. *Journal of Verbal Learning and Verbal Behavior*, 2, 217–228.

Miller, G. A. and Nicely, P. (1955) An analysis of perceptual confusions among some English consonants. *Journal of the Acoustical Society of America*, 27, 338–352.

Milner, A. D. and Goodale, M. A. (1995) *The visual brain in action*. New York: Oxford University Press.

Milner, B. (1963) Effects of different brain lesions on card sorting. *Archives of Neurology*, 9, 90–100.

Milner, B., Corkin, S. and Teuber, H. L. (1968) Further analysis of the hippocampal amnesic syndrome: A 14 year follow-up study. *Neuropsychologia*, 6, 215–234.

Minsky, M. L. (1975) A framework for representing knowledge. In: P. H. Winston (ed) *The Psychology of Computer Vision*. New York: McGraw Hill.

Mitchell, S. W. (1871) Phantom limbs. *Lippincott's Magazine for Popular Literature and Science*, 8, 563–569.

Miyawaki, K., Strange, W., Verbrugge, R., Liberman, A. M., Jenkins, J. J. and Fujimura, O. (1975) An effect of linguistic experience. The discrimination of [r] and [l] by native speakers of Japanese and English. *Perception and Psychophysics*, 18, 331–340.

Monsell, S. (1984) Components of working memory underlying verbal skills: A 'distributed capacities' view—A tutorial review. In: H. Bouma and

D. G. Bouwhuis (eds) *Attention and Performance X* (pp. 327–350). Hove, UK: Lawrence Erlbaum Associates.

Monsell, S. (1996) Control of mental processes. In: V. Bruce (ed) *Unsolved Mysteries of the Mind*. Hove, UK: Erlbaum (UK) Taylor and Francis.

Moore, B. C. J. (1995) *Hearing*. San Diego, CA: Academic Press.

Moray, N. (1959) Attention in dichotic listening: Affective cues and the influence of instruction. *Quarterly Journal of Experimental Psychology*, 11, 56–60.

Morgan, M. J. (1996) Visual illusions. In: V. Bruce (ed) *Unsolved Mysteries of the Mind: Tutorial Essays in Cognition* (pp. 29–58). Hove, UK: Lawrence Erlbaum Associates Ltd.

Morris, C. D., Bransford, J. D. and Franks, J. J. (1977) Levels of processing versus transfer appropriate processing. *Journal of Verbal Learning and Verbal Behavior*, 16, 519–533.

Morton, J. (1967) A singular lack of incidental learning. *Nature*, 215, 203–204.

Muller, J. (1842) *Elements of Physiology* (translated by W. Baly). London: Taylor and Walton.

Navon, D. (1977) Forest before trees: The precedence of global features in visual perception. *Cognitive Psychology*, 9, 353–383.

Neisser, U. (1967) *Cognitive Psychology*. New York: Appleton Century Crofts.

Neuman, O. (1987) Beyond capacity: A functional view of attention. In: H. Heuer and A. F. Sanders (eds) *Perspectives on Selection and Action*. Hillsdale, NJ: Lawrence Erlbaum Associates Inc.

Neutzel, J. M. and Hafter, E. R. (1981) Lateralisation of complex wave forms: Spectral effects. *Journal of the Acoustical Society of America*, 69, 1112–1118.

Newell, A. and Rosenbloom, P. S. (1981) Mechanisms of skill acquisition and the law of practice. In: J. R. Anderson (ed) *Cognitive Skills and Their Acquisition*. Hillsdale, NJ: Lawrence Erlbaum Associates Inc.

Norman, D. A. (1968) Towards a theory of memory and attention. *Psychological Review*, 75, 522–536.

Norman, D. A. (1981) Categorization of action slips. *Psychological Review*, 88, 1–15.

Norman, D. A. and Bobrow, D. G. (1975) On data-limited and resource-limited processes. *Cognitive Psychology*, 7, 44–64.

Norman, D. A. and Shallice, T. (1986) Attention to action: Willed and automatic control of behaviour. In: R. Davison, G. Shwartz and D. Shapiro (eds) *Consciousness and Self-Regulation: Advances in Research and Theory*. New York, Plenum Press.

Ooi, T. L. and He, Z. J. (1999) Binocular rivalry and visual awareness: The role of attention. *Perception*, 28, 551–574.

Oshawa, I., De Angelis, G. C. and Freeman, R. D. (1990) Stereoscopic depth discrimination in the visual cortex: Neurons ideally suited as disparity detectors. *Science*, 249, 1037–1041.

Pallis, C. A. (1955) Impaired identification of faces and places with agnosia for colours. Report of a case due to cerebral embolism. *Journal of Neurology and Psychiatry*, 18, 218–224.

Palmer, S. E. (1975) The effects of contextual scenes on the identification of objects. *Memory and Cognition*, 3, 519–526.

Palmer, S. E., Rosch, E. and Chase, P. (1981) Canonical perspective and the perception of objects. In: J. Long and A. D. Baddeley (eds) *Attention and Performance IX*. Hillsdale, NJ: Lawrence Erlbaum Associates Inc.

Parkin, A. J. (1997) *Memory and Amnesia: An Introduction* (2nd ed). Oxford: Blackwell.

Parkin, A. J. (2000) *Essential Cognitive Psychology*. Hove, UK: Psychology Press.

Pashler, H. (1990) Do response modality effects support multi-processor models of divided attention? *Journal of Experimental Psychology: Human Perception and Performance*, 16, 826–842.

Pashler, H. (1998a) *The Psychology of Attention*. Cambridge, MA: MIT Press.

Pashler, H. (ed) (1998b) *Attention*. Hove, UK: Psychology Press.

Passingham, R. E. (1996) Attention to action. *Proceedings of the Royal Society of London, B* 351, 1473–1479.

Paivio, A. (1986) *Mental Representations: A Dual Coding Approach*. New York: Oxford University Press.

Pedzek, K., Finger, K. and Hodge, D. (1997) Planting false childhood memories: The role of event plausibilty. *Psychological Sciences*, 8, 437–441.

Penfield, W. and Rasmussen, T. (1950) *The Cerebral Cortex of Man: A Clinical Study of Localisation of Function*. New York: MacMillan.

Perret, E. (1974) The left frontal lobe of man and the suppression of habitual responses in verbal categorical behaviour. *Neuropsychologia*, 12, 323–330.

Poggio, G. and Poggio, T. (1984) The analysis of stereopsis. *Annual Review of Neuroscience*, 7, 379–412.

Poggio, G. F. and Fischer, B. (1977) Binocular interaction and depth sensitivity in striate and prestriate cortex of behaving rhesus monkey. *Journal of Neurophysiology*, 40, 1392–1407.

Pollack, I. and Pickett, J. M. (1964) Intelligibility of excerpts from fluent speech: Auditory vs. structural content. *Journal of Verbal Learning and Verbal Behavior*, 3, 79–84.

Pollack, I., Pickett, J. M. and Sumby, W. (1954) On the identification of speakers by voice. *Journal of the Acoustical Society of America*, 26, 403–406.

Posner, M. I. (1978) *Chronometric Explorations of Mind*. Hillsdale, NJ: Lawrence Erlbaum Associates Inc.

Posner, M. I. (1980) Orienting of attention. *Quarterly Journal of Experimental Psychology*, 32, 3–25.

Posner, M. I. and Badgaiyan, R. D. (1998) Attention and neural networks. In: R. W. Parks, D. S. Levine and D. L. Long (eds) *Fundamentals of Neural Network Modelling* (pp. 61–76). Cambridge, MA: MIT Press.

Posner, M. I. and Boies, S. J. (1971) Components of attention. *Psychological Review*, 78, 391–408.

Posner, M. I. and Petersen, S. E. (1990) The attentional system of the human brain. *Annual Review of Neuroscience*, 13, 25–42.

Posner, M. I. and Snyder, C. R. R. (1975) Attention and cognitive control. In: R. L. Solso (ed) *Information Processing and Cognition: The Loyola Symposium*. Hillsdale, NJ: Lawrence Erlbaum Associates Inc.

Posner, M. I., Snyder, C. R. R. and Davidson, B. J. (1980) Attention and the detection of signals. *Journal of Experimental Psychology: General*, 109, 160–174.

Posner, M. I., Walker, J. A., Friedrick, F. J. and Rafal, R. D. (1984) Effects of parietal injury on covert orienting of visual attention. *Journal of Neuroscience*, 4, 1863–1874.

Prince, M. (1914) *The Unconscious*. New York: Macmillan.

Pylyshyn, Z. W. (1981) The imagery debate: Analogue media versus tacit knowledge. *Psychological Review*, 86, 16–45.

Ramachandran, V. S. (1988) Perceiving shape from shading. *Scientific American*, 259, 76–83.

Ramachandran, V. S. and Blakeslee, S. (1998) *Phantoms in the Brain. Human Nature and the Architecture of the Mind*. London: Fourth Estate.

Reason, J. (1979) Actions not as planned: The price of automatization. In: G. Underwood and R. Stephens (eds) *Aspects of Consciousness, Vol. 1*. London: Academic Press.

Reason, J. T. (1984) Absentmindedness and cognitive control. In: J. E. Harris and P. E. Morris (eds) *Everyday Memory, Actions and Absentmindedness*. London: Academic Press.

Reason, J. T. and Mycielska, K. (1982) *Absentminded? The Psychology of Mental Lapses and Everyday Errors.* Englewood Cliffs, NJ: Prentice Hall.

Reber, A. S. (1967) Implicit learning of artificial grammars. *Journal of Verbal Learning and Verbal Behavior*, 6, 855–863.

Reisberg, D., Rappaport, I. and O'Shaughnessy, M. (1984) Limits of working memory: The digit-digit span. *Journal of Experimental Psychology: Learning Memory and Cognition*, 10, 203–221.

Rensink, R. (2000) The dynamic representation of scenes. *Visual Cognition*, 7, 17–42.

Rensink, R. A., O'Regan, K. O. and Clark, J. J. (1997) To see or not to see: The need for attention to perceive changes in scenes. *Psychological Science*, 8, 368–373.

Rhodes, G. (1987) Auditory attention and the representation of spatial information. *Perception and Psychophysics*, 42, 1–14.

Richardson, J. T. E. (1999) *Imagery*. Hove, UK. Psychology Press.

Riddoch, M. J. and Humphreys, G. W. (1987a) A case of integrative agnosia. *Brain*, 110, 1431–1462.

Riddoch, M. J. and Humphreys, G. W. (1987b) Picture naming. In: G. W. Humphreys and M. J. Riddoch (eds) *Visual Object Processing: A Cognitive Neuropsychological Approach*. London: Lawrence Erlbaum Associates Ltd.

Rinkenauer, G., Mattes, S. and Ulrich, R. (1999) The surface-weight illusion: On the contribution of grip force to perceived heaviness. *Perception and Psychophysics*, 61, 23–30.

Rizzolatti, G. and Carmada, R. (1987) Neural circuits for spatial attention and unilateral neglect. In: M. Jeannerod (ed) *Neurophysiological and Neuropsychological Aspects of Spatial Neglect*. Amsterdam: North Holland.

Rizzolatti, G. and Gallese, V. (1988) Mechanisms and theories of spatial neglect. In: F. Boller and J. Grafman (eds) *Handbook of Neuropsychology, Vol. 1*. Amsterdam. Elsevier.

Rizzolatti, G., Gentilucci, M. and Mattelli, M. (1985) Selective spatial attention: One centre, one circuit or many circuits. In: M. I. Posner and O. Marin (eds) *Attention and Performance, XI*. Hillsdale, NJ: Lawrence Erlbaum Associates Inc.

Rizzolatti, G. and Matelli, M. (2003) Two different streams for the dorsal visual system: Anatomy and functions. *Experimental Brain Research*, 153, 146–157.

Rock, I. and Victor, J. (1964, February 7) Vision and touch: An experimentally created conflict between the senses. *Science*, 143, 594–596.

Rosch, E. (1973) On the internal structure of perceptual and conceptual categories. In: T. E. Moore (ed) *Cognitive Development and the Acquisition of Language*. New York: Academic Press.

Rosch, E. and Mervis, C. B. (1975) Family resemblances: Studies in the internal structure of categories. *Cognitive Psychology*, 7, 573–605.

Rumelhart, D. E. (1975) Notes on schema for stories. In: D. G. Bobrow and A. Collins (eds) *Representation and Understanding* (pp. 211–236). New York: Academic Press.

Rumelhart, D. E. and Norman, D. A. (1985) Representation of knowledge. In: A. M. Aitkenhead and J. M. Slack (eds) *Issues in Cognitive Modelling*. Hove, UK: Lawrence Erlbaum Associates Ltd.

Rumelhart, D. E., Smolensky, P., McClelland, J. L. and Hinton, G. E. (1986) Schemata and sequential thought processes in PDP models. In: J. L. McClelland and D. E. Rumelhart (eds) *Parallel Distributed Processing: Explorations in the Microstructure of Cognition. Vol. 2. Psychological and Biological Models*. Cambridge, MA: MIT Press.

Rundus, D. (1971) Analysis of rehearsal processes in free recall. *Journal of Experimental Psychology*, 89, 63–77.

Salame, P. and Baddeley, A. D. (1987) Noise, unattended speech and short-term memory. *Ergonomics*, 30, 1185–1193.

Salame, P. and Baddeley, A. D. (1989) Effects of background music on phonological short-term memory. *Quarterly Journal of Experimental Psychology*, 41A, 107–122.

Schacter, D. L. (1987) Implicit memory: History and current status. *Journal of Experimental Psychology: Learning Memory and Cognition*, 13, 501–518.

Schacter, D. L., Harbuck, J. L. and McLachlan, D. R. (1984) Retrieval without recollection: An experimental analysis of source amnesia. *Journal of Verbal Learning and Verbal Behavior*, 23, 593–611.

Schacter, D. L., Israel, L. and Racine, C. (1999) Suppressing false recognition in younger and older adults: The distinctiveness heuristic. *Journal of Memory and Language*, 40, 1–24.

Schacter, D. L. and Tulving, E. (1994) What are the memory systems for 1994? In: D. L. Schacter, and E. Tulving (eds) *Memory systems, 1994* (pp. 1–38). Cambridge, MA: MIT Press.

Schacter, D. L. and Tulving, E. (1982) Amnesia and memory research. In: L. S. Cermak (ed) *Human Memory and Amnesia*. Hillsdale NJ: Lawrence Erlbaum Associates Inc.

Schank, R. C. (1975) *Conceptual Information Processing*. Amsterdam: North Holland.

Scharf, B. (1988) The role of attention in speech perception. *Journal of the Acoustical Society of America*, 84, S158 (A).

Scharf, B. (1998) Auditory attention: The psychoacoustical approach. In: H. Pashler (ed) *Attention*. Hove, UK: Psychology Press.

Scharf, B. (1999) Auditory attention: The psychophysical approach. In: H. Pashler (ed) *Attention*. Hove, UK: Psychology Press.

Scharf, B., Magnan, J. and Chays, A. (1994) On the role of the olivo-cochlear bundle in hearing: A case study. *Hearing Research*, 75, 11–26.

Scharf, B., Magnan, J. and Chays, A. (1997) On the role of the olivocochlear bundle in hearing: Sixteen case studies. *Hearing Research*, 103, 101–122.

Schiffman, H. R. (1994) The skin, body and chemical senses. In: R. L. Gregory, and A. M. Colman (eds) *Sensation and Perception*. Harlow, UK: Longman.

Scoville, W. B. and Milner, B. (1957) Loss of recent memory after bilateral hippocampal lesions. *Journal of Neurology, Neurosurgery and Psychiatry*, 20, 11–21.

Selfridge, O. (1959) Pandemonium: A paradigm for learning. In: *Symposium on the Mechanisation of Thought*. London: HM Stationery Office.

Shaffer, L. H. (1975) Multiple attention in continuous verbal task. In: P. M. A. Rabbitt and S. Dornic (eds) *Attention and Performance V*. New York: Academic Press.

Shallice, T. (1982) Specific impairments of planning. *Philosophical Transactions of the Royal Society of London*, B298, 199–209.

Shallice, T. (1988) *From Neuropsychology to Mental Structure*. Cambridge: Cambridge University Press.

Shallice, T. and Burgess, P. W. (1993) Supervisory control of action and thought selection. In: A. D. Baddeley and L. Weiskrantz (eds) *Attention: Awareness Selection and Control. A Tribute to Donald Broadbent*. Oxford: Oxford University Press.

Shallice, T. and Warrington, E. K. (1970) Independent functioning of verbal memory stores: A neuropsychological study. *Quarterly Journal of Experimental Psychology*, 22, 261–273.

Shallice, T. and Warrington, E. K. (1977) The possible role of selective attention in acquired dyslexia. *Neuropsychologia*, 15, 31–41.

Shepard, R. N. and Metzler, J. (1971) Mental rotation of three-dimensional objects. *Science*, 171, 710–703.

Shiffrin, R. M. and Schneider, W. (1977) Controlled and automatic information processing: II. Perception, learning, automatic attending and a general theory. *Psychological Review*, 84, 127–190.

Simons, D. J. and Levin, D. T. (1998) Failure to detect changes to people during a real world interaction. *Psychonomic Bulletin and Review*, 4, 644–649.

Skinner, B. F. (1938) *The Behaviour of Organisms: An Experimental Analysis.* New York: Appleton-Century-Crofts.

Sloboda, J. A. (1999) *The Musical Mind: The Cognitive Psychology of Music.* Oxford: Oxford University Press.

Smith, E. E., Shoben, E. J. and Rips, L. J. (1974) Structure and process in sematic memory: A featural model for semantic decisions. *Psychological Review*, 81, 214–241.

Smith, S. M., Glenberg, A. and Bjork, R. A. (1978) Environmental context and human memory. *Memory and Cognition*, 6, 342–353.

Spence, C. J. and Driver, J. (1996) Audiovisual links in covert spatial attention. *Journal of Experimental Psychology: Human Perception and Performance*, 22, 1005–1030.

Spence, C. J., Pavani, F. and Driver, J. (2000) Cross-modal links between vision and touch in covert endogenous spatial attention. *Journal of Experimental Psychology: Human Perception and Performance*, 26, 1298–1319.

Sperling, G. (1960) The information available in brief visual presentations. *Psychological Monographs*, 74, (Whole number 498).

Stern, L. D. (1981) A review of theories of human amnesia. *Memory and Cognition*, 9, 247–262.

Stevens, S. S. (1936) A scale for the measurement of a psychological magnitude: Loudness. *Psychological Review*, 43, 405–416.

Stevens, S. S. (1956) The direct estimates of sensory magnitudes—loudness. *American Journal of Psychology*, 69, 1–25.

Stevens, S. S. (1957) On the psychophysical law. *Psychological Review*, 64, 153–181.

Stirling, J. (2000) *Cortical Functions.* Routledge Modular Psychology series. London: Routledge.

Stoffer, T. H. (1993) The time course of attentional zooming: A comparison of voluntary and involuntary allocation of attention to the levels of compound stimuli. *Psychological Research*, 56, 14–25.

Stroop, J. R. (1935) Studies of interference in serial-verbal reaction. *Journal of Experimental Psychology*, 18, 643–662.

Styles, E. A. (1997) *The Psychology of Attention.* Hove, UK: Psychology Press.

Styles, E. A. and Allport, D. A. (1986) Perceptual integration of identity, location and colour. *Psychological Research*, 48, 189–200.

Talland, G. (1965) *Deranged Memory.* New York: Academic Press.

Tanaka, J. and Farah, M. J. (1993) Parts and wholes in face recognition. *Quarterly Journal of Experimental Psychology*, 46A, 225–246.

Tanner, W. and Norman, R. (1954) The human use of information: II Signal detection for the case of an unknown signal parameter. *Transactions of the Institute of Radio Engineering, Professional Group on Information Theory*, 4, 222–227.

Tarr, M. J. (1995) Rotating objects to recognise them: A case study of the role of viewpoint dependency in the recognition of three-dimensional objects. *Psychonomic Bulletin and Review*, 2, 55–82.

Thomas, A. K. and Loftus, E. (2002) Creating biarre false memories through imagination. *Memory and Cognition*, 30, 423–431.

Treisman, A. (1986) Features and objects in visual processing. *Scientific American*, November, 106–115.

Treisman, A. (1988) Features and objects: The fourteenth Bartlett memorial lecture. *Quarterly Journal of Experimental Psychology*, 40A, 201–237.

Treisman, A. (1999) Feature binding, attention and object perception. In: G. W. Humphreys, J. Duncan and A. Treisman (eds) *Attention space and action: Studies in cognitive neuroscience* (pp. 91–111). Oxford: Oxford University Press.

Treisman, A. and Schmidt, H. (1982) Illusory conjunctions in the perception of objects. *Cognitive Psychology*, 14, 107–141.

Treisman, A. M. (1960) Contextual cues in selective listening. *Quarterly Journal of Experimental Psychology*, 12, 242–248.

Treisman, A. M. (1964a) Monitoring and storage of irrelevant messages in selective attention. *Journal of Verbal Learning and Verbal Behavior*, 3, 449–459.

Treisman, A. M. (1964b) Verbal cues, language and meaning in selective attention. *American Journal of Psychology*, 77, 206–219.

Treisman, A. M. (1964c) Effect of irrelevant material on the efficiency of selective listening. *American Journal of Psychology*, 77, 533–546.

Treisman, A. M. and Gelade, G. (1980) A feature-integration theory of attention. *Cognitive Psychology*, 12, 97–136.

Tulving, E. (1966) Subjective organisation and effects of repetition in multi-trial free-recall learning. *Journal of Verbal Learning and Verbal Behavior*, 5, 193–197.

Tulving, E. (1972) Episodic and Semantic memory. In: E. Tulving and W. Donaldson (eds) *Organisation of Memory*. New York: Academic Press.

Tulving, E. (1983) *Elements of Episodic Memory*. Oxford: Oxford University Press.

Tulving, E. and Osler, S. (1968) Effectiveness of retrieval cues in memory for words. *Journal of Experimental Psychology*, 77, 593–601.

Tulving, E. and Schacter, D. L. (1990) Priming and human memory. *Science*, 247, 301–306.

Tulving, E., Schacter, D. L. and Stark, H. A. (1982) Priming effects in word fragment completion are independent of recognition memory. *Journal of Experimental Psychology: Learning Memory and Cognition*, 8, 336–342.

Tulving, E. and Thomson, D. M. (1973) Encoding specificity and retrieval processes in episodic memory. *Psychological Review*, 80, 352–373.

Turvey, M. T. and Kravetz, S. (1970) Retrieval from iconic memory with shape as the selection criterion. *Perception and Psychophysics*, 8, 171–172.

Ungerleider, L. G. and Mishkin, M. (1982) Two cortical systems. In: D. J. Ingle, M. A. Goodale and R. J. W. Mansfield (eds) *Analysis of Visual Behaviour*. Cambridge MA: MIT Press.

Vallar, G. and Baddeley, A. D. (1984) Fractionation of working memory. Neuropsychological evidence for a phonological short-term store. *Journal of Verbal Learning and Verbal Behavior*, 23, 151–161.

Vitevitch, M. S. (2003) Change deafness: The inability to detect changes between two voices. *Journal of Experimental Psychology: Human Perception and Performance*, 29 (2), 333–342.

Volpe, B. T., Ledoux, J. E. and Gazzaniga, M. S. (2000) Information processing of visual stimuli in an 'extinguished' field. In: M. S. Gazzaniga (ed) *Cognitive Neuroscience: A Reader*. Oxford: Blackwell.

Von Helmholtz, H. (1866) *Treatise on Physiological Optics, Vol. III*. New York: Dover (translation published 1962).

Von Holst, E. (1954) Relations between the central nervous system and the peripheral organs. *British Journal of Animal Behaviour*, 2, 89–94.

Von Wright, J. M. (1969) Selection in visual immediate memory. *Quarterly Journal of Experimental Psychology*, 20, 62–68.

Von Wright, J. M. (1970) On selection from immediate memory. *Acta Psychologia*, 33, 280–292.

Warren, R. M. (1970) Perceptual restoration of missing speech sounds. *Science*, 167, 392–393.

Warrington, E. K. and Taylor, A. M. (1973) The contribution of the right parietal lobe to object recognition. *Cortex*, 9, 152–164.

Warrington, E. K. and Taylor, A. M. (1978) Two categorical states of object recognition. *Perception*, 7, 695–705.

Warrington, E. K. and Weiskrantz, L. (1968) New method for testing long-term retention with special reference to amnesic patients. *Nature*, 217, 972–974.

Warrington, E. K. and Weiskrantz, L. (1970) Amnesic syndrome: Consolidation or retrieval? *Nature*, 228, 628–630.

Watson, J. B. (1916) The place of the conditioned reflex in psychology. *Psychological Review*, 23, 89–116.

Waugh, N. C. and Norman, D. A. (1965) Primary memory. *Psychological Review*, 72, 89–104.

Weber, E. H. (1834) *De pulsu, resorptione, auditu et tactu. Annotationes anatomicae et psychologicae*. Leipzig: Loeler. [Trans. H. E. Ross and D. J. Murray (1978) *The Sense of Touch*. London: Academic Press.]

Welford, A. T. (1952) The psychological refractory period and the timing of high speed performance: A review and a theory. *British Journal of Psychology*, 43, 2–19.

Wertheimer, M. (1923) Untersuchungen zur Lehre von der Gestalt II. *Psychol. Forsch.*, 4, 310–350.

Wheatstone, C. (1838) Contributions to the physiology of vision, Part 1: On some remarkable and hitherto unobserved phenomena of binocular vision. *Philosophical Transactions of the Royal Society of London*, 128, 371–394.

Wheeler, M. A., Stuss, D. T. and Tulving, E. (1997) Toward a theory of episodic memory: The frontal lobes and autonoetic consciousness. *Psychological Bulletin*, 121, 331–354.

White, B. (1960) Recognition of distorted melodies. *American Journal of Psychology*, 73, 100–107.

Williams, J. M. G. and Broadbent, D. E. (1986) Autobiographical memory in suicide attempters. *Journal of Abnormal Psychology*, 95, 145–149.

Wolfe, J. M., Cave, K. R. and Franzel, S. L. (1989) Guided search: An alterative to the feature integration model for visual search. *Journal of Experimental Psychology: Human Perception and Performance*, 15, 419–433.

Wood, N. and Cowan, N. (1995) The cocktail party phenomenon revisited: How frequent are attention shifts to one's name in an irrelevant auditory channel? *Journal of Experimental Psychology, Learning Memory and Cognition*, 2, 255–260.

Wundt, W. (1873) *Outlines of Psychology*. [Trans. C. H. Judd (1907) Leipzig: Wilhelm Engelman.]

Young, A. W., Hay, D. C. and Ellis, A. W. (1985) The faces that launched a thousand slips: Everyday difficulties and errors in recognising people. *British Journal of Psychology*, 76, 495–523.

REFERENCES

Young, A. W., Hellawell, D. J. and Hay, D. C. (1987) Configural information in face perception. *Perception*, 16, 747–759.

Zeki, S. (1980) The representation of colours in the cerebral cortex. *Nature*, 284, 412–418.

Subject Index

353

Author Index